MW00562356

The Shame Factor

The Shame Factor

How Shame Shapes Society

edited by
ROBERT JEWETT

with
WAYNE L. ALLOWAY JR. *and* JOHN G. LACEY

CASCADE *Books* · Eugene, Oregon

THE SHAME FACTOR
How Shame Shapes Society

Copyright © 2011 Wipf and Stock Publishers. All rights reserved. Except for brief quotations in critical publications or reviews, no part of this book may be reproduced in any manner without prior written permission from the publisher. Write: Permissions, Wipf and Stock Publishers, 199 W. 8th Ave., Suite 3, Eugene, OR 97401.

Scripture quotations are from the New Revised Standard Version of the Bible, copyright © 1989 by the Division of Christian Education of the National Council of the Churches of Christ in the U.S.A. and used by permission.

Cascade Books
An Imprint of Wipf and Stock Publishers
199 W. 8th Ave., Suite 3
Eugene, OR 97401

www. wipfandstock.com

ISBN 13: 978-1-60899-987-3

Cataloging-in-Publication data:

The shame factor : how shame shapes society / edited by Robert Jewett with Wayne L. Alloway Jr., and John G. Lacey.

xii + 238 p. ; cm. 23 — Includes bibliographical references and index.

ISBN 13: 978-1-60899-987-3

1. Shame. 2. Shame in the Bible. 3. Shame—Religious aspects—Christianity. 4. Shame in literature. I. Jewett, Robert. II. Alloway, Wayne L., Jr. III. Lacey, John G. IV. Title.

BF575 .S45 S525 2011

Manufactured in the U.S.A.

Contents

Contributors

WAYNE L. ALLOWAY JR., Senior Pastor of St. Mark's United Methodist Church in Lincoln, Nebraska.

DAVID A. DESILVA, Trustees' Distinguished Professor of New Testament and Greek at Ashland Theological Seminary, Ashland, Ohio.

ROBERT JEWETT, Guest Professor of New Testament at the University of Heidelberg, Germany, and Theologian in Residence at St. Mark's United Methodist Church, Lincoln, Nebraska.

JAMES W. JONES, Professor of Religion and Adjunct Professor of Clinical Psychology at Rutgers University, New Brunswick, New Jersey, and Senior Research Fellow, Center on Terrorism at John Jay College of Criminal Justice, New York, New York.

JOHN G. LACEY, Executive Pastor of St. Mark's United Methodist Church, Lincoln, Nebraska.

BRUCE J. MALINA, Professor of New Testament and Early Christianity at Creighton University, Omaha, Nebraska.

VICTOR H. MATTHEWS, Professor of Religious Studies and Dean of the College of Humanities and Public Affairs at Missouri State University, Springfield, Missouri.

STEPHEN PATTISON, Professor of Religion, Ethics and Practice at the University of Birmingham, United Kingdom.

DAVID M. RHOADS, Professor of New Testament Emeritus at the Lutheran School of Theology, Chicago, Illinois.

SANDRA ROBERTS Rhoads has served as a prison counselor in Wisconsin.

THOMAS J. SCHEFF, Professor of Sociology Emeritus at the University of California, Santa Barbara, California.

ANNE E. STREATY WIMBERLY, Professor of Christian Education at the Interdenominational Theological Center, Atlanta, Georgia.

EDWARD P. WIMBERLY, Professor of Pastoral Care and Vice President of Academic Affairs/Provost at the Interdenominational Theological Center, Atlanta, Georgia.

Introduction

WAYNE L. ALLOWAY JR.

YEARS AGO, IN ONE of the first churches I served following my ordination, there was an old World War II veteran who always sat in the back pew and refused to come forward to receive communion. While shaking my hand on his way out of the sanctuary the last Sunday of my tenure, he broke down in tears and asked if we could speak privately. He came to my office and unburdened himself through sobs of sadness and shame. He told me he had been an Army sergeant in the Philippines during the war, and one of his job duties was to pull the lever on the hangman's platform at the execution of convicted Japanese war criminals. The memory had haunted him ever since. "I'm ashamed," he said. "I don't feel worthy of God's love."

At another church, years later, a young man in his early thirties came to me and confessed that his swimming coach had sexually molested him while he was in middle school. He said the "shameful secret" had burdened him for many years, but he had been too afraid to tell anyone for fear of what they might think of him. At still another church, a woman declined to serve on the worship planning committee for fear that church members might discover her daughter was an exotic dancer, and label her a bad or incompetent mother. She believed her daughter's career choice was a reflection on her character, and felt deeply ashamed.

I've also known numerous people over the years who have refused to acknowledge the suicide of a loved one or family member because they feel guilt-ridden and ashamed by it. People are ashamed of their past, and their present. They're ashamed of what they've done and they're ashamed of what's been done to them. They're ashamed of their appearance, their perceived intelligence, their job, their social status, and even their families, but—if they are Christian—they are seldom, if ever, ashamed of their faith or the gospel.

In today's culture, with churches standing prominently on street corners and crosses worn proudly around necks, we find Paul's remark, "I am not ashamed of the gospel," (Rom 1:16) almost strange. But for those who heard Paul's letter read aloud in early Christian congregations, shame was a key issue. Recall the words in 1 Corinthians where Paul claims the "Jews demand signs and Greeks seek wisdom, but we preach Christ crucified, a stumbling block to Jews and folly to Gentiles" (1 Cor 1:23). Early congregations met in secret, and the cross of Christ was never openly displayed. Moreover, the cross was a sign of shameful failure for the Jews; a "stumbling block" for those who expected their Messiah to be a victorious warrior who would free them from Roman authority. And the message of the crucified Christ seemed "folly" to the Greeks who wanted proof of wisdom in their religion; a crucified savior seemed anything but wise to them. Then, there's the shame of crucifixion itself. Crucifixion was the humiliating death suffered by slaves, bandits, pirates, and revolutionaries. The crucified were stripped of their clothes, nailed naked to crossbars, and hung where their helplessness was visible to all. Crucifixion was the ultimate act of shaming someone.

Yet Paul was unashamed. He and other early Christians believed the gospel was the ultimate revelation of God's grace. They understood that Christ was crucified because he took the side of marginalized members of society, and demonstrated they were acceptable to God. With Christ, there was no need for shame.

The essays in this book were delivered as lectures in a conference, "The Shame Factor," sponsored by St. Mark's United Methodist Church in Lincoln, Nebraska, in October 2010. They explore the impact and the transformation of shameful status in a variety of arenas. William Paul Young lectured on his experiences of sexual, familial, and educational abuse in Irian Jaya that led to the writing of *The Shack*, the best-selling religious novel. Our interview about his book opens this volume. In *Shame: Theory, Therapy, Theology,* Stephen Pattison has written the definitive study of "toxic unwantedness," the ultimate form of social shame. His essay here explains the psychological function of chronic shame and suggests theological resources in dealing with it. Thomas Scheff has written *What's Love Got to Do with It? Emotions in Popular Songs,* and contributes an essay that examines how shame is largely hidden in our society, yet many Top 40 song lyrics imply the shame and humiliation of rejection. James Jones is a pioneer in studying the impact of shame on terrorism, including *Blood That Cries Out From the Earth: The Psychology of Religious Terrorism.* He continues this work by discussing the link between humiliation and violence, offering a new understanding of the impact of narcissism. Anne Streaty Wimberly's essay describes the remarkable use of texts from the Epistle to the Hebrews in spirituals that deal with overcoming shame. Her studies in African American culture include *Soul Stories: African American Christian Education.* David Rhoads and Sandra Roberts have developed a new way to relate the doctrine of justification to shame. Combining her experience as a jail chaplain and his mastery of the New Testament, they adapt Reformation theology to the shame of crime and incarceration. Edward Wimberly breaks new ground in linking Wesleyan theology to the experience of blacks in America. His essay extends the analysis in his book *Moving from Shame to Self-Worth: Preaching and Pastoral Care.*

Victor Matthews has led the paradigm shift on shame issues in his field through many publications, including *More Than Meets the Ear: Discovering the Hidden Contexts of Old Testament Conversations.* In our volume, he shows how the avoidance of shame functioned in the ethical system of ancient Israel. Bruce Malina initiated the study the New Testament texts in the light of anthropological investigations of honor and shame. Having written *The New Testament World: Insights from Cultural Anthropology,* his essay analyzes the role of envy in the hostility of the high priests against Jesus. David deSilva is a leader in applying classical references to honor and shame to biblical writings. Having written *Despising Shame: Honor Discourse and Community Maintenance in the Epistle to the Hebrews,* his essay in our volume analyzes how 1 Peter employs honor in dealing with the experience of social shame in the early church. The Jewett essay offers new insights about praying on the street corner and similar behavior, motivated by the desire to earn social status and the triumph of one's sect. The volume concludes with a sermonic essay by John Lacey that connects biblical texts with Billy Joel's song "Shameless."

In presenting this book, we are indebted to our Lincoln copyeditor, Nancy Hammel, to the staff of St. Mark's church for administering the conference, to our Theologian-in-Residence, Robert Jewett, for inviting the contributors, and to K. C. Hanson, Jim Tedrick, and their staff at Wipf and Stock for timely publication. We offer this collection of essays as a modest contribution to the emerging interpretation of religious issues related to social shame and honor. While traditional theology has restricted its understanding of shame to the sphere of individual guilt, these essays join an emerging recognition that very different forms of shame arise from social traumas imposed by others and by the tragic dimensions of life. We are convinced that the church needs to take the varied forms of shame into account when it proclaims that "nothing can separate us from the love of Christ."

Interview with William Paul Young,
author of *The Shack*

Why did you write *The Shack*?

I've been a writer most of my life. It was one of those survival things. The first part of my life I wrote to get the pain out. The second part of my life I wrote as creative gifts: poems, short stories, songs to give away. Kim, my wife, appreciated my writing and so she had been pestering me—actually she would say "encouraging me"—for about four years to write something as a gift for the kids. We have six children, my youngest is seventeen and my oldest is just turning thirty. She said, "Could you just put in one place how you think as a gift for our children? Because you think outside the box." By the way, when the book came out she told me she had imagined only four to six pages! I've never written something of this volume, but I love "story." Story has a way—actually any kind of creative work—whether as art or music, or looking at God's creation. Creativity penetrates to the heart without asking for permission. And I think fiction does that. It can get past your watchful dragons.

So in 2005, that was my goal. I felt I was healthy enough to write something for my children, and I tried to get it done by Christmas. I then went down to Office Depot and made fifteen copies. That was my only vision for *The Shack*. I've never published anything and never really thought about it. Fifteen copies at Office Depot and I went back to work. I said to myself, "Look, 2005 is the year I turn fifty and I really want to communicate with you, my children, about the God who healed me, not the God I grew up with." I think there's a Western God who watches from a distance, untouchable, unreachable, and that's the God I grew up with. You know, Gandolf with an attitude! Plato's God.

So I was trying to communicate with my children that God is a God of relationship, the Father, the Son, and the Holy Spirit in a circle of relationship, and mutuality and love. The intent of God's purpose was always to include us into that love and affection, and in exchange God enters into our stuff, to heal us from the inside out. That's the story of Mackenzie, which is really my story.

How did you come to that realization, for you, that view of the Father, Son, and Holy Spirit?

Boy, that's a great question, and it comes from a lot of different rivers and little streams that have merged, because my relationship with my own father is reflected in the book, and it has been a difficult one, and not all his fault either. It took me fifty years to wipe the face of my father off the face of God. Part of that process in my own healing was dealing with the damage from my relationship with my father. That's probably one of the longest processes; to begin to realize that God is full of affection—relentless and ferocious—toward us. And so that's one stream. Another stream is that I spent twenty-five years working on gender issues, and that's also a matter of relationship. I talk about the shack as a metaphor for the heart of a human being, the house on the inside that people help us build. I think every person is unique in how they've been created. Every person is incredibly, intricately designed, that we're each damaged uniquely so our process of healing must also be unique. And I think the core of it is going to be relationship. Relationship is what damages us and I think relationship is what heals us.

How will what you have to say to the conference audience fit in with the theme of shame?

Mackenzie spends a weekend in the shack. That weekend represents eleven years of my life. I grew up a shame-based person and part of my "Great Sadness" is sexual abuse. Sexual abuse will drive you into the jaws of shame faster than anything else on this planet. So my experience in dealing with shame will be one of the focuses in what I'll have to say.

How do you think shame in your life held you back?

Let me tell you one of the most powerful things that shame does. Shame destroys your ability to distinguish between a value statement and an observation. For example, when I was first married to Kim, she would say things like "Paul, don't mix the colored with the whites." You know, talking about laundry, right? But I heard her say, "I don't know why I married such a loser of a human being as you!" I had this thin layer of perfectionist performance that covered up this Ocean of Shame. And shame destroyed my ability to distinguish between a value statement and an observation. She was just making an observation. But any time that my perfectionist performance was tampered with, all I heard was a value statement. And that was true in reading Scripture as well as with relationships with anybody. I was always on edge, needing to be perfect so that I could be one of those people that somebody could have affection for, approval for.

What do you hope the audience can take away from your appearance at the conference?

That's a good question. Actually, I don't come in with any expectations. All I have is the desire to be present in the grace of the day, and trust that the Holy Spirit knows who will be there. I don't really know exactly where we're going to go when I stand up. God has been very faithful in that. If there are any hopes, I would desire that people, these magnificent human beings, would begin to get a bigger view of the character and nature of God, one that pushes us away from religion and back into relationship. And have a sense of that ferocious, relentless affection with which God pursues us. And then, to face our own darknesses in certain ways and to understand that we're in a process. It's not an event, you know. We are in the process of the healing of our souls, and that it is a process only indicates what amazing creations we are. That journey is an important one and a good one.

I suppose I could start thinking my way through the book and finding all kind of pieces: issues of forgiveness and relationships with those we love in which much of our experiences of damage occurred, for example.

You just said, "... pushes away from religion into relationship ..." Do you think it's possible to have that relationship within the context of

organized religion?

When I say religion, I'm talking about any kind of system that tells you that you have to earn your way into God's affection. And I don't care what it is. Human beings will organize themselves in one way or another. Organizations were always meant to serve the people, not the people the system or organization. A lot of what we call "church" today is really a parachurch organization. The church is the people, and if you take the people out of that building, that program, then the church has left the building. I don't have an agenda to change systems. Systems exist, and you'll just replace one with another sometimes worse one. But I would like to place the value where it needs to be, which is on the people. Systems should be an expression of the life of those individuals, fluid and changing, rather than individuals having to conform to a system that exists to placate God or someone's agenda.

True life is independent of systems. If I'm in a prison cell, the system that put me there says nothing about my relationship with God. Not at all! And while I don't want to equate prison cells with religious institutions, they both can be very destructive and hurtful. As everybody knows, most religious systems exist because of division. So the answer is obviously, "Yes." I'm inside institutional religious systems probably more than anybody I know, which my friends think is quite funny. But I have no problem being there. Freedom's got nothing to do with the structure or system unless you think it does. It is about being "in" it but not "of" it.

At our church, several Bible study groups have read and discussed your book. I'm sure that's the case at a lot of churches around the country. Why do you think this book has caught on the way it did?

I think in part because it asks a lot of the questions that a lot of us have, as human beings and not just as spiritual people. Also it has given people a language, a way to have a conversation about God, about life, about pain, about suffering, about issues of forgiveness. It has given people a language to have that conversation and it's a relational language, not a religious language. So the book has tampered with some of the paradigms that exist and I think that's been very helpful in terms of conversation. I have heard lots of stories where "believers" were given the book by "unbelievers" who said, "You need to read this!" I think that is hilarious but sad too. The book seems to speak to issues and fundamental questions that exist in every kind of religious and non-religious environment. It has had a huge impact, and I never intended any of it. To me, it's all a God thing.

That was my next question, if you think this was God working through you?

I'm a person who believes in participation, and participation is a word of relationship. I don't believe that God uses us. I believe that he heals us because he loves us and invites us to play and participate. So this is participation. I did something for one reason, you know, and obviously God has utilized whatever I did for one reason for a totally different purpose. For me it goes back to a conversation I had in early 2005. My prayer was—because this was after the eleven years when my life was pretty much dismantled—the prayer I had left was, "Papa, I'm never going to ask you again to bless anything that I do, but if you've got something you're blessing and if it'd be OK for me to be a part of that, then I'd be all over it. I don't care if I'm cleaning toilets or shining shoes or holding the doors open. I just want to know at the end of the day that you did this." I was praying this—and I still do—the whole time I was writing the story for my kids. And it's almost like he said, "Well, Paul, how about if I bless this little story? You give it to your kids and I'll give it to mine." And that's kind of what's happened. And I'm just thrilled to be a part of it. But my identity is not impacted by it. Everything that matters to me was in place before I wrote this story. And I'm grateful for that. I'm grateful that I didn't know what I was doing.

You talk about being "... well enough ..." to write this story. How did you get to that point where you were well enough?

Oh my! That's an hour and a half conversation. You know, as much as we would like some magic bullet, it's not like that. We'll save that until I get to Lincoln. That's probably a good part of the conversation. It's a long and involved conversation.

People want to know ... is this story true?

I tell them it's true but it's not real. Right? Parables are true, but they're not real. And I think the book's a parable. It's a metaphor for the heart of a human being. To answer the question from another side, a writer out of Nashville put it best, "I don't know your history but my sense is that Missy represents something murdered in you as a child, probably your innocence, and Mackenzie is you as an adult trying to deal with it." I showed that to Kim and she said, "She nailed it!" You know, we've had deaths in our family but not exactly like the novel. We've known situations like this. We had a six-month period where Kim's mom at fifty-nine died suddenly, but on each end of those six months my eighteen-year-old brother was killed and my five-year-old niece was killed the day after her birthday. So you have that kind of pain and loss, but *The Shack* really goes much more deeply into my own history.

Some might say it's a feel-good sort of faith . . .

Then they haven't read the book. Papa doesn't let Mackenzie off on anything. We're just used to the idea that God has a disapproving heart, watching from a distance, being placated by Jesus. It suggests that God has a different agenda from Jesus: Jesus came to love us but God is on the justice side. People have asked me, "Where's the wrath?" But that's because we've defined wrath through a judicial lens, through a mostly Platonic, Western form of Enlightenment theology. We think that somehow holiness is the fundamental reality of God, where it's really relationship. Everything in Scripture tells you it's relationship, and holiness is actually the description of the otherness of the love that exists between Father, Son, and Holy Spirit. So wrath is motivated by love. And this book is indicative of the fact that God will pursue Mackenzie for Mackenzie's good. But sin and choices and the destructive things that remain unforgiven keep us from being free. So God will pursue destroying those things. And unfortunately, we identify with them to such a degree that sometimes we consider the destruction of such things very personal. And we see it as wrath, which it is. But does God do anything that is not motivated by love? The answer is "No!" Everything that God does is motivated by love, which has to include wrath.

As a child of missionary parents, you knew the Bible. When you were going through your experiences of abuse, did you question where God

was in all that?

You know, as a child—and I'm sure this is not the experience of every-body—even though I felt shameful in my relationship with God, God was the only person who was there all the time. That was comforting for me, so even in the midst of all the transitions and as far back as I remember, God was present. Even though I learned early on, in very involved ways, how guilty and unworthy I felt, God was a comfort. Later, I questioned, but you know what? I never had the experience of Mackenzie's rage against God. His rage was really my rage at human beings. I always sensed that God was not responsible for all the crap we brought to the table. We would love to say that God was responsible, because then we're off the hook. But for me it was people who did this damage, who made the choices to do what they did. So God was a person of comfort for me as a child. But I totally understand how God becomes the easy target for our fury. It's sometimes easier than to express our rage against people who should have been there and weren't.

God was the target of Mack's rage. Do you think that's a common perception for a lot of folks?

Yes, and I think it's an OK direction to aim your fury, because fundamen-tally the questions are there and I was able easily to enter into Mack's rage and to ask the basic human question: "How come you didn't stop it?" That's a question for me too. God's big enough to deal with such questions. It's an OK place to direct your anger because it's a legitimate question: "If you are good all the time, why did you allow this?" And the story is true to my history.

What was the process of writing?

I actually started with the conversations, and was writing on the train that goes into town forty minutes each way. So I had forty minutes on the train with my yellow pad and these conversations started coming alive to me. I was working three jobs and was fitting in the writing at differ-ent places. It was like I was following the characters, once the characters emerged. But the questions were ones I was not allowed to ask, growing up in a religious environment, and they fill the book. I did have a day, a Saturday, when Kim and the kids were gone and there was no job to take my time. I started at eight in the morning and in eight and a half hours, I wrote four complete chapters. The fourth of those is "Festival of Friends," which is in the book the way I wrote it. It's never been touched by any rewrite process. I told Kim when she got home that I got swept along by this river and got tossed out twenty miles downstream.

Did you publish any other books? Are you working on other projects?

No, no. But I'm working on stuff. I didn't even intend to publish this. But I'm working on a narrative, biographical piece and some fiction. There's some science fiction that is waiting. And probably stories that have happened around *The Shack*. I have well over a hundred thousand e-mails from all over the world and I've met so many people who have told me their stories. They're remarkable. You just say, "Who would have thought?" You know? Not me. Again, the grace of being allowed to participate in something.

Any other points you'd like to make?

Well, in terms of the controversy, I think it's really healthy. I think it's good. It's part of the conversation. It doesn't bother me. The only time it has bothered me is when it has been an attack against my children, when people have really stepped over the line. But you know, people are people and they bring to the table what they have. I think the controversy indicates that even religious people are involved in the conversation. Which is good.

Questions posed by Brad Penner
Transcribed and edited by Robert Jewett

2

Shame and the Unwanted Self

SHAME IS ONE OF the most difficult aspects of the human condition to understand and to live with.[1] In this chapter, I want to argue that it touches on the very nature of what it is to be human in society. Shame is familiar to most of us in one way or another, both individually and socially. For better, and often for worse, the capacity to experience shame is part of what makes us the humans that we are, individually and collectively. And this experience or phenomenon is not entirely without its important positive and helpful effects. However, shame can and often does connote misery, diminishment, and discomfort, especially if it comes to dominate a person's or group's attitude to itself. It is not an easy subject to deal with either in theory or in practice. Even thinking about it can make us feel uneasy, as if we might be contaminated by this acutely uncomfortable condition just by considering it. The idea of shame, let alone the experience of it, can seem defiling or polluting. At first blush, then, shame seems to be an unwanted phenomenon which figures unwantedness—toxic unwantedness at that.

I want here to do several things. First, I will try to get a handle on the understanding and experience of ordinary, reactive psychological shame or the kind that most of us experience in Western society. After a short diversion to consider some complexifying theoretical factors like the changing nature and objects of shame over time and cultures, I then turn to the main type of shame which I want to address here, chronic shame. This is the kind of shame that becomes a habitual character trait and which can form a lifelong blight for individuals and communities.

9

I consider the factors that bring this kind of shame into existence and maintain it, and the pernicious and damaging effects that it can have. I then look at the possibilities of countering it and achieving healing and integration. Unfortunately, churches and religious communities are themselves places where, mostly unwittingly, chronic shame can be engendered and reinforced. So I turn to suggest some of the ways in which Christian ideas and practices may be involved in this. I then suggest some ways in which Christian believers and theologians might be able to re-orient themselves to live more responsibly and creatively with shame. Shame is not something that lies only outside the church; this needs to be owned by Christians if we are to provide balm, not blame, for those individuals and groups who are crippled by it—including many church members. Finally, I make some suggestions as to how Christian theology and practice might be re-oriented to line up better with the mission of the man Jesus, apostle to the shamed, who came to seek and save the lost and to restore their image and face in the kingdom of God.

NORMAL, PSYCHOLOGICAL SHAME

It is possible that everyone has some basic and perhaps unconscious experience of ontological shame or shame of existence—a kind of shame that arises in infancy simply from coping with the fact that one is small, naked, weak, and powerless.[2] Beyond this, most people have some conscious experience of acute shame, often in their early life. Often the incident that caused the shame reaction to arise, and which can still cause it to recur years after the event, seems trivial. Standing in the wrong place, wearing the "wrong" clothes, having a different lunch box, saying something stupid, or failing to understand a game can all make a young child feel deeply ashamed and embarrassed.

I can still remember, and even now feel a reddening of my cheeks and a cold sweat threatening, at an insensitive remark I made to a boy whose birthday party I was attending more than fifty years ago. Having made it, I wished that the heavens would fall in, that I would disappear, or that I could hide somewhere, never to be seen again. This vivid, early experience of shame captures something important about the essence of the condition. The shamed person realizes that in some way they have dropped out of the realm of normal behavior and expectations as seen through the eyes of critical others. In a minor, and hopefully temporary way, they have become less than acceptable and fully human in the context of the community that surrounds them.

Shame, then, brings the person experiencing it up short. Psychologically, it acts like a kind of brake, making the person freeze for a moment and reconsider their position. The shamed individual is suddenly vividly aware of the workings of their self and feels inadequate, inferior, exposed, small, and weak in such a way that they are temporarily paralyzed and disabled. They may well turn their face away from others, slump downward, and avoid eye contact. Significantly, they may lose the capacity to speak to or communicate with others—they become literally speechless and banished from the social realm of language.

Shame returns us into ourselves in a way that makes us self-conscious, self-pre-occupied, and deeply dissatisfied with the suddenly naked, "noisy," and all-too-visible inadequate self, seen, as it were, through the eyes of judgmental others. Indeed, it exposes us to a sense of ourselves as vile, defiled, rejected, unwanted, and unwantable. We become dirt to ourselves and may literally feel like shit. It may take a while for this sense of self-rejection, isolation, and paralysis to dissipate, and for the person to feel accepted and accept himself or herself again and resume unselfconscious functioning as a full member of the human community and resume normal relations with self and others.[3]

Early experiences of shame like this may be quite disproportionate to the amount of offense or inhumanity committed or threatened. Indeed, from an objective point of view, no real offense may have been committed at all—it is not morally wrong or damaging to others if a child comes to school in clothes or with food unlike those of other children. I very much doubt that the boy I inadvertently offended remembers me now, let alone the event that seared itself into me half a century ago.

What I have described is what might be called a normal, contemporary psychological experience of shame in reaction to a specific event. This kind of "normal," individual and psychological reaction is appropriate because it stops people from ploughing on with acts of possible deviance or inhumanity to others and makes them consider what is happening very carefully. It may be quite momentary and brief; it functions as a temporary disrupter of action that sharply reminds individuals of a threat to their relations with other members of the human race and community. Their sense of belonging is brought into focus and into question. Sometimes, it might point toward a possibly important breach in relations with others, such as when one is in danger of treating some group or individual very badly. In this sense, shame can be a great preserver of respect for others. At other times, shame might emerge over quite trivial things, like not wearing the appropriate clothes for attending a dinner or a garden party. But one way and another, reactive shame is an important way of reminding people of their connections to others and to society and getting them to assess their behavior and expectations so that they do not lose significant bonds and connections.[4]

The reactively shamed person is powerfully reminded that they need to get back in contact with the humans around them, or at least to think carefully about the threatened state of the bonds and relationships that surround them. Even in reactive shame, restoring these bonds may not be easy because the feeling of retreat and deprivation of agency evoked by shame takes away people's sense that they can do anything about their situation. This is in strong contrast to the state of guilt, where a person can commit a clear offense, have a sense of conscious responsibility about it, apologize, and then undertake direct reparative action to put things right with the offended person.[5] A guilty person is a responsible self who has committed an offense. Their whole identity is not impaired by this so they can act to make amends. Shamed persons feel that it is their whole identity and self that is inadequate and impaired. They therefore cannot act to remedy their situation. Shame is a judgment on the whole self, not just on an aspect of action of behavior.

The person who experiences reactive shame can be left speechless, powerless, and uncomfortable without having committed any kind of moral offense and with no form or remedy for undoing the shame, whether it is trivial or profound. Hence the memory of shaming experiences and acts can hang around for years even if no real offense of significance has been committed. Some people who complain of feeling perpetually guilty about small things then are really talking about a sense of irredeemable shame. Unfortunately, shame like this is not amenable to apology, reparation, and forgiveness. Even more seriously, it can act as a distorting lens that stops people from being able to recognize and address their real guilt. Of course, guilt at real offense and shame at acting in a less-than-human way often go closely together and occur simultaneously. But if they are not carefully distinguished, shamed people may label their condition as one of guilt; they may then wonder why their attempts at repentance and reparation do little to restore their sense of self-acceptance and belonging within their reference communities and relationships.

UNDERSTANDING SHAME:
SOME THEORETICAL OBSERVATIONS

I have already begun to move away from the basic experience of reactive shame to discuss some of the pathologies that can accompany and complexify shame in human life, e.g., the way in which guilt and shame can be conflated. To pursue this further, having distinguished normal, reactive, psychological shame, I now want to discuss the nature of chronic shame.[6] This is not normal, functional, specific, contextual, and possibly helpful at times. It denotes a habitual approach to self and to life. It is the condition of the "unwanted self" of my title and it represents a condition of lasting alienation, toxic unwantedness, and defilement that is deeply damaging to self and others.[7]

But before doing that I want to make a few important theoretical observations about understanding shame of all kinds. First, shame is not just something that can be understood in one way. Many disciplines bear on the understanding of shame—from literature to biology, psychology, philosophy, and sociology.[8] There is no one way of understanding shame and it can mean many things to different disciplines and people.

Secondly, shame is not just an individual matter. In the culture of ancient Palestine, and indeed in many nonindividualistic cultures today, shame is not regarded so much as an individual psychological condition but as a social one.[9] Thus shame represents a breach in social relationships and is categorized as being the opposite of honor. The breach of honor produces shame, and this disruption in social relations is deeply felt and requires action to remove dishonoring pollution. Sometimes this takes the form of revenge, as in the case of honor killings where family honor is restored and stain of shame removed by the person who has induced the shame being murdered. So shame can be seen as an unwanted, polluting condition for groups that has a kind of objectivity that is not merely temporary, psychological, or emotional—and this can lead to profound, important, and sometimes very unpredictable social effects. Arguably, it was the shaming of the whole German nation at the end of the First World War that contributed to the rise of Hitler and the persecution of the Jews. [10]

Just because shame is not individual does not mean that it is not intolerable, and I will return to the negative effects of shame soon. A final point to make here, though, is that shame does not only vary in nature, understanding, and effects over cultures, it, and the things that bring it about, may also change significantly. A collection of letters about shame and sex assembled by researchers in Finland reveals that in the 1950s women were ashamed of having had pre-marital sex while their granddaughters are more likely to feel ashamed of not having had sex before marriage.[11] All of which should make us even more aware of the slippery and changing nature and understandings of shame. So it is important to try to understand exactly what is meant by shame and what causes it in particular times, contexts, and circumstances.

With that caveat in mind, I would like to return to the nature, experience, and understanding of shame that is found in Western capitalist society where shame is seen principally as a very personal emotional matter of the individual psyche. While it is generally true that shame is regarded an immediate, urgent, and reactive thing, I will argue that shame is not just an immediate emotional experience and also that it can be exacerbated and used by society in various ways. So, for example, some governments believe that naming and shaming groups and individuals so they compare themselves unfavorably with others is a good way of getting them to change their unsatisfactory ways. But let us in the first instance return to the situation of individuals who find themselves experiencing chronic or pathological shame.

UNDERSTANDING CHRONIC SHAME

For many people shame is an immediate, sharp, acute, but temporary experience of self-failure. However, for some people self-failure, or the experience of being a toxically unwanted or impaired self, seems to become an integral aspect of their lives, not just an occasional unpleasant event. It becomes a character or personality trait. Such people appear to experience the whole of life as potentially or actually shame productive, and habitually manifest such traits as withdrawal, self-contempt, inferiority, and gaze-aversion. In this context, shame becomes pathological and chronic, and the people affected by it can be described as shame-bound and shame-prone. They manifest a deeply engrained habitual mode of reacting to self and others.[12] They therefore live diminished and fearful lives, unable to enter fully into responsive and responsible relations with others that might provoke further shame experiences. Some such shame-bound or shame-prone people may be conscious of their condition, but it is also possible for shame to manifest itself in an indirect or unidentified form in which the person just feels bad but does not recognize this as shame.[13] Some people do not even feel shame directly at all, and simply live in a world of "bypassed" shame that can only be recognized in, for example, a persistent tendency to compare oneself unfavorably with others.

What causes people to become chronically shamed? There is probably no single factor that brings it about. However, any experience that constitutes a rejection, objectification, or boundary invasion of the person so he or she feels social or individual inferiority, worthlessness, alienation, or abandonment is likely to contribute to it, especially if such experiences are multiplied or prolonged. Some writers think there may even be biological and genetic factors involved here, citing, for example, the perception that women seem to be more shame-prone than men.[14] Beyond this, if infants do not have their narcissistic needs met within the loving gaze and attention of a parent, it is suggested that they may come to have an incurable sense of worthlessness, inferiority, and alienation.[15] Children who experience emotional, physical, and psychological abuse and neglect in so-called shame-bound families are likely to come to see themselves as worthless, particularly if their boundaries are physically or psychologically invaded so they see themselves as powerless.[16] Toxic parenting that breaks the will of the child and so makes them feel inferior and weak is relevant here.[17] And similar boundary-breaking events such as rape can also produce a sense of habitual shame in which individuals hate themselves rather than their violators. Education and schooling can reinforce feelings of inferiority and incompetence, as can incarceration and bullying. And then wider social factors such as not having a worthwhile job or not being able to provide for or protect others can help to create or amplify a sense of hopeless shame, whether overt or bypassed. Belonging to a despised or suspected social group, such as an ethnic or sexual minority, can also help to buttress the habitual sense of inferiority, worthlessness, and alienation.

It is not difficult to imagine a person who might experience all of these individual, familial, and social factors; indeed many people experience many or most of them. This makes the point indirectly that there is a politics to shame. Even if chronic shame is located in the individual, social circumstances, habits, and opportunities can have an enormous impact on its development or alleviation. Any experiences or circumstances that induce a sense of persistent inferiority, worthlessness, abandonment, weakness, abjection, unwantedness, violation, defilement, stigmatization, and unlovability are likely to contribute to chronic shame. And chronically shamed individuals, whether they are conscious of their condition or not, will probably have endured much that is very difficult and destructive in their lives. They are unlikely to have a well-founded sense of worth and may be very unclear about boundaries between self and others. Unable to respect themselves, they may also disrespect and distrust those around them as well as having little sense of personal agency and power.

"Almost any affect feels better than shame."[18] So painful is the effect of shame, the sense of failed, defiled, or toxically unwanted self, that chronically shamed people learn to defend against experiencing it and develop defensive scripts. Don Nathanson talks about four possible main responses in what he calls The Compass of Shame.[19] These are:

- Withdrawal (literal and physical and/or psychological and internal), often interpreted as depression;

- Attack Self (e.g., by ritual humiliation and putting down the self, or by masochistic and self-harming practices that deprive others of the chance to damage the self);

- Avoidance (deceiving the self about its defective nature by, e.g., being grandiose and perfectionist, or associating with the power and influence of others, even God, or flight into addiction and behaviors that allow forgetting of the self);

- Attack others (engaging in contempt or rage against others, putting them down, bullying them, blaming them, etc., to provide the self with a sense of its own goodness and power).

The outworkings of these responses are often, as implied above, destructive to self, to groups, and to others.[20] Depression, addiction, abuse, violence, eating disorders, compulsive behaviors, and many other pathological and self- and other-harming habits and conditions can all be linked to shame and the fundamental experience of the defiled and unwanted self: "I am a flawed and defective human being. I am a mistake."[21]

Perhaps one of the most serious implications for shame-prone, toxically unwanted people is that they are unable to behave truly morally with efficacy, freedom, responsibility, and choice. If you are not really a member of the human community, even if you conform to some norms (perhaps to please people and so avoid shame), you remain in a pre- or amoral state, focussed fundamentally on yourself and not on others and the acts or courses of action that might really help them. In my opinion, shame often gets in the way of people experiencing and responding to true guilt, e.g., with reparation and repentance because they remain fundamentally trapped in wanting to avoid further self-humiliation and hurt to the whole of their wounded global self. They act a part so they can retain a sense of self-respect rather than being able to see that offense and action is just part of what constitutes human behavior. Shamed people need to grow up into full membership of the human community to become guilty people whose whole selves are not implicated in any sense of criticism or offense, however small and insignificant. It is thus that I call for more guilt and less shame as a sign of development and health.

Because shame is so amorphous and unstructured, and because, like miasma or slime, it can so easily seep into people's fundamental sense of their own value, threatening their global sense of self (you do not have shame, you are ashamed), I believe it is very dangerous for people to think that shame is a good tool for controlling criminals and others in society. It's much better to have a clear system of crimes, offenses, punishments, and reparative demands that can be met by guilty individuals with an intact sense of self. However, bullying, humiliation, stigmatization, scapegoating, and other practices and structures that challenge and weaken the sense of the responsible and responsive self are widespread in contemporary organizations as mechanisms of social control, either deliberately or inadvertently. Shame and humiliation form some of the most powerful tools for social influence; after all, shamed people may be unhappy, but like depressed people (which they might also be), they are often malleable, quiescent, and biddable, wanting to be seen as "good" and acceptable through the eyes of others. Unfortunately, the deployment of these methods is likely to create and exacerbate shame and lead to an increase in amoral or immoral behavior in the long run. This is a tragic state of affairs.

Sadly, Christian churches are among those groups who fail to understand how shame works and how it can be counteracted. I will move on to discuss this and the theological and practical responses that might be more appropriate for changing this, but first a little bit about whether chronic shame can in fact be "cured" or dealt with effectively, either in individuals or groups.

HEALING CHRONIC SHAME AND RE-INTEGRATION

Shame denotes alienation, isolation, defilement, depletion, and pain, both individual and social. Chronic shame casts a baleful and toxic miasmic shadow across individuals, families, groups, even whole societies. To deal with it, re-integration is required so people can face up to it and to themselves. However, given the depth and gravity of the causes and sustaining factors in shame, it can be very difficult to address effectively. In the first place, it is often to recognize or wish to recognize shame and its effects as it is such a slippery and polluting condition. On the individual level, a combination of visual (face cast down), linguistic (hard on self, hard on others), and paralinguistic factors (addictive behaviors) may have to be recognized as constituting a chronically shamed identity.[22] There are various informal methods such as integrating ritual and humor that can enable individuals to escape from shame. Loving personal relations can help a lot. But in all these instances, the means of healing may also be a way of denying or even deepening shame. Consider the potential of wrongly directed or interpreted laughter and humor for deepening humiliation, and rituals can be a way of excluding as much as including people. Leon Wurmser points out that creativity, self-loyalty, and masking can be ways of heroically transcending shame for individuals, as in the cases of people like Beethoven and Ibsen, but again, failure to engage with the world may even weaken a person's sense of efficacy.[23] Within the self-help literature for individuals, John Bradshaw suggests that shamed people need to come out of hiding, to externalize and recognize their condition and engage with the human race in something like the twelve-step programs advocated by Alcoholics Anonymous.[24] Once again, this is far more easily said than done because shamed people may have great difficulty in meeting and trusting the people they need to gain the healing they seek. In psychotherapy, which some individuals may seek, it is recognized that shame is a difficult condition to diagnose, live with, and heal. Shamed individuals may evoke the shame of their psychotherapist, and even the attention of the therapist may seem invasive and shame-reinforcing. Even the fact that the therapist may seem to have knowledge and skill may make a shamed person feel inferior, envious, and humiliated. Carl Goldberg acknowledges that the "the treatment of shame . . . at best . . . is a creative and compassionate art." [25] Change, if it occurs, will be gradual and requires the surrendering and rebuilding of identity—a very tall order for those who feel powerless and without efficacy in their lives.

Turning to groups and society, we have noted that shame is a very effective way to control and manipulate people, even as it makes clear the boundaries of groups in a tribal way. It is difficult to conceive of an earthly society or institution that can exist without boundaries and sense of insiders and outsiders. So shame in some ways is inevitable. However, it may be possible to create a critical ethical attitude of recognition that goes alongside a determination to create decent institutions that do not unnecessarily or casually humiliate and alienate people.[26] Richard Sennett suggests that it is possible to help individuals and groups recognize the dynamics of domination, submission, and abuse so they can be made overt and can be transcended as autonomy, freedom, and proper responsibility are developed.[27] More immediately, people who work with those who are likely to be humiliated can offer recognition, negotiation, collaboration, celebration, relaxation, validation, and facilitation. Organizational and societal life structured around an ethic and practice of personal and social recognition is neither unimaginable, nor unattainable, but it clearly requires attention, work and commitment if it is to become a reality so that shame is not reproduced and reinforced in individuals and groups.[28]

CHRISTIAN PRACTICE AND THEOLOGY IN RELATION TO SHAME

The Western Protestant Christian tradition, the bit of Christianity that I know best, has not devoted much attention to shame either in theory or in practice. While salvation and atonement have been central to Protestantism, the alienation that humans experience from God, sin, which is healed in Jesus Christ, is predominantly understood in terms of willed offense, guilt, and reparation. This follows Lutheran and Augustinian understandings of the human condition. Like many secular systems and world views, contemporary Western Christianity tends to bracket out and shy away from shame, particularly chronic shame. While the language of dirt and defilement is often used in relation to sin, the real locus of this abjection and pollution within groups and individuals is shame, not guilt. And shame, unlike guilt, is not nearly so amenable to remedy and change as overt, conscious offense against others. So you might say, the church talks dirty to get the attention of the shamed, the polluted and unwanted, but because of its focus on guilt as the main component of sin, it fails to offer the real means of cleanliness and acceptance that might move shamed people from amoral marginalization to communal belonging and responsibility.

Even in the sphere of pastoral theology, where there has been a flurry of books on understanding and dealing with shame over the past couple of decades, there is not much sense of how you might help people to overcome shame that does not really come from psychological and other secular literature (which as already noted, is not really very strong on how to "cure" chronic shame).[29] A few twentieth-century theologians have given some general attention to shame (Bonhoeffer, Tillich, Barth) but here again there tends to be a lack of specific help and guidance on how chronic, dysfunctional shame might be healed. It is only recently that some thinkers have begun to revise the Augustinian view of the New Testament to see shame and honor as main categories for understanding Jesus' work and early Christian life and thought rather than guilt and offense.[30] Overcoming fundamental shame establishes basic belonging and the possibility of honor and respect in the human community. Overcoming guilt establishes and maintains ongoing relations of respect and responsibility within the community. So both are necessary, but the overcoming of shame and primary alienation must come first. So overall, Christians, along with many of our non-Christian contemporaries it must be said, start from a low base in trying positively to address the experience of shame and alienation.

Worse than that, however, because we have not much considered the nature, theology, and healing of shame, many of our ideas and practices may actually contribute to it. For some people, their experience of Christianity has actually heightened their sense of shame. (Of course, others have found Christianity very helpful—but what I am pointing to here is a profound ambivalence in the effects of this religious tradition on its adherents.) Theologically, the idea that God is an all-perfect, all-powerful, and all-seeing "King" can heighten their sense of insignificance and being seen as unworthy.[31] The Old Testament picture of God as a despot who laughs his enemies to scorn and shame or who sees people wherever they are is still part of the Christian tradition of public worship and can contribute to some people feeling terror, inadequacy, or shame. That God is disembodied can also lead to a devaluing of the human body (despite the doctrine of the incarnation), and the purity and holiness of God can lead to an increased sense dirt and defilement. That this God is also unbiddable, apparently arbitrary, and often apparently absent in times of need, and despite exhortation, can also lead to powerlessness and humiliation among God's vulnerable children. This idealized God can be powerfully attractive to the shamed who want to be healed, identified with power, and included within the loving parental gaze. But their encounter with this deity and the ideas and practices surrounding God in theology and worship can all too often reinforce the sense of powerlessness, defilement, unworthiness, and alienation.

Such people can find their experience of this kind of God tormenting.[32] They may also find that Christian understandings of sin continue to trap them in a perpetual feeling of worthlessness with no end. And even the idealizing example of Jesus as perfect man can exacerbate feelings of futility, humiliation, and lack of identification.[33] Christianity continually condemns the sin of pride and advocates humility. But destructive over-assertion can often be confused with having and sense of self and agency. Shamed people need a sense of self-esteem and self-worth. Too much teaching on sin and pride can be misunderstood as the condemnation of having an identity or pleasure in oneself and one's own proper talents, wishes, and achievements. This is perhaps particularly pernicious when the objects of teaching on pride and selfishness are children who have still to establish a firm sense of self. But, of course, the self itself is problematic in Christian teaching. From Augustine onward, the individual person has often been seen as a degraded site of resistance to the will of God. It is, then, difficult for some Christian people to have a sense that it is right to value one's own flesh, spirit, and intentions rather than denying it and trying to dispose of it. And this sort of attitude plays straight into the hands of shame.

I am by no means trying to suggest here that Christian theology and practice inevitably has a shame-inducing or shame-maintaining effect on people. The tradition is pluralistic and multivalent in the meanings it generates, and those meanings are received in very different ways by different Christians. But I do want to suggest that it can have equivocal, perhaps unintended, effects on believers in bolstering their shame. Later, I will suggest that this ambivalence needs to be owned and managed. But let me first say a little about the kinds of practices that might exacerbate or at least not help people to overcome their shame. Again, I am not arguing that any particular practice inevitably causes or exacerbates shame, but simply suggesting that our good intentions in practice can produce strange and possibly baleful consequences for some people.

One set of practices has to do with liturgy. Here, not only do people routinely have to acknowledge their faults (real and imagined), they also often kneel before God, acknowledging the unequal, dependent relationship that an inferior may have with a superior in a traditional, hierarchical society. Some liturgical practices in churches are also overtly excluding: not everyone is allowed to take communion, for example, and those who cannot read may feel they are made to feel unwanted. The language of power, royalty, domination, obedience, submission, and humility to be found in many hymns, prayers, and sermons may also serve to buttress the sense of inferiority and unwantedness experienced by the chronically shamed.

Outside formal Christian worship, believers' child-rearing practices that focus on obedience, self-control and self-denial, reflecting the "will of God," and sometimes supplemented by physical beating and punishment can help to make children feel shamed and alienated from self and others. It is not uncommon to hear Christians advocating smacking and corporal punishment along the lines of "spare the rod and spoil the child."[34] Unfortunately the child is often not so much spoiled as shamed and ruined, partly in the name of obeying God's will.

Christian moral attitudes and teaching can also have a baleful effect on creating and maintaining shame. Much Christian moral teaching proclaims ideals or purity and perfectionism that are far beyond what many shamed people can manage. Of course, they are attracted to such ideals in the hope of relinquishing their stained and inadequate identity, but their failure to live up to them can reinforce a sense of powerlessness, exclusion, and self-rejection. A main locus for the production and reinforcement of shame is in teaching about the body, sex, and gender, often taken as boundary issues for Christian identity and belonging.[35] In general terms, there is a long history in Christianity of distrusting and disparaging the body and its desires and appetites. Bodily weakness is feared and despised. Many churches still talk about women as second-class citizens whose presence is somehow defiling and polluting in ministry. And their teaching on homosexuality and sex both within and outside marriage can be crushing to those who find themselves on the wrong side of it. The church may regard itself as a community of sinners, but some of those sinners can be very good at excluding others from the fellowship of grace, sometimes with disastrous effects on individuals and groups. This is perhaps particularly evident in disciplinary processes with clergy and others. Often, real wickedness in terms of clerical misbehavior is tolerated unless it becomes public. But if such offenses become known, the guilty person is often then treated as an outcast and excluded from the community. This maintains communal boundaries and purity, but once again it colludes with mechanisms of shame that downplay responsibility and forgiveness. Churches that run on the dynamics of the preservation of "face," honor, and respect rather than on the principles of guilt, repentance, and forgiveness risk discouraging honesty along with personal and communal growth.

So, it would seem that churches are far from immune to the influence and use of shame. This is not confined to any one church or religious community. Furthermore, shame is implicated in religious life in complex and subtle ways—it is not usual for churches consciously to seek to foster shame and not all church members will have their lives affected by it. Shame emerges from a complex ecology of personal psychology and circumstances, parental, family, and communal attitudes, and religious beliefs and practice. So it cannot be said that religion is always a direct and primary cause of shame. However, Christian beliefs and practices can fail to challenge shame-causing factors and practices, such as child abuse and neglect, and the slippery vocabulary of guilt, shame, humility, disgust, and redeeming victimization can in many ways help to buttress shame in individuals and groups. Too often, theological ideas and religious practices can be recruited into an idealizing system that contributes inadvertently to low self-esteem, rejection, humiliation, and alienation that chronically shamed individuals and groups experience. And there are still Christians who argue for the value and benefits of shame as a fundamental orientation to life. That being said, it must also be acknowledged that for some, perhaps many Christians, their faith has been a source of healing from shame. Some of these Christians would say that their engagement with faith had sometimes created shame and then sometimes healed it at different points in their lives.

The relationship between shame and Christianity, as with other human institutions, is an ambivalent one. For my own part, I don't think churches can ever be entirely free of shame and potential shame-generating ideas and practices. Wherever a group of people gathers together and defines itself over against others, there will always be the possibility of exclusion, particularly if a group pursues stretching ideals. Shame is part of human life and it cannot therefore be eliminated. However, it may be possible for Christians to become a little bit more aware of the unintended consequences of shame and the practices and ideas that might engender and buttress it, and thus better represent more adequately a commitment to incarnational healing. So in the final part of this paper, I want to make a few suggestions for how Christians might live more responsibly and responsively with shame.

LIVING RESPONSIBLY AND RESPONSIVELY WITH SHAME

First, it would be helpful if churches became more conscious of their own use of possible shaming practices and ideas. Shame is a powerful tool for maintaining conformity and order and it is doubtful that any human organization can eliminate it as a way of holding the community together and differentiating it from the outside world. However, it is qualitatively different to be consciously aware of, and take responsibility for tendencies such as bullying, abuse, and exclusion than just accepting these things as an inevitable part of life. Christians need to examine the mechanisms of "pastoral power" that are used in their communities and consider whether they are appropriately exercised.[36] Related to this, Christians might like to consider the use of the language of dirt, defilement, and corruption in their liturgies and theologies. While these may be a powerful attraction to the shamed who seek cleansing and acceptance, if used carelessly they can simply trap people in an endless circle of self-denigration and rejection. Does the church, then, exploit people and keep them in a position of dependence by deploying this kind of language and thought? Are there other languages and concepts that might be more empowering and liberating?

Beyond recognizing the shaming potential of practices, ideas, and languages that can be used to control and exploit people, it would also be helpful perhaps if Christians were to develop a less idealized view of

God and of themselves as the children of God or the body of Christ. If the community over-identifies with and even fuses itself with a perfect, all-good, all-powerful deity, then it will find it difficult to accept and recognize impurity and evil within itself, as well as insisting on an idealized practice which may well be beyond many of its adherents. Idealizing dualism helps to create demonized and impure "others" who may then be despised, victimized, scapegoated or rejected, e.g., Jews, homosexual people. Ecclesiastical self-idealization and over-identification with God help create a sense of cohesion, efficacy, and value within the church. But they can negate attempts to recognize and respond to shame, alienation and victimhood, both within and outside the church. It is surely time to turn from the illusory purity of a tribal church to face the needs and hurts of all God's children.

On a more specific level, Christians can try to be more aware of the workings of shame within themselves, and also attempt to listen to the experiences of the shamed rather than pushing these people away or encouraging them to dissemble and cloak their shame with lies and appearance. There are implications here for pastoral workers, but it would also be possible for worship leaders to be more sensitive about the kinds of words and attitudes they include in worship.

The interests and needs of children might also be more carefully thought about. Abused and shamed people do not need a sense of sin, they need a sense of loved and valued self; this should be at the forefront of Christian education. Too many children have been made to walk the way of the cross and self-denial in the valley of the shadow of death as they have been abused; often, religious groups have either condoned or ignored their situation, sometimes, tragically, they have provided and effectively sustained the abusers.[37] Perhaps the inclusion of contemporary stories of shame and abuse might be allowed a place in the Christian community to re-balance a system of idealized thought and practice that appears to marginalize the neglected and alienated. If the purpose of Christianity is to allow people to help people to love God and their neighbour as themselves, then working toward inclusion and identification for all is of vital importance if shame is to be kept in its place as a response to temporary breach of social bonds rather than a lifelong role or character disposition.

Theologically, there is a further re-dressing of the balance of shame and humiliation that might be of assistance. Theologians could aim to emphasize and explore the fundamental goodness and value of creation and of humanity. The emphasis on the redemption through Christ being attained though his crucified victimhood might be modified by a more holistic approach to the salvation as part of creation and the whole life and work of Jesus so that shame-producing victimhood is not the exalted model for Christian self-understanding and living. Thus redemption could be seen less as the exaltation of historical victimhood and more as part of an active, ongoing, creative, and reconciling process in the contemporary world whereby the living are raised into membership of the living body of Christ. Within this general theological framework it might be more helpful to see the alienation that exists between God and humanity as the brokenheartedness of frail humans rather than sin, guilt, and offense against a divine despot. The reconstruction of what we mean by discovering the face and image of God might be a further implication of the quest to find a more inclusive, practical, and less shaming set of theological concepts. Let me finish, then, by talking a little about Jesus as the image of a God who is courteous, respectful, and inclusive in healing relationships that overcome shame.

JESUS: APOSTLE TO THE SHAMED

Jesus is the apostle of a kingdom that inverts the relationships of this world so that the first come last, the poor are rich, and the excluded and misfits are guests of honor. His ministry subverts the tribal systems of shame and honor that conferred membership, identity, and humanity in the ancient social world. Two particular incidents represent this inclusive subversion powerfully and poignantly.

In Luke 13:10–16 a crippled woman comes to Jesus in the synagogue on the Sabbath. She is bent double and unable to stand upright. Thus, presumably, she could not look into the faces of those around her. Jesus heals her so that she can stand straight and see into the faces of others once again. The others in the synagogue, however, are disgusted with Jesus' action. He then rebukes them, at which point they are ashamed. One takes it that they were the ones who then had to cast their eyes to the ground before the woman whose dignity had been restored. It is when we collude with the shaming of others as a group that shame properly belongs to us and we lose our humanity.[38] If we are lucky, this kind of shame of realizing our inhumanity might cause us to repent and turn back on our wicked ways. Thus, shame can be a catalyst for change.

A second story from Luke also bears upon shaming and inclusion here. Luke 19:1–10 recounts the encounter of Jesus with Zacchaeus, a tax gatherer, therefore a sinner and social outcast, one of the shamed. When Jesus visits Jericho, Zacchaeus climbs a tree to see him. Coming to the tree, Jesus looks upward and addresses him, calling him down so he can stay in his house. Zacchaeus hurries down and welcomes him joyfully. He takes Jesus to his house and then announces that he proposes to give half his property to the poor and pay back those whom he has cheated. The story ends with Jesus rejoicing in Zacchaeus's salvation; "For the son of man is come to seek and save that which was lost" (Luke 19:10).

This is a wonderful example and paradigm for the overcoming of shame and alienation. Jesus looks up into Zacchaeus's face from below, thus being anything but invasive, bullying, or dominating. He calls Zacchaeus by name, showing respect for him. He then asks something of Zacchaeus that he can easily give, demonstrating that he does not despise or reject him and affirming his efficacy and agency. The recognition of personhood and inclusion and affirmation that Jesus offers makes Zacchaeus want to include himself further. From alienated and despised immoral pariah, he becomes a moral person who aims to take responsibility for the needs and rights of others, someone who can feel guilt and offer reparation. A lost, outcast, immoral man, rejected by the community becomes integrated into Jesus' community by the conferral of respect and love that removes the stain and power of shame. He then starts to behave like a responsible person.

It seems to me that the shame-removing and morally empowering process figured in this story forms both parable and process for Christians to begin to explore how they might combat the pernicious effects of chronic shame in individuals, groups, and society. For those who follow the one who came to seek and save the lost, this story provides both warrant and inspiration for doing likewise.

ENDNOTES

1. This chapter is substantially based on my study, *Shame*.

2. Nussbaum, *Hiding from Humanity*, 177–89.

3. For more on the symptoms of individualized psychological shame mentioned here see, e.g., Pattison, *Shame*, 71–82. My characterization there is informed by Block Lewis, *Role of Shame*; Kaufman, *Psychology of Shame*; Lewis, *Shame*; Lynd, *On Shame*; Scheff, *Emotions*.

4. See further Scheff, *Emotions*, for the importance of shame as a marker of social and emotional bonds.

5. For a discussion of the differences between guilt and shame, see e.g., Pattison, *Shame*, 43–45.

6. For more on different "types" of shame, positive and negative, see Schneider, *Shame, Exposure and Privacy*.

7. For this characterization of shame, which situates it within the metaphorical ecology of dirt and stain, rather than that of offense, see Pattison, *Shame*, 88–92. My discussion there draws on, e.g., Douglas, *Purity and Danger*; Parker, *Miasma*.

8. See further Pattison, *Shame*, 39–64.

9. See Jewett, *St. Paul Returns, Romans*; also Malina, *Social World*.

10. See Scheff, *Emotions*.

11. I owe this knowledge to Teemu Ratinen, a Finnish research student who is working on the letters.

12. See Pattison, *Shame*, 93.

13. See further Block Lewis, *Role of Shame*, 197; Pattison, *Shame*, 85–86.

14. See, e.g., Block Lewis, *Role of Shame*.

15. See, e.g., Nussbaum, *Hiding From Humanity*, 177–203.

16. See Donaldson-Pressman and Pressman, *The Narcissistic Family*; Fossum and Mason, *Facing Shame*.

17. See further, e.g., Miller, *For Your Own Good*; Pattison, *Challenge of Practical Theology*, chapter 13, which considers child abuse and its implications for Christian thought and practice.

18. Nathanson, *Shame and Pride*, 312.

19. Ibid., 303ff.

20. See Kaufman, *Psychology of Shame*, 113ff.

21. Bradshaw, *Healing the Shame*, 16.

22. See further, e.g., Pattison, *Shame*, 156–58.

23. See Wurmser, *Mask of Shame*.

24. See Bradshaw, *Healing the Shame*.

25. Goldberg, *Understanding Shame*, 257.

26. Margalit, *Decent Society*, 1.

27. Sennett, *Authority*, 129ff.

28. For more on possible responses to shame, see e.g., Pattison, *Shame*, chapter 7.

29. For some interesting pastoral theological responses to shame, see e.g., Capps, *Depleted Self*; Goodliff, *With Unveiled Face*; McNish, *Transforming Shame*.

The most interesting and suggestive book in this connection in my view remains Patton, *Is Human Forgiveness Possible?*

30. See, e.g., Jewett, *St. Paul; Romans;* Malina, *Social World.*

31. Nietzsche in *The Gay Science,* 38: "Is it true God is present everywhere?" a little girl asks her mother; "I think that's indecent . . ."

32. See Capps, *The Child's Song.*

33. See further Pattison, *Challenge of Practical Theology,* chapter 17, which deals with the shadow side of Jesus and the ambivalent effects understandings of Jesus may have on believers.

34. For a good treatment of punishment and violence in Christian "nurture" of the young, see, e.g., Greven, *Spare the Child.*

35. See further, e.g., Pattison, *Challenge of Practical Theology,* chapter12, which deals with Christian attitudes to the body and sexuality.

36. For more on Foucault's notion of "pastoral power" see Kritzman, *Michel Foucault,* 57ff.

37. See further Pattison, *Challenge of Practical Theology,* chapter 13, which deals with child abuse and Christian practice and theology.

38. For appropriate corporate and social shame which we assign to ourselves and which leads to changes in behavior, see Nussbaum, *Hiding From Humanity.*

3

Shame as the Master Emotion

Examples from Popular Songs

Thomas J. Scheff

I**T IS DIFFICULT TO** understand the importance of shame in modern societies because we live inside an ethos that is highly individualistic and focused on exteriors, especially the material world, but also, in humans, their behavior. In the interior, thought and perception are recognized, but hardly a thought is given to emotions and relationships. This essay attempts an explanation of why shame should be considered to be the master emotion. This idea will be illustrated by pop song lyrics chosen from the most popular, the Top 40 over the past eighty years. Finally, a brief discussion of steps toward managing shame in a way that might change the direction that our civilization is moving.

TAKING THE ROLE OF THE OTHER

Humans, like other mammals, are social creatures first. Not even a close second, they are also stand-alone, self-reliant individuals. There is a deep, virtually automatic link between humans, but it is more or less invisible. As C. H. Cooley, a Protestant minister and early American sociologist, put it: "we live in the minds of others, *without knowing it*."[1]

The literal content of ordinary speech and gesture is so fragmented and contextual as to be confusing if not completely incomprehensible. A whole school of thought, deconstructionism, has been built on this fact. However, their analysis is misleading, since it leaves out a key ingredient

30

in social transactions, role-taking.[2] By an early age, most children have learned to understand speech not only from their own point of view, but also from the point of view of the speaker. Comprehension depends on success in taking the role of the other, in reading their minds, so to speak.

Although there are many misses, some not even close, modern societies depend on a high rate of successful mind reading. Considerable success must occur not only in conversation, but in most other settings as well. A bank, for example, depends on it in making loans, and an automobile driver, for getting through traffic without collisions.

Gradually the child gets so apt at guessing the other's viewpoint and at going back and forth between the two points of view as to forget what he or she is doing. In forgetting, the child becomes the kind of adult that modern societies imagine us all to be, a self-contained individual.

CONNECTEDNESS

Perhaps various degrees of connect and disconnect are both cause and effect of most emotions. Human beings need to be connected with others as much as they need air to breathe, a social oxygen. Disconnected from others, one is alone in the universe. Deep connection, even if only momentary, can feel like union, not only with the other(s) but also with groups, even large groups. Varying degrees of disconnect at the level of individuals and of groups lead to a vast array of problems, large and small.

An example that implies disconnect at all three levels is provided by President Bush's comment after an Iraqi reporter threw his shoes at him in Bagdad: "I don't know what his beef is." This response suggests the failure of connection by one individual with another individual and with another group. It further implies the same lack by one group (the U.S. government) toward another group (the people of Iraq).

Being overconnected can be a problem also. One can be so engulfed in the other(s) as to give up vital aspects of one's self, such as one's creativity. The stasis of traditional societies may be largely due to engulfment. The rabid nationalism that occurs in modern societies has similar results in the long run.

I will treat degree of connectedness and emotion as the main dimensions of *the social-emotional world* (SEW). Although these domains are closely linked, they are separate entities. The first dimension is harder to envision than the emotions, because it is usually taken for granted. The idea of an intersubjective component in consciousness has come up frequently in philosophy and the social sciences, but the implications are seldom explored. As Cooley suggested, mind-reading is so primitive that we usually take it for granted, to the point of invisibility. Cooley's idea is profoundly significant. We have many, many names for connectedness: *intersubjectivity*, and *shared* or *mutual awareness*, are examples from a long list. The term *joint attention* was used by the psychologist Jerome Bruner,[3] when he explained how an infant learns to *read the mind* of its caretaker. The mother, he says, is only trying to teach a new word. She places an object (such as a doll) in her own and the baby's line of sight, shakes it to make sure of the baby's attention, saying "See the pretty DOLLY." In this situation, the baby is encouraged to learn not only the meaning of a word, but also, since both parties are looking at the same object, how to have, jointly with the mother, *a single focus of thought and attention*, to use Erving Goffman's phrase.[4]

John Dewey used still another term, *shared experience*. He proposed that it formed the core of communication and therefore of humanness: "Shared experience is the greatest of human goods. In communication, such conjunction and contact as is characteristic of animals become endearments capable of infinite idealization; they become symbols of the very culmination of nature."[5] This formulation by Dewey, because of its expansive reach, reminds us of the individualist ethos of modern societies, with its emphasis not only on solitary individuals, but also on thought and the material world, rather than the social-emotional one.

SHAME IS SOCIAL AND INDIVIDUAL IN EQUAL MEASURE

Shame, like most emotions, is more or less hidden in modern societies. It is too shameful to even think about, much less discuss. When shame is addressed, even by experts, it is usually considered to be completely internal. However, a brilliant psychoanalyst, Helen Block Lewis, has provided a conception of shame that is equally social and individual.[6] She proposed that shame is a signal of *threat to the bond*. This idea would give shame a social dimension as well as an internal one. Similarly, genuine pride (as contrasted with false pride, egotism) is a signal of a secure bond (connectedness). This idea includes the individualist one, since most of our positive feelings about ourselves involve reaching goals that are also held by others.

Shame can be considered to be the master emotion for several reasons. First, it is probably ubiquitous in human experience and conduct. Cooley suggested why: "[The self] seems to have three principal elements: the imagination of our appearance to the other person; the imagination of his judgment of that appearance, and some sort of self-feeling, such as pride or mortification."[7]

In this passage he restricts self-feelings to the two emotions he thought the most significant, pride and shame (considering "mortification" to be a shame variant). To make sure we understand, he mentions shame three more times in the passage that follows:

> The comparison with a looking-glass hardly suggests the second element, the imagined judgment, which is quite essential. The thing that moves us to *pride or shame is* not the mere mechanical reflection of ourselves, but an imputed sentiment, the imagined effect of this reflection upon another's mind. This is evident from the fact that the character and weight of that other, in whose mind we see ourselves, makes all the difference with our feeling. We are *ashamed* to seem evasive in the presence of a straight-forward man, cowardly in the presence of a brave one, gross in the eyes of a refined one and so on. We always imagine, and in imagining share, the judgments of the other mind. A man will boast to one person of an action—say some sharp transaction in trade—which he would be *ashamed* to own to another.[8]

The way in which Cooley linked intersubjective connectedness, on the one hand, with pride and shame, on the other, suggests ubiquity of both pride and shame. However, his examples, many of which are not included above, all involve shame rather than pride.

Modern societies, built as they are upon a foundation of the mobile, self-reliant individual, rather than the group, are highly alienated, and therefore rife with shame or its anticipation: there is no interaction in which participants do not take an appreciable chance of being slightly embarrassed or a slight chance of being deeply humiliated.[9]

If this sentence is taken literally, it means that shame and/or the anticipation of shame haunts *all* social interaction. Avoidance of shame/embarrassment/humiliation is the driving force behind Goffman's central idea of *impression management*: much of our life is spent anticipating, experiencing, and /or managing shame. That would mean that genuine pride, the signal of connection with the other, would be fairly rare.

In addition to its haunting presence, shame can be considered the master emotion for other reasons as well. One is that shame could be the driving force in our moral lives: it is a sense of shame that propels conscience. Moral thoughts not backed up by a sense of shame have little weight because they are mere thoughts, lost in the galaxy of other thoughts.

Finally, shame can be considered to be the master emotion because it controls the expression and even our recognition of our other emotions, and surprisingly, of shame itself. This idea with respect to other emotions will be illustrated in the discussion of pop song lyrics that touch on the taboo against men crying. The idea of shame about shame turns out to be important for understanding violence, which will also be discussed below.

To sum up, I will treat shame as the master emotion because of its ubiquity in human experience, its role as the force behind conscience, and as the regulator of all of our emotions, including shame itself.

SHAME IMPLIED IN POP SONG LYRICS

The lyrics of the most popular of all pop songs, the Top 40, are designed to elicit emotions, but usually don't name them. The emotion of love is obviously crucial, and almost as visible, the grief and/or anger resulting from what I call heartbreak, the loss of a lover.[10]

Although the word shame is seldom mentioned, pop lyrics also often convey the private and public shame, embarrassment, and humiliation of being rejected. Usually heartbreak songs imply shame indirectly, *sub rosa*: "I thought that bein' strong meant never losin' your self-control / But I'm just drunk enough to let go of my pain, / To hell with my pride, let it fall like rain . . ."[11]

The phrase about pride is a common way of implying shame indirectly. It refers to the embarrassment most men experience if they cry or even feel like crying. Men are trained to believe that crying is unmanly, as is the expression of fear, shame, and even anger. More anger is expressed by men then other emotions because it is least shameful. Even so, for most men, most of their anger is probably suppressed.

In this lyric, shame is implied more strongly: "I pretended I'm glad you went away, / these four walls closin' more every day / And I'm dying inside, / and nobody knows it but me."[12] The phrase "dying inside" is one of many ways to refer to shame without naming it. The pain of rejection is so shameful that it must be hidden from others. One is ashamed both of being rejected and of being ashamed.

An early Beatles song (1968) is a virtual workshop on implying shame without actually mentioning it:

> Here I stand head in hand
> Turn my face to the wall
> If she's gone I can't go on
> Feeling two foot small
> Everywhere people stare
> each and every day
> I can see them laugh at me
> And I hear them say
> Hey, you've got to hide your love away ... [13]

Since the actual word shame sometimes occurs in Top 40 lyrics, even in titles, one might think the emotion of shame is being represented. However, "Ain't It a Shame" and similar phrases do not actually refer to emotion. A similar phrase "What a shame!" occurs in everyday conversation, but it is without specific emotional content, since the same meaning can be conveyed by "What a pity!" In modern societies, direct references to the emotional meaning of shame are infrequent.

The song "Shame is the Shadow of Love" (2004) is a rare exception, written and performed by the English punk-rock singer P. J. Harvey:

> I don't need no rising moon
> I don't need no ball and chain
> I don't need anything with you
> Such a shame, shame, shame
> Shame, shame, shame
> Shame is the shadow of love
>
> You changed my life
> We were as green as grass
> And I was hypnotized
> From the first 'til the last
> Kiss of shame, shame, shame
> Shame is the shadow of love
>
> I'd jump for you into the fire
> I'd jump for you into the flame
> Tried to go forward with my life
> I just feel shame, shame, shame

Shame, shame, shame
Shame is the shadow of love

If you tell a lie
I still would take the blame
If you pass me by
It's such a shame, shame, shame

Although shrewd and attractive, this song never made it to the Top 40, even in England, and probably never will, since it is explicit about shame. It implies that feelings of shame inevitably accompany genuine love. This song names the emotion that so many songs hide, and hints at its close association with love.

SHAME AS THE SHADOW OF LOVE

This lyric by Harvey refers to heartbreak, the pain of being left by one's lover. But unlike other heartbreak lyrics, this one does not suggest grief or anger. Rather it openly refers to shame as the emotion that is causing suffering. Cleverly, the song also uses the word shame in a vernacular way, "It's a shame."

The main emotional risk of loving may be not only the desperate grief of dramatic loss. The song by Harvey recognizes shame, as well as grief, as the main emotions in romantic relationships. Shame is the shadow of love. This observation may point to the answer to a difficult question concerning emotional pain. How can it be experienced as unbearable? This quotation provides a hint. "Since there is shame about shame, it remains under taboo."[14]

Although Gershen Kaufman didn't expand on the idea of "shame about shame," it suggests an explanation of unbearable emotional pain. The idea that one can be ashamed of being ashamed implies that shame, particularly, can loop back on itself, amplifying the original feeling with no natural limit, a chain reaction.

The predicament of persons who blush easily provides an illustration. Students who blush easily when they are embarrassed have told me that whatever the source of the original feeling, their blush further embarrasses them; they become acutely self-conscious. Although the reaction may stop after only one loop, some of them have experienced lengthy cycles of continuing self-amplification. Indeed, I once heard the actor Ian Holm recounting an incident that got out of hand. During a rehearsal, he began blushing because of mistakes he was making in his lines. The more self-conscious he became, the more he blushed, ending in paralysis to the point he had to be carried off stage.

A shame-shame loop can be come a doomsday machine, leading also to lethal endings as well as paralysis or other types of withdrawal and silence. The psychiatrist James Gilligan (1997) spent many years as a prison psychiatrist. He noted that all of the most violent of the prisoners were also imprisoned in shame: The emotion of shame is the primary or ultimate cause of all violence . . . The different forms of violence, whether toward individuals or entire populations, are motivated (caused) by shame.[15]

It is important to know that in all his writing, Gilligan was referring to a certain kind of shame as causing violence. He called it secret shame: the violent prisoners were ashamed of being ashamed, it was unmanly. Helen B. Lewis introduced a similar idea, based on her study of emotion episodes in psychotherapy sessions: shame caused trouble when it went *unacknowledged*.[16] A recent study of 211 cases of family killings[17] strongly supports Gilligan's theory.

MANAGING SHAME

To end this discussion, I will very briefly indicate what I consider to be the steps toward managing shame so that it doesn't cause disaster. It follows from the discussion of secret or unacknowledged shame above that the first step would be to reveal one's shame, rather than hiding it. This one step would probably avert the recursive loops of shame about shame.

The second step is less obvious. Once shame has been acknowledged to self or self and other, what would be the best way of resolving it? This idea has two parts.[18] The first is freely talking about the feeling of shame, sometimes at great length. The second step, which may come quickly or only after much talk, is laughing about the incident. Deep humiliation, particularly, often requires a great deal of talk about the shameful events before one can see the humor in them.

It is important to note that a particular kind of laughter is required to resolve shame. I call it a good laugh, parallel to a good cry. It must be involuntary, and directed at self (Silly me!). Laughing at others is usually an expression of ridicule and anger, rather than a resolution of shame. I have seen many instances of good laughs in my classes on emotion, by asking students to tell the group about their most embarrassing moments. Many of the students get so convulsed with laughter that they can hardly finish the story.

Unfortunately, the hiding of shame in song lyrics provides a language for the listeners that can help them deny their own shame and that of others in real life. This practice seems to both reflect and reinforce the denial of emotion in the larger society.

In pop song lyrics, emphasis on extreme situations and disguising shame ignores the many subtle emotional risks that accompany even requited love. For example, whether the relationship is short or long, loving someone more, even slightly more, than they love you can give rise to shame. Another possibility is that in loving another person, one becomes more susceptible to their disdain.

Jealousy is one obvious example of the risks involved in loving. The slightest hints of detachment can trigger it. For example, you and your lover are talking to your friend at a party about a film all three of you have seen. For a few seconds, you notice that your lover and your friend are making eye contact with each other as they excitedly talk about the film, more than with you. You feel excluded, if only briefly, but enough to trigger your jealousy. For that brief period, you feel intense pains of betrayal by your lover, and anger, even hatred, toward the friend.

In the same situation, if you are very secure in your relationship, you probably wouldn't feel jealousy. However, it might still be painful. Being excluded from eye contact can evoke momentary shame, no matter how secure the relationship.

Close relationships can be much more comforting, but also much more upsetting than other relationships. Most Top 40 pop songs provide an idealized and therefore unrealistic picture of love. It is portrayed as a safe haven from all pain, which it is not. It both protects from and generates emotional pain.

CONCLUSION

This essay has briefly explored the shame world in modern societies, with examples from the lyrics of pop songs. It seems that shame is largely hidden, and that the act of hiding is profoundly damaging to individuals, groups, and our whole civilization. Some suggestions for bringing shame into the open are briefly discussed.

ENDNOTES

1. Cooley, *Human Nature*, 1; emphasis added.
2. Mead, *Mind*.
3. Brunner, Child's Talk, 71.
4. Goffman, *Presentation*.
5. Dewey, *Experience*, 202.
6. Lewis, *Shame*.
7. Cooley, *Human Nature*.
8. Ibid., 184–85; emphasis added.
9. Goffman, *Presentation of Self*, 243; emphasis added.
10. Scheff, *What's Love*.
11. Urban, "Tonight I Wanna Cry," 2004.
12. Rich, "Nobody Knows," 1996.
13. Lennon/McCartney, "You've Got to Hide Your Love Away," 1968.
14. Kaufman, *Psychology of Shame*.
15. Gilligan, *Violence*, 110–11.
16. Lewis, *Shame*,
17. Websdale, *Familicidal Hearts*.
18. Scheff, *Catharsis*.

4

Shame, Humiliation, and Religious Violence

A Self-Psychological Investigation

JAMES W. JONES

FOR MANY DECADES, RESEARCHERS have been studying the link between humiliation and violence. A review published in 1971 in *The
American Psychologist* concluded that "violations of self esteem through
insult, humiliation . . . [are] probably the most important sources" of
anger and aggression.[1] Scheff and Retzinger claim that "shame is first
evoked, which leads to rage and violence."[2] In the 90s James Gilligan produced his monumental study based primarily on his work in prison in
which he concluded: "The emotion of shame is the primary or ultimate
cause of all violence, whether towards others or towards the self. Shame
is a necessary but not a sufficient cause of violence. . . . The different
forms of violence, whether toward individuals or entire populations, are
motivated (caused) by the feeling of shame. The purpose of violence is
to diminish the intensity of shame and replace it as far as possible with
its opposite, pride."[3]

More recently a study of the rise of the insurgency in Iraq after the
American invasion underscored the importance of "the commitment
felt by individuals to fight as the result of their perceived humiliation,
and the processes related to colonial humiliation in the formation of
political violence."[4] This study found a direct link between experiences
of humiliation on the part of the Iraqi population (often at the hands
of American forces) and the growth of the insurgency in post-Saddam
Iraq. Another contemporary example involves jihadi recruitment videos

and websites. A common theme in many of these videos, designed to evoke an identification with a worldwide Muslim *umma*, is the humiliation of Muslims around the world. The same theme can be found on the websites of the Aryan Nations and other neo-Nazi groups. Whether it's Muslims throughout the world or the white race in North America, portrayals of their humiliations appear to serve as powerful motivators to join fanatical and violent groups.[5]

None of this is new. The two greatest group humiliations of the modern age produced the two greatest movements of genocide and terrorism in the modern world: the collapse of the Ottoman Empire along with the imposition of European colonialism on the Arab world leading to the rise of the jihad; and the Treaty of Versailles at the end of the First World War and the appeal of Nazism in Germany.

The defeat of the Ottoman Empire ended a multinational Muslim caliphate. On the heels of this defeat came the imposition of European colonial rule, subjecting and further humiliating the Arabic world. The failure of secular nationalism to create a pan-Muslim civilization and return it to power further humiliated the Muslim world. And the Muslim world's inability to influence world events was further exemplified by the imposition of the state of Israel without any negotiations with Arab leaders and their defeat in the 1967 war. These collective humiliations still cast a shadow over the Muslim world and are an important background for the rise of militant and violent Islamic groups who seek to restore the ancient caliphate and with it the pride and power of the Muslim civilization. Sayyid Qutb, the intellectual forefather of the jihadi movement, insists on the moral and spiritual superiority of the past Muslim civilization and that the Muslim world has nothing to learn from a decadent West. Rather this glorious past must be restored by the use of violence. Osama bin Laden's speeches make clear he too desires to undo the humiliation of the Muslim world at the hands of the "crusaders" and restore it to greatness through violence. Virtually all the interviews I have seen with jihadis and recruits to fanatical Muslim groups in Europe and the Middle East, as well as the recruiting videos put out by al Qaeda, have mentioned humiliation. The same is true of many interviews with members of Christian Identity and white supremacist groups in the United States.[6]

The Treaty of Versailles removed all of Germany's colonies from its control, laid on Germany onerous sanctions that decimated its economy, and demanded its disarmament. All of these had been sources of pride and their loss was a total humiliation for the Germans. These humiliations along with the virtual collapse of the weak Weimar government and the German economy laid the groundwork for Hitler's rise to power. German veterans returning to a defeated and destabilized nation reported "as a Front-fighter, the collapse of the Fatherland in November 1918 was to me completely incomprehensible," or "a great hopelessness was in me," or "I had believed adamantly in Germany's invincibility and now I only saw the country in its deepest humiliation—the entire world fell to the ground."[7] People holding such sentiments became the core of the Nazi movement. National humiliation caused by military defeat, internal political weakness, and economic collapse had at least two disastrous results for Germany and for the rest of the world: it set off a furious search for scapegoats, for someone or some group to blame and to punish for all this suffering; and it unleashed a ferocious drive to undo the humiliation by defeating those who had humiliated Germany. Many citizens were vulnerable to someone who could explain which group was to blame and could offer a way to overcome the humiliation. That person was obviously Adolph Hitler who pointed the finger of responsibility at Jews and other "non-Aryans" and had a plan to restore German prominence through military conquest.

These two historical examples make clear that a nation, a transnational group, or a subgroup within a society that experiences profound humiliation is exceedingly vulnerable to radicalization and *recruitment* into movements and cultures of violence.[8]

Psychological studies of political violence reinforce this point.[9] Psychiatrist Jerrold Post who spent a career studying political violence describes those whom he calls "nationalist-separatist" groups such as the Palestinian Liberation Organization and the Irish Republican Army.[10] They express devotion to a national (or sometimes ethnic) identity. Such groups tell and retell a history of national or ethnic humiliation and use violence in the hope of correcting injustices experienced by previous generations. The repetition of this lineage of humiliation is a major feature of these groups. Vamik Volkan makes the same point when he writes that a violent group is characterized by what he terms the group's "chosen trauma."[11] "Chosen trauma" refers to the "collective memory" of a humiliation from the past, experienced by the group's forbearers. "Chosen" describes the large group organizing its self-definition around an injustice or wrong done to its ancestors. Thus the group's identity becomes bound with the intergenerational transmission of humiliation. Making a past trauma central to group identity requires that the experience of humiliation be re-evoked in each succeeding generation through rituals, stories, beliefs, and ideologies that develop in relation to this ancestral wrong. These evoke feelings and attitudes in later generations that serve to nurture and reinforce the large group's identity as a wronged party.[12] The idea of the "chosen trauma" points to this continually reinforced sense of group humiliation.

SHAME, HUMILIATION, AND RELIGIOUS VIOLENCE[13]

Feelings of humiliation on the part of Arab populations has been one of the most frequently cited "root causes" of the turn to fundamentalism.[14] One Palestinian trainer of "human bombers" has said, "Much of the work is already done by the suffering these people have been subject to. . . . Only 10 percent comes from me. The suffering and living in exile away from their land has given the person 90 percent of what he needs to become a martyr."[15] Mohammed Hafez in his study of "human bombs" makes the same point: "In Palestine, intense feelings of victimization underpin societal support for suicide bombings."[16] A Palestinian psychiatrist reports that "humiliation is an important factor motivating young suicide bombers."[17] By one estimate, over 90% of the recruits to militant Palestinian groups come from the villages and camps suffering the most from the Israeli presence, where the humiliation is greatest and the struggle is most intense.[18] Nasra Hassan reports: "Over and over I heard them [militants] say, 'The Israelis humiliate us. They occupy our land, and deny our history.'"[19] In a 2006 lecture, Jessica Stern, author of *Terror in the Name of God*, said in no uncertain terms that in the Muslim communities, the greatest cause of terrorism is the feeling of humiliation.[20]

A very different example of the same theme of humiliation is that, like many New Religious Movements, the Japanese cult Aum Shinrikyo (the group that unleashed sarin gas in the Tokyo subway and also murdered several people) regularly engaged in rituals of shaming and humiliation of its members. Members were often harangued by the guru, kept in isolation, made to wait hours for their leader to appear while chanting over and over, "Master, please appear."[21]

While often rooted in social and political circumstances, shame and humiliation are profoundly psychological, and often spiritual, conditions. By holding out an absolute and perfect ideal—whether it's a divine being or a perfect guru or master—against which all mortals inevitably fall short and by insisting on the "infinite qualitative difference" (in the words of Soren Kierkegaard) between human beings and the ideal, religions can easily exacerbate and play upon any natural human tendency toward feelings of shame and humiliation.[22] I suggest that the more any religion exalts its ideal or portrays the divine as an overpowering presence and emphasizes the gulf between finite human beings and that ideal so that we must feel like "worms, not human" (in the words of the Psalms), the more it contributes to and reinforces experiences of shame and humiliation.

In addition, many writers have noted the connection between feelings of shame and disgust with the body and embodiment. One of the Muslim leaders of the 9/11 attacks wrote some years earlier in his will that no woman or other unclean person should touch his body and that his genitalia be washed with gloved hands. A classic example in the West is St. Augustine, who virtually single-handedly made the doctrine of original sin central to the Western Christian understanding of human nature. It is not coincidence that this proponent of the idea that we are born sinful and impure continually (in his book *Confessions*) expresses revulsion at anything associated with his body. But such a theological linkage of the body with feelings of shame is (unfortunately) not unique to Augustine but can be found in the traditional texts of many religions. And even the very secular, science fiction-based Heaven's Gate cult—whose members committed suicide in an act of violence against themselves—recommended castration for all the men involved.

Much psychological research suggests that there is a linkage of shame, humiliation, and violence; religion then can contribute to violence by creating and/or reinforcing and potentiating feelings of shame and humiliation, which in turn increase the likelihood of violent outbursts. While much of the humiliation that fuels certain acts of terrorism might begin in social and cultural conditions, fanatical religions may build upon that and establish a cycle in which their teachings and practices increase feelings of shame and humiliation which intensifies aggressive feelings. Then, in turn, the religion provides targets for that aggression. By fomenting crusades, dehumanizing outsiders, and encouraging prejudices, fanatical religions provide ready, religiously sanctioned targets for any increase in aggression.

To understand contemporary religiously motivated terrorism, it is important to emphasize that the humiliation that leads to violence does not have to be experienced directly and personally; for example, it may be the humiliation of a family member or the whole Muslim community with which Islamic terrorists identify. The rise of mass media and the Internet throughout the Muslim world has extended the range of this identification.[23] Mohammad Sidique Khan, thought to be the leader of the group that bombed the London underground in July 2005, said in his last video shown on TV by Al Jazeera on September 1, 2005: "Your democratically elected governments continuously perpetuate atrocities against my people all over the world. And your support makes you directly responsible, just as I am directly responsible for protecting and avenging my Muslim brothers and sisters . . . Until you stop the bombing, gassing, imprisonment, and torture of my people, we will not stop this fight."[24] Pictures from Abu Ghraib prison in Iraq or the demolition of family homes in Palestine evoke these identifications and feelings of humiliation that can lead directly to terrorist acts. Farhad Khosrokhavar calls this "humiliation by proxy."[25]

This expansion of the feeling of humiliation illustrates the way in which the experience humiliation can be theologically potentiated. A conquered, imprisoned, subjugated population experiences humiliation directly. But that is not the only source of humiliation now. An Arab citizen in Europe does not have to experience humiliation directly; mass communications can generate feelings of humiliation through empathy with fellow Muslims thousands of miles away.[26] Religious ideology can play a major role here too. Throughout the Muslim diaspora, commentators and preachers strengthen this empathic link with coreligionists around the world, established by the mass media. The role of Muslim preachers of hate, living in England and throughout Europe, in stirring up the passions of their hearers, sometimes to the point of committing terrorist acts, has been well documented.[27] On the other side, Jewish settlers describe feeling humiliated because Palestinians are living on "their land" in the occupied West Bank.[28] No United Nations mandate gave them title to that land; the "might makes right" philosophy of conquest has been illegal in international law for a century or more. The only claim the settlers have on the land is through religion—"that God gave us this land forever." Their feelings of humiliation because Palestinians are living there are derived entirely from a set of religious convictions about it being their land. Both the Muslims living in diaspora in Europe and the settlers living on the West Bank use religious ideologies and interpretations to construct and intensify a sense of humiliation. For another example, Shoko Asahara felt that Aum Shinrikyo was being humiliated by the Japanese press inquiring into his activities, even though that is well within the accepted role of the press. And some American Christians claim to feel humiliated by the separation of church and state, the teaching of evolution, or images in movies. In his book, "*America Right and Wrong,*" Anatol Lieven speaks of the humiliation that the white Christian American nationalistic cohorts felt during the 60s—the groups that form the backbone of the Christian religious right whose apocalypticism is suffused with violence.[29] The same point is made by Chris Hedges in his account of the radical Christian right in America.[30]

In all these instances, a set of religious beliefs generates these feelings of humiliation on the part of many in the Muslim diaspora, in the Jewish settlements, or among the American apocalyptic Christians. The fact that these various forms of humiliation are ideologically driven does not mean they are not real. Quite the contrary. Such feelings of humiliation are just as able to fuel terrorist acts as the humiliation arising from military occupation. Thus religions fuel humiliation not only by subjecting devotees to humiliating rituals or beliefs or by playing on experiences of humiliation by occupying powers; religions also cast an ideological net that enables devotees to feel humiliated in circumstances when no direct humiliation is present.

In addition, globalization and "the new world order," do in fact result in a homogenization of societies and their economies—a McDonaldization of the world. With this comes the loss of local cultures and values. In ways that are apparently hard for those in the West who benefit from globalization to comprehend, many indigenous cultures experience this loss of local culture as a cultural imperialism on the part of the West, and especially the United States. Rather than a military invasion and occupation, this is felt to be a cultural invasion and occupation. Like all occupations by foreign powers, this one too can be experienced as a humiliation. And fanatical religions can and do play on these widely held feelings of humiliation caused by globalization's cultural imperialism.

Feelings of humiliation thus appear common in many of the groups that produce violence and terrorism. Such feelings of humiliation may indicate a self that feels threatened, and a self that feels threatened may dream of violence and revenge. So a religion that emphasizes divine vengeance (which either the true believer carries out with divine sanction or the true believer fantasizes about God carrying out in the near future) appeals to those feeling humiliated. And many religious terrorists see themselves explicitly as agents of divine vengeance. The theme of divine vengeance runs throughout the writings of contemporary American Christian apocalyptic literature and the literature of other religions' texts of terror.[31] To the origin of that connection between violence and humiliation we now turn.

WHY HUMILIATION LEADS TO VIOLENCE

I want to argue that part of the origin of this violence lies in either threats to the self or threats to cherished institutions, beliefs, and world views that the believer feels are necessary to maintain self-esteem and identity. Heinz Kohut is one who has explicated this connection between humiliation and rage. For Kohut, humiliation is an injury to a person's sense of self and their self-esteem, a threat to the self. The *psychologically* threatened self responds with violence, just as the physically threatened self sometimes does, especially if the self is inclined toward violence and lacks empathy for others. This parallels a finding from forensic psychology: men who batter or kill their wives or girlfriends often say openly that they felt they were losing control over their partners (when the partners talked about leaving them, for example, or had other friendships). This need for control often covers a psychological vulnerability that leads to violence when the self feels threatened, in this case threatened by the loss of control.

Kohut suggests that "destructive rage, in particular, is always motivated by an injury to the self."[32] The injury that evokes this destructive rage can be a direct threat or, more commonly, a threat to some ideal, ideology, or institution on which the individual depends for his identity and self-esteem. Such objects, which the self needs to sustain its sense of coherence and vitality, are called by Kohut "selfobjects." Selfobjects are the people, places, and things that maintain and enhance an individual's self-esteem, creativity, and self-efficacy and in which the individual can invest her energies. If identity and sense of self-worth are inextricably bound to identification with a religious, political, ethnic, or professional community, when they are threatened, Kohut says, we feel threatened at the most basic level as a person.

One of the most relevant aspects of Kohut's theorizing for the psychology of religion is the way he shows that beliefs, institutions, and ideals can become part of the sense of self. A person then becomes dependent on them to maintain that sense of self. A threat to a cherished belief, ideal, or institution can feel like as much (if not more) of a threat than a direct physical threat. The response is what Kohut calls "narcissistic rage."[33] Such rage is to be expected if a person's entire sense of self is built on a single identity as a religious devotee, a patriot, the partisan of a cause, or a rational scientist. Under such conditions, individuals are set up for "narcissistic rage" when those foundations of selfhood appear threatened. The main characteristic of such rage is that "those who are in the grip of narcissistic rage show total lack of empathy toward offender."[34] Such a total lack of empathy is one of the most striking traits frequently seen in those who bomb innocent noncombatants, assassinate reproductive health care providers, and imagine (and sometimes plot) apocalyptic genocidal violence in the name of their deity.

Kohut distinguishes such narcissistic rage from ordinary aggression by its totalistic qualities and complete lack of empathy. Here there is a limitless, insatiable quality to the desire for revenge, like that seen in the apocalyptic fanatics who want to purge the world of all evil-doers, sinners, and nonbelievers. In contrast to normal aggression or even normal desire for revenge, narcissistic rage "in its typical form is an utter disregard for reasonable limitations and a boundless wish to re-dress an injury and to obtain revenge."[35] While some religiously motivated terrorists may employ violence purely tactically in the pursuit of limited and achievable political goals (as Robert Pape and others describe), others dream of complete purification and the apocalyptic eradication of all unholy people. Such totalistic schemes of divine vengeance reek of narcissistic rage born of threats to cherished beliefs and institutions. As Kohut says: "Aggressions employed in the pursuit of maturely experienced causes are not limitless. However vigorously mobilized, their goal is definite: the defeat of the enemy who blocks the way to a cherished goal. The narcissistically injured, on the other hand, cannot rest until he has blotted out a vaguely experienced offender who dared to oppose him, to disagree with him, or to outshine him."[36] The terroristic religious imagination can even conceive of a God of narcissistic rage who "cannot rest until he has blotted out a vaguely experienced offender who dared to oppose him, to disagree with him."

Such totalistic dreams of vengeance on the unrighteous do not necessarily coincide with a loss of cognitive functioning. Rather, Kohut accurately observes, "the irrationality of the vengeful attitude becomes even more frightening in view of the fact that . . . the reasoning capacity, while totally under the domination and in the service of the overriding emotion, is often not only intact but even sharpened."[37] Devotees motivated by narcissistic rage can still fly planes, make sophisticated bombs, and author brilliantly rhetorical texts in the service of their visions of terror.

Central to all living religions is the idealization of particular ideas, beliefs, institutions, books, codes of conduct, or various leaders.[38] This can easily set one up for narcissistic rage if the idealized object is threatened. Kenneth Pargament and his group investigated exactly that possibility in a study of what they call "desecration" which involves the perceived violation of something held sacred.[39] As distinct from the loss of something held sacred (a belief, commitment, or object) which usually leads to depression, the desecration of something held sacred most likely leads to rage. While "post-traumatic growth" and increased self-reported "spiritual development" can follow the loss of something sacred when the loss is "worked through," psycho-spiritual development most often goes in the opposite direction following the desecration of something held sacred. The desecration of something held sacred is most often experienced as a significant trauma bringing with it intense emotional distress. Desecration is usually associated with decreased mental health and increased anger. In another study Pargament and his colleagues found that Christians who believed Jews were responsible for Jesus' crucifixion and other desecrations of Christian values displayed higher than average levels of anti-Semitism. Even when all other predictors of anti-Semitism were controlled for, belief that Jews desecrated Christian values was a robust predictor of anti-Semitism.[40] Such results fit neatly with Kohut's model of narcissistic rage.

There is now a significant body of related empirical research that connects narcissism and violence. Narcissists seem exquisitely sensitive to slights and threats to their self-image and are very likely to respond with anger, that "narcissism combined with ego threat [yields] the highest levels of aggression."[41] In addition, narcissists seem weak in those characteristics that often act as a break on aggression—empathy and the capacity to regulate and inhibit affect. Some research suggests that the narcissist's high sense of entitlement correlates most significantly with aggression.[42] This research has not found narcissists to be more aggressive in general, but rather that "narcissists were exceptionally aggressive toward anyone who attacked or offended them."[43] As Kohut suggests, this narcissistic rage has an interpersonal component. It is a specific response to a threat to the self and is specifically directed at the person or persons who threaten the self, that is "narcissists mainly want to punish or defeat someone who has threatened" their sense of themselves.[44]

Narcissism here is not equated with self-esteem. Research finds no particular correlations between high self-esteem and aggression. But this apparently applies only to people with relatively stable levels of self-esteem. Empirical research suggests that people whose self-esteem is quite high but also unstable are exceptionally prone to violence. People whose self-esteem regularly fluctuates from high to low show the greatest tendency toward hostility and anger. This too fits nicely with the psychoanalytic view of narcissism as expressing a fragile, easily threatened sense of self.

Some studies have questioned this view of narcissism as involving a fragile sense of self. A study using both explicit and implicit measures (measures designed to test more unconscious beliefs) found that narcissists had high self-regard both explicitly and implicitly (i.e., both consciously and unconsciously).[45] This raises the question of how narcissism is conceptualized in this research. The studies I have reviewed all rely on the Narcissistic Personality Inventory developed by Robert Raskin and colleagues in the late '70s and early '80s. This instrument measures characteristics such as perceiving oneself as destined to be leader, exhibitionist tendencies, feelings of entitlement and superiority, being manipulative. Narcissism is thus conceptualized as a set of interrelated traits. Most of which involve an inflated sense of self. Here narcissism inevitably appears as pathological. This is a slightly different focus from clinical self-psychology which theorizes narcissism as a necessary, nonpathological part of human psychology and which concentrates on narcissism's developmental history and the psychological processes that underlay and connect these traits. For our purposes, the mere existence of these traits says little about their possible connections with violence and the reasons for any such connections.

There is only one place where I found this link of humiliation and violence questioned. In a study published in 2008, Jeremy Ginges and Scott Atran report that humiliation reduces support for violence and increases resistance to comprise.[46] They studied Palestinians in the occupied territories and found that Palestinians who responded with feelings of humiliation to signs of Israeli occupation (e.g., held at checkpoints, land expropriated, etc.) were less likely to feel joy or pride at reports of suicide bombings. Palestinians who did not report feeling humiliated were more likely to feel joy at these violent acts done by their compatriots. Feelings of joy and pride were taken as measures of support for violent actions.

In these studies individuals either reported their responses or were primed with a reminder of Israeli checkpoints and the majority reported either humiliation or insult as the primary or secondary feeling. But they are no more likely than others to respond with joy at the report of a martyrdom operation. If it is the case that there is a broader cultural context of humiliation in the background of all these situations, the fact that individuals feeling humiliation at a specific moment are no more overjoyed at martyrdom operations than others who do not report feeling humiliation at that moment may not sufficiently differentiate the two groups on this variable of humiliation—momentary episodic feelings of humiliation may not tap into or represent the more longstanding and encompassing, and perhaps ideologically maintained, sense of humiliation that many report as characteristic of these groups. Also, it is not clear that feelings of joy at the report of a suicide bombing can represent the larger condition of level of support for violence in general. Hafez reports that many Palestinians feel rather ambivalent about suicide bombing as a tactic in their struggle with Israel.[47] There are Muslim groups that support armed actions for the liberation of Palestine who do not necessarily support suicide bombing as a tactic.

But there is a deeper issue. As the authors note, some research suggests that the connection between being insulted and the recourse to violence can be moderated by narcissism. We have seen that some research finds that people low on a narcissism index are less likely to be violent in response to an insult than those who are higher on narcissism who are more likely to resort to violence when insulted. So perhaps the connection between humiliation and violence is more robust for those narcissistically oriented, but that hardly means there is no connection; at most it means the connection is multidetermined in some instances.

Also in the videos and websites of fanatical religious groups that appeal to humiliation as a vehicle for recruitment, the reference is less to the potential recruit's personal experience of humiliation and more to his identification with his religious, ethnic, or national group that is being humiliated. It may be that the individuals who respond to these radicalizing appeals are not themselves humiliated but rather identify with the humiliation of their group.

BEYOND SHAME, HUMILIATION, AND VIOLENCE IN RELIGION

The most important message to take away from this research is that to reduce the level of violence in the world, we must work to reduce the level of humiliation and desecration in our cultural and religious systems and political policies.[48] But in addition, are there ways we might break the connection between humiliation and violence and reduce the recourse to violence even when shame and humiliation are present?

There is some research relevant to this question too. Two factors—empathy and a sense of connection—have been found to reduce the recourse to violence. One series of studies dealing specifically with narcissists and their proclivity for aggression toward those who threaten their sense of self found that if a sense of connection can be established between the narcissist and the person who appears to threaten them, the potential for violence can be reduced.[49] These studies involved the simplest markers of connection (sharing a birthday, sharing a fingerprint type) with someone who harshly criticized the narcissistic subjects. But even these very simple markers of connection were enough to almost completely eliminate the subjects' aggressive response in comparison with narcissists who were criticized by those with whom they shared no traits in common. The researchers conclude: "across studies, the results support the conclusion that the narcissistic-aggression relationship can be attenuated if participants can be made to believe that they share a characteristic with the ego threatener . . . this result suggests that a lack of connection with other individuals is a key contributor to narcissistic aggression."[50]

This is similar to a secondary finding from Stanley Milgram's obedience experiment where subjects often inflicted what they thought were intense, sometimes near fatal, electric shocks on a "victim" (who actually did not receive any shocks).[51] Proximity to the alleged "victim" was a major factor in muting the administration of these shocks. Subjects who could see the "victim," hear their screams, etc., were less likely to inflict shocks or at least inflict the most intense shocks. So some research suggests that a sense of connection can reduce the recourse to violence.

A review of more than fifty studies in 1988 concluded that "empathy is negatively related to aggression."[52] While other research on empathy as a antidote to violence is complex and sometimes contradictory,[53] there appears a general consensus that (in the words of a review that is quite critical of the research) "more recent lines of research provide clearer support for the idea that empathy-induced altruistic behavior can inhibit aggression".[54] In addition, research on forgiveness finds that empathy may be a necessary step in moving to forgiveness rather than revenge.[55] So research finds that a sense of connection to and empathy with others, even those who oppose us, are major inhibitors of the recourse to violence. Of course, such a project is close to the heart of all the world's religions.

However, in keeping with the focus of this paper, we must also ask about the deeper psychological dynamics that might be involved in engendering a greater sense of connection to and empathy with other members of the human species, even those who are our enemies. In his essay, "Forms and Transformations of Narcissism,"[56] Kohut calls one such transformation "cosmic narcissism" which is a shift from a concentration on the self to a "participation in a supraindividual and timeless existence."[57] Here individuals move from a life centered on the maintenance of the individual self, which is the self on which self-psychology focuses, to a life centering on a "supraordinate Self" and their narcissism expands to embrace the cosmos at large.[58]

Enlarging one's narcissism and identifying with a supraordinate Self enables one to achieve "the outlook on life which the Romans called living *sub specie aeternitatis* [from the perspective of eternity] which is characterized not by "resignation and hopelessness but a quiet pride."[59] The latter comment may be an aside at Freud whose outlook was often characterized by resignation and hopelessness. For example, in reference to death Freud writes in *The Future of an Illusion*, "As for the great necessities of Fate, against which there is no help, they [humankind] will learn to endure them with resignation."[60] Freud insists that the only alternatives in the face of death are either religious illusions or stoic resignation to the twin Gods of "reason and fate."[61] Kohut is suggesting a third alternative—seeing life from the perspective of eternity. About this he writes, "I have little doubt that those who are able to achieve this ultimate attitude towards life do so on the strength of a new, expanded, transformed narcissism: a cosmic narcissism which has transcended the bounds of the individual."[62]

Kohut contrasts his concept of cosmic narcissism with Romain Rolland's idea of an oceanic feeling. "In contrast to the oceanic feeling, however, which is experienced passively (and usually fleetingly), the genuine shift of cathexes toward a cosmic narcissism is the enduring, creative result of the steadfast activities of an autonomous ego, and only very few are able to attain it."[63] Cosmic narcissism is not a transitory "peak experience" but is rather an abiding attitude toward life and a deeper insight into the nature of reality. As a psychological definition of religion, such an expansion of empathy to include the cosmos is an alternative to both the oceanic mysticism of Rolland in which the self disappears into the Absolute and the legalistic monotheism of Freud in which the self must continually struggle to conform itself to a set of prohibitions.

Cosmic narcissism, unlike the "oceanic feeling," is not a regression to the fusion of infancy in which individuality and intentionality vanish. Rather it is the result of disciplined activity because "a genuine decathexis of the self can only be achieved slowly by an intact, well-functioning ego; and it is accomplished by sadness as the cathexis is transferred from the cherished self to the supraindividual ideals and to the world with which one identifies."[64] In these brief and suggestive remarks, it would seem that Kohut is referring to some kind of psycho-spiritual practice in which "the span of the ego here is not narrowed; the ego remains active and deliberate" resulting in "a rearrangement and transformation of the narcissistic libido."[65]

Kohut is clear that intellectual activity and discursive reason alone cannot bring about this transformation and transcendence of individual egoism, for "I believe that this rare feat rests, not simply on a victory of autonomous reason and supreme objectivity over the claims of narcissism, but on the creation of a higher form of narcissism."[66] Whereas psychoanalysis is often associated with an unswerving faith in autonomous reason alone, Kohut here implies that other forms of knowing and being are also required. While never elaborating further on this idea of cosmic narcissism, in an essay, "On Leadership," he writes in reference to the late secretary-general of the United Nations, Dag Hammarskjold, whose posthumously published diary revealed a mystical orientation:

> The survival of Western man, and perhaps of mankind altogether, will in all likelihood be neither safeguarded by 'the voice of the intellect' alone, that great utopian hope of the Enlightenment and Rationalism of the 18th and 19th centuries; nor will it be secured through the influence of the teachings of the orthodox religions. Will a new religion arise which is capable of fortifying man's love for its old and new ideals . . . the transformation of narcissism into the spirit of religiosity . . . could it be that a new, rational religion might arise, an as yet uncreated system of mystical rationality . . . ?[67]

Again, Kohut does not elaborate on the meaning of his calling for the "amalgamation [of psychoanalysis] with mystical modes of thinking."[68] In these brief remarks, however, he is clearly doing two things. First, he is pointing toward a new goal for psychoanalysis to supplement Freud's dictum of reason controlling instinct by calling for a more universal or cosmic love, "a higher form of narcissism."[69] Second, he is underscoring that such a cosmic narcissism will not come through ego rationality alone but will require something analogous to a spiritual practice built upon "a constructive mysticism."[70] Since neither intellectual argument nor assertions of willpower alone are sufficient, Kohut is clear that religion can be a major (perhaps the primary) force in this transformation of individual narcissism into a universal embrace.

A religious practice is often an important ingredient in the transformation of egoism and individual narcissism into this cosmic love and universal attitude. Religious teachings often focus on the transitoriness of human existence and call to mind our connection to a greater reality that dwarfs and encompasses our individual concerns. Religious disciplines like meditation, communal worship, and devotional activities can evoke an experience of connection to a greater and more encompassing reality, that "supraordinate Self" that constrains and limits our individual selfishness. Thus religion can serve to reduce the egoism that interferes with a more universal sensibility.

CONCLUSION: SACRED HUMILIATION, RELIGION,
AND VIOLENCE

So religion plays a very ambiguous role in relationship to this connection between humiliation and violence. Religions can potentiate this connection in two ways. Religious spokespersons can play upon feelings of humiliation generated by social and political factors. For example, recruiters of human bombers in the occupied territories play upon the feelings of humiliation experienced by the Palestinians, or al Qaeda in Iraq plays upon the feelings of humiliation experienced by the Iraqis under American occupation, or Christian Identity groups play upon feelings of humiliation experienced by marginalized men in post-industrial America. Here fanatical religions rhetorically draw upon and channel for their own (often violent) purposes feelings of humiliation arising from social and political conditions.

However, religions can also generate experiences of humiliation in their own right. Some religions teach that human life is to be regarded as something unclean and despicable. Some religions have rituals of self-deprecation and self-humiliation. Some religions continually deploy the rhetoric of judgment and condemnation. In these, and many other ways, religion can make its own, independent contribution to the experience of humiliation, separate from the humiliation generated by social conditions.

The combination of these two processes is lethal. When religions of humiliation interact with people who are shamed, humiliated, and alienated (especially in the context of a culture of violence where the implements of violence and the know-how to deploy them are available), conditions are ripe for a turn to religiously motivated violence and terrorism.

Again, however, religion's relationship to the connection between humiliation and violence is very ambiguous. Religions can exacerbate this connection. But religion also can transform experiences of humiliation into constructive movements for the betterment of humankind: as the Dalai Lama is doing with the oppressed people of Tibet, as Gandhi did with the masses of India, as Martin Luther King did with those bearing the stigma of slavery in the United States. A task for the future is to understand better the psychological and spiritual dynamics involved in these movements of social and personal transformation by which humiliation is transfigured into humility.

ENDNOTES

1. Feshbach, "Dynamics," 285; Gilligan, "Shame"; Hartling and Luchetta, "Humiliation"; Pattison, *Shame.*

2. Scheff and Retzinger, *Emotions and Violence,* 3.

3. Gilligan, *Violence,* 110–11.

4. Fontan, "Polarization," 236.

5. For the past few years I have been doing research on jihadi recruitment videos and recruitment over the Internet by studying jihadi websites and those of the Aryan Nations, Christian Militias, and violent antichoice groups. My comments here reflect some of that research.

6. Jones, *Blood*; Juergensmeyer, *Terror*; Khosrokhavar, *Suicide Bombers*; Stern, *Terror.*

7. The quotations in this paragraph are from Redles, "Ordering Chaos."

8. My special thanks to Professor David Redles who supplied the examples from WWI German veterans who became Nazis and Professor Charles Strozier and Dr. David Terman with whom I have had many productive discussions on the role of humiliation in violent, apocalyptic movements.

9. Lindner, *Making Enemies*; Miller, *Humiliation.*

10. Post, *Terrorist*; Post, Ruby, and Shaw, "Radical Group."

11. Volkan, *Bloodlines,* 48.

12. Ibid., 81–82.

13. Much of this section is taken from Jones, *Blood,* and is used with permission from Oxford University Press. A more in-depth discussion of these issues with many more examples can be found there.

14. Abi-Hashem, "Peace and War"; Davis, *Martyrs*; Hassan, "Arsenal"; Khosrokhavar, *Suicide Bombers.*

15. Davis, *Martyrs,* 154.

16. Hafez, *Human Bombs,* 7.

17. Quoted in Victoroff, "Mind of the Terrorist," 29.

18. Post, Sprinzak and Denny "Terrorists," 173.

19. Hassan, "Arsenal," 38.

20. Stern, "Anatomy of Terror."

21. Lifton, *Destroying*; even more horrific acts of humiliation are described in Reader, *Religious Violence,* 137–41.

22. McNish, *Transforming Shame*; Pattison, *Shame.*

23. For examples, see Atran, "Imagination;" Atran and Stern, "Small groups"; Hoffman, *Inside Terrorism*; Khosrokhavar, *Suicide Bombers*; Rosenthal, *Jihad*; Weimann, *Terror.*

24. British Government, "Intelligence," 19.

25. Khosrokhavar, *Suicide Bombers.*

26. Rosenthal, *Jihad.*; Khosrokhavar, *Suicide Bombers.*

27. Khosrokhavar, *Suicide Bombers.*

28. Juergensmeyer, *Terror*, chapter 3.

29. Jones, "Eternal Warfare"; Strozier, *Apocalypse*; Lieven, *America.*

30. Hedges, *Fascists.*

31. Jones, "Eternal Warfare"; Jones, *Blood*; Strozier, *Apocalypse.*

32. Kohut, *Restoration,* 117.

33. Kohut, "Narcissistic Rage," 379.

34. Ibid., 386.

35. Ibid., 382.

36. Ibid., 385.

37. Ibid., 382.

38. Jones, *Terror.*

39. Pargament, et al., "Sacrilege"; Bushman, et al., "God Sanctions Killing."

40. Pargament et al., "They Killed."

41. Bushman and Baumeister, "Threatened Egotism," 227.

42. Bushman and Baumeister, "self-love."

43. Bushman and Baumeister, "Threatened Egotism," 227.

44. Ibid., 227.

45. Campbell, et al., "Narcissists;" Raskin and Terry, "Principal-Components."

46. Ginges and Atran, "Humiliation."

47. Hafez, *Human Bombs.*

48. Lindner, *Making Enemies.*

49. Konrath, et al., "Attenuating the Link."

50. Ibid., 1000.

51. Milgram, *Obedience*; Blass, *Obedience.*

52. Miller and Eisenberg, "Relation of Empathy," 338.

53. Batson, et al., "Benefits"; Eisenberg, et al., "Empathy-Related."

54. Batson, et al., "Benefits," 364.

55. Worthington, "Unforgiveness."

56. Kohut, "Narcissism."

57. Ibid., 456.

58. Jones, *Terror.*

59. Kohut, "Narcissism," 455.

60. Freud, *Illusion*, 82.

61. Ibid., 88.

62. Kohut, "Narcissism," 455.

63. Ibid., 456.

64. Ibid., 458.

65. Ibid., 457.

66. Ibid., 454.

67. Kohut, *Self Psychology*, 70.

68. Ibid., 71.

69. Ibid., 72.

70. Ibid., 71.

5

Overcoming Shame in Slave Songs
and the Epistle to the Hebrews

ANNE E. STREATY WIMBERLY

I've been 'buked and I've been scorned;
I've been talked about, sho's you're born.
Dere is trouble all over dis world.
Ain't gwine to lay my 'ligion down.[1]

WHAT MAKES IT POSSIBLE for people to continue on in life amidst unfathomable circumstances and the threat of shame? How would we deal with humiliation or shame resulting from the treatment of another or from the self's action? Where is hope found in difficult and shame-producing situations? These questions lay at the core of the life experiences of black people in bondage during the era of slavery in America, of Jews in Nazi Germany, of black people who lived through apartheid in South Africa, of the poor who are identified as "slum dogs" in India, and those on the receiving end of ethnic cleansing in various parts of the global village, for example. Yet, dare we add unseen victims of human trafficking, rape and abuse, those suffering from HIV and AIDS, and the hundreds of thousands of long-term and new homeless and unemployed persons across the U.S. in an era of economic disaster?

In the throes of life's hard trials and tribulations, whatever the source, the answers to the questions of how persons continue on, deal with shame, and find hope do not always come easily. My purpose here is to invite us to explore two sources for discerning answers to the questions. One source is found in the musical narratives called the *spirituals* of black people who were in bondage during the era of slavery in this country. We will explore what is communicated in these songs about a way of "traveling" over the tough road of life and overcoming indignity and shame with hope that comes from God and Jesus, the friend who accompanied them on the journey.

The other source for addressing the questions is the Epistle to the Hebrews, which we will explore side-by-side with the spirituals. The importance of this biblical source lies in the realization that, in slavery, black Christians readily connected with the biblical worldview that was communicated to them. Black people identified with biblical stories and themes, and drew on this material as means of living out their own stories. Particularly regarding the spirituals, John Lovell Jr., stated that the slaves drew on experiences in the Bible that paralleled their own.[2] They internalized central metaphors in the Bible and somehow heard the intent behind biblical narratives and thematic material; and they were somehow able to see the applicability of biblical narratives and thematic material for Christian religious experience and the formation of life meaning and life direction that overcame shame.

The parallels between the messages of the spirituals and the content of the Epistle to the Hebrews suggest that, perhaps Hebrews may have been part of the biblical worldview of the slaves or became a mirror through which they viewed and sang about their journey. What is clear is that both give attention to journeying beyond shame by acknowledging the one who knows and accompanies us on the journey, forming a communal identity, inviting faithful participation in God's unfolding story, and confessing hope *in Jesus* and that *is Jesus*. The intent is to grasp connections between the spirituals and Hebrews for their import for our ongoing journey of life.

I will begin with an overview of the story of black people in slavery and the circumstances out of which the Epistle to the Hebrews emerged as means of centering us on experiences of deep trials and crises that challenge persons' ability to hold onto courage, dignity, and hope. I will then invite us to explore three resources for the journey beyond shame appearing both in the spirituals and in Hebrews—namely, (1) the embrace of life as a journey that is neither frozen nor unchangeable; (2) acknowledgment of Jesus, the Son of God and kingly Christ who was tested and, therefore, knows all about our troubles, intercedes on our behalf and journeys with us as divine friend; and (3) the formation of a communal identity bestowed by God shown in the images of family membership and language of belonging in a divine household.

The final section will focus on the centrality of hope in moving beyond shame. The emphasis will be placed on the meaning of a confession of hope and implications of a confession of hope for twenty-first-century sojourners.

OVERVIEW: BLACK PEOPLE IN SLAVERY AND HEBREWS UNDER SIEGE

This section will begin with an overview of the situation of black people in slavery in this country and will conclude with the place and critical circumstances that the Epistle to the Hebrews addresses.

Black People in Slavery

We are reminded that, in this country, slavery began in 1619, reached a high point from 1763 to 1775, and continued until its end was signaled by the Emancipation Proclamation of January 1, 1863, followed by the enactment of the Thirteenth Amendment of the Constitution on December 18, 1865. The number of black people in slavery increased from 575,000 in 1781 to four million by 1860.[3] Further statistics show that those who were put on slave ships for delivery to the New World were between sixteen and thirty years old. In fact, census figures reported by Lovell indicate that, "in 1850, for example, 45 percent of the slaves in the southern United States were under 15 years of age; 56 percent were under 20 and almost 74 percent were under age 30."[4] These figures are important because it is often thought that the spirituals were songs created primarily by older people when, in fact, they were the songs of the young.

Slavery was a wholly degraded state of being that was circumscribed by total subordination, physical and psychological abuse carried out with threats and actual uses of punishments and torture from whippings to brandings, to amputations of fingers and toes, to castration of men and rape of women, to separation of family members.[5] Shame was intensified by the realization that the slaves had no status in the law and that the slaveholder would not be held accountable even for maiming them.[6] The following stories are indicative of the brutal conditions of slavery that were designed to denude persons of honor and reduce them to shame by stripping them of the power to exercise their own will effectively.[7]

Harriet Jacobs: "Incidents in the Life of a Slave Girl"[8]

In my childhood I knew a valuable slave, named Charity, and loved her, as all children did. Her young mistress married, and took her to Louisiana. Her little boy, James, was sold to a good sort of master. He became involved in debt, and James was sold again to a wealthy slaveholder, noted for his cruelty. With this man he grew up to manhood, receiving the treatment of a dog. After a severe whipping, to save himself from further infliction of the lash, with which he was threatened, he took to the woods. He was in a most miserable condition—cut by the cowskin, half naked, half starved, and without the means of procuring a crust of bread.

Some weeks after his escape, he was captured, tied, and carried back to his master's plantation. This man considered punishment in his jail, on bread and water, after receiving hundreds of lashes, too mild for the poor slave's offence. Therefore, he decided, after the overseer should have whipped him to his satisfaction, to have him placed between the screws of the cotton gin, to stay as long as he had been in the woods. This wretched creature was cut with the whip from his head to his foot, then washed with strong brine, to prevent the flesh from mortifying, and make it heal sooner than it otherwise would. He was then put into the cotton gin, which was screwed down, only allowing him room to turn on his side when he could not lie on his back. Every morning a slave was sent with a piece of bread and bowl of water, which were placed within reach of the poor fellow. The slave was charged, under penalty of severe punishment, not to speak to him.

Four days passed, and the slave continued to carry the bread and water. On the second morning, he found the bread gone, but the water untouched.

When he had been in the press four days and five nights, the slave informed his master that the water had not been used for four mornings, and that a horrible stench came from the gin house. The overseer was sent to examine into it. When the press was unscrewed, the dead body was found partly eaten by rats and vermin. Perhaps the rats that devoured his bread had gnawed him before life was extinct. Poor Charity! Grandmother and I often asked each other how her affectionate heart would bear the news, if she should ever hear of the murder of her son. We had known her husband, and knew that James was like him in manliness and intelligence. These were the qualities that made it so hard for him to be a plantation slave. They put him into a rough box, and buried him with less feeling than would have been manifested for an old house dog. Nobody asked any questions. He was a slave; and the feeling was that the master had the right to do what he pleased with his own property. And what did he care for the value of a slave? He had hundreds of them. When they had finished their daily toil, they must hurry to eat their little morsels, and be ready to extinguish their pine knots before nine o'clock, when the overseer went his patrol rounds. He entered every cabin, to see that men and their wives had gone to bed together, lest the men, from over-fatigue, should fall asleep in the chimney corner, and remain there till the morning horn called them to their daily task. Women are considered of no value, unless they continually increase their owner's stock. They are put on a par with animals. This same master shot a woman through the head, who had run away and been brought back to him. No one called him to account for it. If a slave resisted being whipped, the bloodhounds were unpacked, and set upon him, to tear his flesh from his bones. The master who did these things was highly educated, and styled a perfect gentleman. He also boasted the name and standing of a Christian, though Satan never had a truer follower.

I could tell of more slaveholders as cruel as those I have described. They are not exceptions to the general rule. I do not say that there are no humane slaveholders. Such characters do exist, notwithstanding the hardening influences around them. But they are like 'angels' visits—few and far between.

THE TESTIMONY OF SOLOMON BRADLEY

The most shocking thing that I have ever seen was on the plantation of Mr. Farraby, on the line of the railroad. I went up to his house one morning from my work for drinking water, and I heard a woman screaming awfully in the door-yard. On going up to the fence and looking over I saw a woman stretched out, face downwards, on the ground her hands and feet being fastened to stakes. Mr. Farraby was standing over and striking her with a leather trace belonging to his carriage-harness. As he struck her the flesh of her back and legs was raised in welts and ridges by the force of the blows. Sometimes when the poor thing cried too loud from the pain Farraby would kick her in the mouth. After he had exhausted himself from whipping her he sent to his house for sealing wax and a lighted candle and, melting the wax,

dropped it on the woman's lacerated back. He then got a riding
whip and standing over the woman, picked off the hardened wax
by switching at it. Mr. Farraby's grown daughters were looking at
all this through the blinds. The punishment was so terrible that I
was induced to ask what offence the woman had committed and
was told by her fellow servants that her only crime was in burning the edges of the waffles that she had cooked for breakfast.[9]

A further example is of a group of enslaved black people in South
Carolina who became objects of research as part of a mid-1800s ethnology project. It is not known how many slaves actually became scientific
objects in the project that centered on the forced photography, called
"daguerreotypes," of slaves. But, the extensive volume by Molly Rogers,
*Delia's Tears: Race, Science, and Photography in Nineteenth-Century
America*, reveals the stories of seven slaves—five men and two wom-
en—whose daguerreotypes were found in a remote spot in the Peabody
Museum of Archaeology in Cambridge, Massachusetts. [10]

Contrary to the typical daguerreotype of that day that entailed "putting on your best and looking as composed and respectable as possible,"
the pictures of Delia, Jack, Alfred, Jem, Fassena, Drana, and Renty revealed minimal or no clothing. Not only had they not been asked whether they wanted their pictures taken, but they had also been stripped of
their respectability. Their forced participation was to assist the scientists'
creation of a typology of desirable or detestable bodies and their answers
to the question, "What is a human being?"[11] In Rogers's words:

> They had somehow become the center of these people's atten-
> tion, the object of their scrutiny and industry. They were, to
> paraphrase the French Caribbean writer, Franz Fanon, dissected
> under white eyes, laid bare, slices of their reality cut away. In this
> place they could not be "themselves," yet neither could they be
> what the environment called for, namely ladies and gentlemen.
> They could only be what they would always be in the presence
> of white people: slaves, negroes, *niggers*. Perhaps at this moment
> they felt the "double-consciousness" described by W.E.B. DuBois:
> "It is a peculiar sensation, this double-consciousness, this sense
> of always looking at one's self through the eyes of others, of mea-
> suring one's soul by the tape of a world that looks on in amused
> contempt and pity."[12]

The importance of these stories lies in what they convey about the realities of slavery that denuded black people of honor by disempowering

them and promulgating images of what an African slave was not—that is, a negative image,[13] while assigning honor to slaveholders based on their ownership of slaves, other property, and material belongings. The stories also present the very real context in which persons who had no say over their entry and treatment in the wretched institution of slavery found a way beyond the shame others assigned to them.

Through the songs called spirituals, black people in slavery passionately responded to the realities of their lives. They expressed their deep emotions and feelings in song and testified against the shame that permeated their lived stories. Moreover, through song, they sought to both reveal the hope within them and nurture that same hope in others.

Hebrews under Siege

The Epistle to the Hebrews is addressed to Christian congregations in the Lycus Valley whose experiences of persecution, loss of honor, and personal and religious dilemmas shook their confidence and threatened their commitment to their identities as Christians. Written around the winter of CE 55–56, the letter was to a people under siege and in crisis.[14] The letter writer's awareness of the severity of the situation appears in references in Heb 10:32–34 to these Christians' endurance of hard struggles and sufferings including public exposure to abuse and persecution even as some of them came to the aid of victims of abuse. Their possessions were looted. Some were imprisoned.

The history of the region was also one of instability. Stuart Sachs' historical overview indicates that, prior to the coming of the Messiah, "revolts and other bloodshed took the lives of more than 100,000 Jews. In 31 BCE, an earthquake had killed another 30,000. Severe famine and pestilence also took their toll. Herod (so-called "the Great") bled the land mercilessly with unrelenting taxation, a blight which continued after his death. Messages of hope were rarely heard; despair was everywhere. The average person felt the bleakness of the times and longed for relief, something to buoy his spirits."[15]

The fledgling Christians interpreted their own and the broader circumstances that unfolded in the region over time as the antagonistic actions and control of hostile cosmic forces. Their response was to engage in cultic activities that ran counter to the Christian faith they espoused in an attempt to mollify "the evil angels and powers responsible for the disagreeable state of the world . . . On the basis of references like

Heb 9:23, the purpose of the esoteric cult being developed in the Lycus Valley was to provide "purification" of the evil elements in the world so that they would lose their threatening qualities."[16]

The essential point of this description of the Hebrews' circumstance of trials and tribulations is that these early Christians required encouragement, a new calling to the meaning of the Christian faith, and a hopeful way forward on life's sojourn in route to the lasting city with the presence of Jesus, the source and embodiment of hope. The writer of the letter to the Hebrews serves as the messenger and guide and brings to the attention of struggling believers the resources they need to continue on amidst the tough, disabling, and dishonoring crises of life. Moreover, the writer of the letter apparently knows the congregations, their fears, troubles, and faults and had likely experienced the same kinds of trials and tribulations as the Hebrew congregants. Consequently, the letter may also show the writer's own impassioned self-disclosure of what it means for Christians to move beyond shame.

Resources for the Journey: The Connected Messages of the Spirituals and the Epistle to the Hebrews

Black people in slavery and the Hebrews under siege both felt the sting of public humiliation and shame, physical abuse, and mental trauma that were intended to denude them of self-respect and honor. Of course, it cannot be denied that enslaved black people exerted the will to resist the denigrating and life-negating exigencies of the slave system. Numerous individual and small group attempts to escape took place over what became known as the Underground Railroad, a clandestine pathway to the presumed northward direction of the honorable existence of freedom. However, many were unsuccessful and the punishment of escapees grim. There were also several notable rebellions that were quelled and that brought execution to the leaders who were regarded as insurrectionists. Of the successes, none is more celebrated than the numerous journeys led by Harriet Tubman, who became known as the "Moses" of black people. Through their every effort to escape, an enslaved people asserted their identities as people of hope and honor—bestowing self-respect in a system where honor was granted to those who bought them, sold them, used them, and profited from them.

But, the religious life of black people in slavery that had its roots in Africa and that was formed from Christian faith stories and scriptures they heard in plantation life and recast in secret meetings, made resistance possible and gave rise to their musical narratives called spirituals. Unlike the letter to the Hebrews that was written by a specific author, though not clearly named, to a specific audience about reliance on God and the presence of Jesus Christ on life's journey through a threatening world, the spirituals have no single authorship or composer. Yet, they are the spontaneous stories of an enslaved people that also attest to a steadfast relationship with God and the person of Jesus along life's treacherous sojourn.

Both the spirituals and the letter to the Hebrews attest to a sojourn beset with threats, but the Christian journey or pilgrimage is lived out by individuals and communities by entering into life-giving dialogue with God. Both exist as spiritual resources that give direction for what is needed to continue on the Christian journey through a threatening world. As resources, they provide an understanding that shame is overcome in a relationship with God who created us and with Jesus Christ as our companion along the way. Moreover, honor is not related to the power of humans over others or even life itself. Rather, honor is related to our regard for others and our fulfilling God's familial household in our relationships with others.

We will turn to a fuller description of the spirituals and Hebrews as spiritual resources in the following sections. As indicated earlier, attention will be given to three resources for the journey beyond shame appearing both in the spirituals and in Hebrews. They include the embrace of Christian life as a journey that is neither frozen nor unchangeable; acknowledgment of Jesus, the Son of God and kingly Christ, who intercedes on our behalf and journeys with us as divine friend; and the formation of a communal identity bestowed by God and shown in the images of family membership and language of belonging in a divine household.

EMBRACE OF CHRISTIAN LIFE AS A JOURNEY

The collections of spirituals reveal that black people in slavery considered themselves to be on a storied pilgrim journey that was not a static one. Rather, they were living out a story plot that was dynamic and that had purpose and directedness. For them, movement meant believing with passionate hope that a different future was possible and that social status was not unchangeable.[17] Overcoming the shame that was forced upon them required their refusal to accept their condition but, rather, to maintain as indicated in the song, "I shall go, I will go, to see what the end will be."[18] Indeed, the journey motif appears in numerous spirituals including "De Ol' Ark's A-Moverin',"[19] "Git On Board, Little Chillun,"[20] "Gwineter Ride Up in de Chariot Soon-a in de Mornin',"[21] "Heaven Boun' Soldier,"[22] "I'm A-Rollin Through An Unfriendly World,"[23] "Keep A-Inchin' Along,"[24] "Walk Together, Children,"[25] "Weary Traveler,"[26] "Great Day, the Righteous Marching,"[27] "Trampin, Trampin, Trying to Make Heaven My Home,"[28] and "We Shall Walk Through the Valley in Peace."[29]

In his book, *Liberation and Reconciliation*, J. Deotis Roberts refers to the historical experience of black people in America as "black pilgrims in progress."[30] His point is that black people in slavery knew, first, what it meant to be "exiled" and to live out a plot of pilgrimage against adversity. For this reason, Bruno Chenu in his book, *The Trouble I See*, indicates that, in the spirituals, we find "the exaltation of movement."[31]

It cannot be said with any degree of certainty that black people in slavery somehow made a connection between their pilgrim journey and the one set forth by the writer of the letter to the Hebrews. However, the "exaltation of movement" in the spirituals coincides with the pilgrimage theme that Robert Jewett identifies in Hebrews. From Jewett's perspective, the letter to the Lycus Valley congregations contains the essence of Christian pilgrimage as a response to the voice of God along the way.[32] The key point here is that, in both the spirituals and Hebrews, we find ways of overcoming shame through movement. Moreover, the journey has particular characteristics. One essential aspect of the character of the journey disclosed in Hebrews is that, through openness to God's voice, remaining in faithful dialogical relationship with God along the wilderness way, and being obedient to God's direction opens the way for God's rest or the experience of a Sabbath rest in route (Heb 3:7–19; 4:1–10). This understanding of rest is not understood as an experience of repose as in the case of reclining and sleep. Neither does it refer to a view of "just compensation" or "time off" from hard work and voluminous projects in which personal and honorific status play important roles.[33] Rather, rest along the way refers to a sense of peace, joy, and concord that comes from God in the throes of hardship.[34] The slaves conveyed a similar message in their first-person musical narrative:

> I shall walk through the valley in peace.
> I shall walk through the valley in peace.
> If Jesus himself will be my leader,
> I shall walk through the valley in peace.[35]

This sense of *sabbatismos* to which both Hebrews and the spirituals point has the character of a present day-by-day reality along the way. It represents a realized eschatological view of rest. However, the rest also connotes an eschatological fulfillment that is understood as the promised land or the eternal "kingdom" where there is eternal rest, freedom from shame, and full provisions of God's bounty (3:17—4:13).[36] For enslaved black people, the peace of this promised land is communicated in the spiritual, "Religion is a Fortune I Really Do Believe":

> Oh, religion is a fortune, I really do believe,
> Oh, religion is a fortune, I really do believe,
> Oh, religion is a fortune, I really do believe,
> Where Sabbaths have no end.
> Gwinter sit down in de kingdom, I really do believe,
> Gwinter sit down in de kingdom, I really do believe,
> Gwinter walk about in Zion, I really do believe.
> Where Sabbaths have no end.[37]

Moreover, the view of a heaven-bound sojourn was revealed in the following spiritual:

> I am seekin' for a city, Hallelujah,
> For a city into de heaven, Hallelujah,
> Oh, bredren, trabbel wid me, Hallelujah,
> Say will you come along wid me" Hallelujah.[38]

Second, an essential character of movement that is also associated with the rest to which Hebrews refers is that rest cannot be manipulated. Rest is arrived at through a sort of striving that is required by the gospel. It is a matter of seeking and holding fast to the kind of dialogue with God that has the power to overcome shame. At its center is complete reliance on God, the source of all life that imbues the wilderness journey with energy and hope.[39] In fact, this kind of striving is what black people in slavery called "striving after God."

A third characteristic of the movement of pilgrims which the letter to the Hebrews sets forth is the necessity of daily mutual exhortation (Heb 3:13). Because of the danger of anxiety versus the embrace of faith along the wilderness way, it is necessary for sojourners to give encouragement or to comfort one another. In so doing, persons become covenant partners with God and ones through whom God speaks.[40] We find this characteristic in the "exaltation of movement" in previously mentioned spirituals such as: "Let us Cheer the Weary Traveler,"[41] and "Walk together children, don't you get weary . . . Oh, get you ready, children, don't you get weary . . . For Jesus is a comin', don't you get weary . . ."[42]

A fourth characteristic of the movement along the wilderness journey that is set forth in Heb 12:1–17 is the requirement of discipline or a sustained "individual and communal effort in coping with the threats of existence in a hostile world."[43] This discipline requires perseverance, courage, and remembering that there are those—a cloud of witnesses—who faced hardship and who cheer persons on the journey beyond shame. The writer of the letter to the Hebrews calls to mind the faith of Abel, Enoch, Noah, Abraham, Moses, and other Israelite heroes (Heb 11:4–39). Black people in slavery also sang about Moses and other Israelite heroes such as Daniel who was delivered from the lion's den, Jonah from the belly of the whale, and the Hebrew children from the fiery furnace.[44] But in their remembrance of the deliverance of Daniel, Jonah, and the Hebrew children, the slaves acknowledged that God was the deliverer; and they asked the rhetorical question, "Then, why not everyone?"

Like the writer of the letter to the Lycus Valley Christians, black people in slavery assigned historical significance to the pilgrim journey. At the same time, even though the difficulties of the slaves and the Lycus Valley Christians bore some similarity to those experienced in earlier generations, they still had to decide to move on, or as the Hebrews letter writer said, to "run with perseverance the race that is set before us looking to Jesus the pioneer and perfecter of our faith (Heb 12:1b–2a). This running theme appears in the spirituals. Two examples include "I'm Runnin' On" and "Yo' Better Run, Run, Run." Lovell states that "in the former, the singer runs to leave the world behind, to cross the "separatin' line," to be free and glad. He promises that he will never turn back. In the latter, the runner has a definitive incentive."[45] The goal is to "keep yo' eyes upon de prize."[46] However, in still another spiritual, there is clear reference to the One who guides the journey:

Guide my feet, Lord, while I run this race;
Guide my feet, Lord, while I run this race.
Guide my feet, Lord, while I run this race,
'Cause I don't want to run this race in vain.[47]

Most of all, in Hebrews and the message of the spirituals, attention is given to Jesus the One who leads the way, who has already experienced shame and insecurities and can, therefore, enable persons to "drop" the burden and go on (12:1–2).[48] The particular message of the writer of Hebrews is that the life of faith is life under the cross, with shame and hostility not unlike that experienced by Jesus. But, weariness and faint-heartedness can be overcome through strong-willed determination and reliance on Jesus, who the slaves said, "knows all about our troubles and will be with us to the end." Enslaved black people also saw Jesus as One who was not meek and mild but, rather, as One who was resistant to undesirable circumstances and resilient after being downed. Thus, their confidence in Jesus resulted in their singing:

And if you meet with crosses
And trials on the way,
Just keep your trust in Jesus
And don't forget to pray.[49]

The slaves' view of the necessity of endurance also points to a journey that is going somewhere as indicated in the words of the spiritual: "Raise up your head with courage bold, for your race is almost run ... I'm bound for Canaan land."[50] However, there is the understanding not simply that Jesus, the enabler and perfecter of their faith is needed, but that there is need to call on Jesus. This view is captured in their invitatory words in the spiritual, "I want Jesus to walk with me all along my pilgrim journey ... In my trials, Lord, walk with me ... When I'm in trouble, Lord, walk with me ... When my head is bowed in sorrow, I want Jesus to walk with me."[51] And, the emphasis of the slaves on ethical behavior in their move-ment amidst hard trials is found in the words, "Can't hate your neighbor when your mind is staid on Jesus."

The spirituals do not reflect in the same sense the emphasis of the writer of Hebrews on God's desire for pilgrims to learn what is necessary from the difficult and painful journey of life for the sake of Christian maturity (Heb 12:7–13). However, the spirituals convey an undeniable message of overcoming tiredness and weakness with the resolve to "keep on the narrow way" to attain something better in the form not simply of freedom from slavery but liberation from all that would bind them emotionally and spiritually. Consequently, they sang: "Don't you let nobody turn you 'round, Turn you 'round, Turn you 'round. Don't you let nobody turn you 'round; Keep straight in the narrow way."[52]

ACKNOWLEDGMENT OF THE SON AND KINGLY CHRIST

We have already seen in the preceding section the attention that both the spirituals and the letter to the Hebrews give to Jesus Christ. In fact, it may be said that the emphasis on Jesus in the spirituals formed the basis for what may be called the Jesusology of black people. Jesus appeared as a generating image in the wilderness sojourn of black people in slavery. James Cone also confirms that the spirituals reflect a Christological perspective.[53] In this regard, Jesus' divinity and his humanity are affirmed in the spirituals. These musical expressions of the slaves' pilgrim plot exhibit no theological argument about how God became man. There is simply the expression of the slave community's story of God and Jesus in their lives. Thus, the slaves sang about the glory of a kingly Christ, yet God made flesh in a manner resembling the writer's claim in the letter to the Hebrews.

Jesus was viewed by the slaves as God made flesh; and, God was the One who took interest in the lowly, who was accessible to them, who spoke to them, and whose presence buoyed up sagging spirits, comforted the heart, and instilled a hope for freedom.[54] According to Cone, the slaves' view of God embraced the whole of life. Their basic belief was that the God of history had not left them alone.[55]

In an extensive study of the spirituals, Chenu identified three levels of titles for Jesus. They included "titles of glory, combat titles, and intimate names. Jesus is, at the same time, the Savior, the Warrior, and the Friend."[56] Chenu also found that two titles of honor—Savior and King emerged strongly within the spirituals. Black people in slavery referred to the high priestly nature of Jesus by singing:

> He is the King of kings, he is the Lord of lords,
> Jesus Christ, the first and last, no one works like Him.
> He built his throne up in the air, No one works like Him,
> And called his saints from everywhere, No one works like Him.[57]

Another spiritual refers to Jesus as King Emanuel:

> Oh, who do you call de King Emanuel?
> I call my Jesus King Emanuel.
> Oh, some call Him Jesus, but I call Him Lord;
> I call my Jesus King Emmanuel.
> *Refrain*
> Oh, de King Emmanuel is a mighty 'manuel;
> I call my Jesus King Emmanuel.[58]

In still another instance, reference is made to King Jesus who has the power to thwart negative influence and treatment:

> Ride on, King Jesus, No man can a-hinder me.
> Ride on, King Jesus, ride on, No man can a-hinder me.[59]

But, it was the kingly Jesus who was also viewed by enslaved black people as the available, knowing friend in "There's not a Friend like the lonely Jesus, No not one, no not one . . . Jesus knows all about our troubles, He'll be 'round 'til the day I die;" and the acting salvific One in the songs, "Slavery Chain" and "The Old Sheep Know the Road":

> *Slavery Chain*
> Now no more weary trav'lin'
> 'Cause my Jesus set-a me free;
> An' dere's no more auction block for me
> Since He give me liberty.[60]
>
> *The Old Sheep Know the Road*
> O, shout my sister, for you are free,
> For Christ has brought you liberty.[61]

Black people also identified with the severity of Jesus' suffering and saw in his test even unto death on the cross a demonstration of honor. Consequently, they sang, "Honor, honor, unto the dying lamb." Jesus was, for them, the sacrificial victim. In Jesus' death, the slaves saw themselves. The Passion meant that Jesus died for them. Jesus' death was a symbol of their journey of suffering, dishonor, and shame.[62] Based on the message of the spirituals, the slaves recognized the significance of the pain and shame of the Christ event. According to Cone, through the blood of slavery, enslaved black people "transcended the limitations of space and time. Jesus' time became their time"[63] They found themselves by Jesus' side; and they recognized that Jesus, the sacrificial victim, was taking their pain upon himself. Jesus was with them. The slaves reckoned Jesus' dishonor on the cross as Jesus' transforming their dishonor and bestowing on them the gift of worth and dignity. This was an affirmation of their overcoming shame. For them, Jesus turned upside down the honor code of the slave system that bestowed honor on the ones who benefited from the status and material gain of slavery.

It is important to note again that the slaves' understanding of Jesus has its corollary in the portrayal of Jesus in Heb 4:14–16; 5:1–10. Specifically, for the writer of Hebrews, Jesus Christ is God's Son, the high priest who is superior over lesser priests or ones among mortals because it is through him that it is possible to draw near to God. Yet, in the letter, Jesus is also the one who is "not unable to sympathize with our weaknesses, but we have one who in every respect has been tested as we are, yet without sin" (Heb 4:15). He experienced unbelievable trials of life with the ability to pass through them in ways that inspire and even awe us. But, he is in the same sense as the slaves portrayed him—friend. This Jesus that God chose paves the way for the Christian's approach to God's throne of grace where God's presence is experienced and God's help is found in time of need.[64] Because of the access made possible through Jesus, the writer admonishes the Lycus Valley Christians to hold boldly and tenaciously their confession, which is what they know to be God's dialogical relationship with them and the response God invites of them.

When we consider the content of the spirituals in light of Hebrews, it might be said that black people in slavery claimed Jesus as their own. Indeed, one might say that, because of the relationship they knew they had with him and of his relationship with them, they conveyed in song an unwavering and courageous confession. This is all the more evident in what appears to be an invitation to the throne of grace in the words of the spiritual:

> "Come to Jesus, come to Jesus, come to Jesus just now; just now come to Jesus, come to Jesus just now . . . He will save you . . . He is able . . . He is willing . . . Come, confess Him . . . Come, obey Him . . . He will hear you . . . He'll forgive you . . . He will cleanse you . . . Jesus loves you . . . Only trust him."[65]

A similar invitation is conveyed in the spiritual: "Come to Me, ye who are hard opprest; Lay your head gently upon my breast. Come to Me, and I will give you rest; Weary one, hither come! God is your home!"[66]

LANGUAGE OF BELONGING IN A DIVINE HOUSEHOLD

The sudden ripping of Africans from the familiar surroundings and re-lationships in their ancestral homes and further severing these ties in slavery were isolating experiences that assaulted personal worth and the African collective consciousness. Because of the shame-invoking experi-ence of being uprooted, relationally separated, landless, without rights, and brutalized, the slaves felt deeply the experience of being relational refugees or persons in exile far away from home.[67] Out of this circum-stance came the wail of loss, "Sometimes I feel like a motherless child, a long ways from home ... Sometimes I feel like I'm almos' gone."[68]

Nonetheless, the slaves' will to overcome loss, indignity, separation, and aloneness resulted in their re-enactment of the African collective value orientation through forming close-knit groups and clandestine church meetings called the "Invisible Institution." In these meetings in cabins or thickets called "brush arbors," black people in slavery became family members in God's house. They overcame the shame of assaults to their individual and communal worth by claiming the unchangeable nature, ever-presence, and freeing work of Jesus, as noted in the ear-lier mentioned song: "Jesus Christ, the first and last, no one works like him."[69] In Jesus, they felt that no one could hinder their building and maintaining relationships.

They referred to themselves as God's children as noted in the spiritual: "O glory, glory hallelujah! O glory, glory to the Lamb; O glory, glory, hallelujah! Child of God, that's what I am!"[70] And, they called one another sisters and brothers. They created a bond of connection that was sealed by this language of belonging in a divine household and by their laying hold of the belief that they would be alright so long as they "hold to God's hand, God's unchanging hand, and build their hopes on things eternal."[71] Further evidence of this re-created family bond is found in the familiar words appearing in the spirituals, "You are my brother, so give me your hand";[72] O brother, O sister, you got a right, I got a right, we all got a right to the tree of life";[73] Not my sister, not my brother, but it's me O Lord, standin' in the need of prayer';[74] and "I'm travelin' through a weary land ... O sister, won't you help me ... O brother, won't you help me to pray?"

Being in the family of God was the mark of being a Christian. As Christians in that family, they knew that God was not ashamed of them as black people in the dishonorable slave system. Likewise, they were not ashamed of God or to be Christian. This view is shown in the words of the spiritual: "Not ashamed to be a Christian; God knows I am a Christian. God knows I'm not ashamed. Well, the Holy Ghost is my witness."[75] It may be said that this view is tied to the dialogical relationship of the slaves with God through Jesus Christ that summoned a response of commitment to be believers, "Lord, I want to be a Christian in-a my heart . . . Lord, I want to be more holy in-a-my heart . . . Lord, I don't want to be like Judas in-a my heart . . . Lord, I want to be like Jesus in-a my heart."[76] At the same time, the slaves were well aware that the ongoing severity of the daily circumstances of slavery had the propensity of making difficult their holding onto their faith. Consequently, they exhorted one another, "My brethren, don't get weary."[77]

It is important to note the attention that is given to communal and family-like relationships by black people in slavery has affinity to the familial language and meanings of its use appearing in the letter to the Hebrews. Although the Lycus Valley Christians were not enslaved, they became, in a sense, relational refugees. They were persons who, in being persecuted for choosing to be Christians, felt a sense of being in exile.[78] In fact, Sachs states that "it is as if they were in the midst of a wilderness experience every bit as intense as the desert wanderings of their ancestors."[79] Becoming Christian separated them from their ancestral Jewish community; and, it was perhaps the case that the hard trials of their becoming followers of Jesus created a longing for their return to Judaism.

The writer of Hebrews picks up the language of family in Heb 3:2–4 by focusing on Christ, the builder of God's house which the entire spiritual family inhabits.[80] Moreover, the writer insists that members become part of God's house insofar as they hold fast their confidence and pride in the hope that comes from God in the person of Jesus Christ who is over God's house (Heb 3:6). Indeed, these family members are part of God's salvation plot and are called for God's purposes with Jesus as leader who is not ashamed to call them brothers and sisters (Heb 2:11). The writer of the letter to the Hebrews also picks up the language of family that is connected to God's house by referring to the Lycus Valley congregants as brothers and sisters: "Take care, brothers and sisters that none of you may have an unbelieving heart that turns away from the living God" (Heb 3:12). In this statement, the writer further tells the Christians to urge one another to hold firmly to their belief to the end (Heb 3:14).

The point here is that Hebrews appears as a mirror for the slaves' understanding that they, like the Hebrews, are part of God's house, are claimed as family members by God unashamedly, and are part of God's salvation plot. Moreover, they must hold one another accountable to maintaining their dialogical relationship with God through Jesus Christ.

CONFESSIONS OF HOPE

Within the songs of black people in slavery, "there breathes a hope—a faith in the ultimate justice of things."[81] These words of W. E. B. DuBois point to the spirituals as songs of hope that helped bring an abused and stigmatized people through unthinkable circumstances. Through their musical narratives, black people in slavery declared that shame was overcome by hope in God and their embrace of the present and lasting hope which was Jesus Christ. Their songs were confessions of hope that in ways answer the call in the letter to the Hebrews to "hold firm the confidence and the pride that belong to hope" (Heb 3:6). These songs seem to respond to the letter's call "to realize the full assurance of hope to the very end so that you may not become sluggish, but be imitators of those who through faith and patience inherit the promises (Heb 6:11–12). Indeed, as though to "seize the hope set before [them] (Heb 6:18b), and make clear the nature of their embrace of "hope, a sure and steadfast anchor of the soul" (Heb 6:19), the slaves sang:

> In de Lord, in de Lord, My soul's been anchored in de Lord;
> In de Lord, in de Lord, My soul's been anchored in de Lord.
> Befo' I'd stay in hell one day, My soul's been anchored in de Lord.
> I'll sing an' pray myself away, My soul's been anchored in de Lord.
> I'm gwinter pray an' never stop, My soul's been anchored in de Lord.
> Until I reach de mountaintop, My soul's been anchored in de Lord
> O, Lord, My soul's been anchored in de Lord.[82]

Importantly Jewett comments that the intent of the letter to the Hebrews is for Christians to embrace hope by entering a dynamic relationship with God. Doing so would provide stability in unstable conditions; buttress mental health amidst sanity defying circumstances; and hold life safe and firm when everything else deteriorates.[83] The significance of this understanding of hope is exceptionally highlighted in the spirituals of black people in slavery. Moreover, we see in the spirituals meanings of confession to which the letter to the Lycus Valley Christians refers. The letter draws attention to confession in Heb 3:1; 10:23; 11:13; and 13:15. The view of confession to which these verses point is not about one's confession of sin. Rather, it is about laying hold of and clinging to a relationship with Jesus, the high priest who, as the slaves sang, "knows all about our troubles." Confession is all about making known or acknowledging the "lonely Jesus who will be with us to the end."

CONFESSION AS INVITATION TO FAITHFUL PARTICIPATION IN GOD'S UNFOLDING STORY

For black people in slavery, the confession of hope was also appended by rousing or making clear to one another the necessity to love, carry out good deeds, and meet together in a manner akin to that conveyed in the letter to the Hebrews (Heb 10:24). In the spirituals, as in Hebrews, this exhortation appears in what may be called a language of mutual pledge or assent to a mutual undertaking for the sake of moving forward with hope and resilience amidst trying, shaming circumstances. The language of mutual pledge appears in the slave's injunction that "you've got to love everybody . . . help everybody when your mind is staid on Jesus." Moreover, in both the spirituals and Hebrews, the language of mutual pledge occurs through use of the words "Let us." In one instance in the spirituals, the mutual pledge is in the form of encouragement:

> Let us cheer the weary traveler, cheer the weary traveler;
> Let us cheer the weary traveler, along the heavenly way.
> I'll take my gospel trumpet, an I'll begin to blow,
> An' if my Saviour helps me, I'll blow wherever I go;
> An' brothers, if you meet with crosses, an' trials on the way,
> Just keep your trust in Jesus, an' don't forget to pray.
> Let us cheer the weary traveler, cheer the weary traveler,
> Let us cheer the weary traveler, along the heavenly way.[84]

A mutual pledge to gather together appears in the words of the spiritual, "Let us break bread together . . . drink wine together . . . praise God together on our knees with our face to the rising sun, O Lord, have mercy on me." In this instance, the mutual pledge of the slaves was to honor their collective membership in God's house and to draw near both to one another and to God in worship. However, some commentators on the spirituals also assert that the reference to facing the rising sun reflected a mutual pledge to communicate secretly to one another the direction for a meeting or location for a planned escape to freedom.[85] The inclusion of the words in the spiritual, "Let us praise God together on our knees" also connotes the meaning of the mutual pledge appearing in Heb 13:15, "Through him, let us continually offer a sacrifice of praise to God, that is the fruit of lips that confess his name." In a real sense, this mutual pledge is a confession that has to do with openly declaring faithfulness to God.

IMPLICATIONS OF CONFESSIONS OF HOPE
FOR THE TWENTY-FIRST CENTURY

No one is exempt from the vicissitudes of life. However, there are extreme cases of individuals and groups who are abused, stigmatized, or shamed in ways that devalue their personal and social identity and that bring physical and psychological harm to them. Why this happens in not fully understood. Jeffrey Jay Hansen, in his article, "Coping Mechanisms of the Stigmatized," cites potential sources as "prejudicial attitudes created by personality variables, such as Authoritarianism and Social Dominance Orientation . . . [and] a more evolutionary perspective, such as competition for resources and the need to bolster self-esteem."[86] Hansen adds that "Terror Management Theory also provides an interesting postulate for the need of an outgroup against whom we must be hostile and aggressive."[87] This last view stems from the idea that someone needs a target. The author goes on the say that "no matter what the reason behind the attitudes, the existence of stigma is unquestionable."[88] And, the need to address shaming attitudes and behavior continues.

The struggle of persons to deal with the trauma of stigmatization and shame is not easy. In truth, it cannot be assumed that black people in slavery did not succumb to their experiences of personal, social, and physical brutalization. In fact, Ronald Salzberger and Mary Turck contend that, for some, the brutalities of slavery resulted in what historian Nell Irvin Painter called "soul murder," insofar as persons experienced an irreversible deadening feeling of self.[89] However, in the very real situation of unspeakable harm faced by black people in slavery, the spirituals were born; and this music attested to the ability of many to overcome shaming attitudes and continue on amidst brutalizing circumstances. How was this possible? What may be useful in twenty-first century situations of shame?

Hansen asserts that "stigmatized individuals do not passively 'soak up' all of the stereotypes and prejudices that they face on a daily basis

... Thus, even if they cannot *avoid* an unpleasant situation, they do have some control over how they *perceive* such a situation."[90] They also can develop active or liberative methods of responding. One of the coping methods that Hansen describes is called "attributional ambiguity." Through this coping method, stigmatized individuals attribute negative attitudes and prejudicial behavior directed toward them to the perpetrator's discriminatory behavior rather than to their own internal or external characteristics.[91] For example, evidence of this coping mechanism among enslaved black people appears in the spiritual that uses words to judge those who participate in the conduct of slavery: "Everybody talkin' 'bout heab'n ain't goin' dere."[92]

Of greater note, however, is the overall use of religion as a coping mechanism. For the slaves, the Christian faith offered a vision of hope resulting in their confession of hope. They took from the Christianity that was presented to them by their captors what was useful for them and left the rest. The music called spirituals became the expressive channel of hope and promise. But, this presentation has also proposed that the themes in the spirituals show great affinity to the letter to the Hebrews. The contributions of this music and Hebrews to twenty-first-century persons who are in need of hope to move beyond shame appear throughout the preceding sections of this presentation. In summary, they include the following:

- See the self as a sojourner. Embrace the view of life as a journey that is neither static nor unchangeable. Decide to move forward believing, with passionate hope, that a different future is possible. Refuse to accept the condition of shame.

- Remain in faithful dialogue with God through the spiritual disciplines of prayer, meditation, worship, and Bible study. Know the self as God's child and as a member of God's house that is cared by Jesus Christ.

- Be open to God's presence and voice along the way as means of experiencing the rest or a sense of peace, joy, and concord in the midst of hardship. Seek after God and rely on God.

- Invite Jesus to walk with you along the pilgrim journey.

- Connect with other sojourners where mutual encouragement can be given and received.

- Don't give up. Persevere. "Don't you let nobody turn you around." Remember, identify, and draw on the stories of exemplars in the faith who have continued on the journey despite hardship.

- Remember the importance of participating in worship where praise of God occurs. Remember to care for others beyond the self. Be unashamedly Christian. Confess hope.

- Name your favorite religious songs. Reflect on the words. Sing or listen to the message. Consider how and why the message shapes your understanding and feelings of hope. Know that it is possible to overcome shame.

ENDNOTES

1. These words to a spiritual that were sung by black people in slavery are found in Chenu, *Trouble*, 255.

2. Lovell, *Black Song*, 197.

3. Zinn, *People's History*, 167.

4. Lovell, *Black Song*, 140.

5. See Douglass, *Narrative*; Rawick, *American Slave*; Lovell, *Black Song*, 144–45; Blassingame, *Slave Community*; Blassingame, *Slave Testimony*; Huggins, *Black Odyssey*; Gates, *Classic Slave Narratives*; Douglass, *Bondage*; Mellon, *Bullwhip Days*; Berlin, *Many Thousand*; Chenu, *Trouble*, 1–25; Salzberger and Turck, *Reparations*, 5–15.

6. Lovell, *Black Song*, 145.

7. See the overview of Harvard sociologist Orlando Patterson's discussion on the degraded status of the slave in: Salzberger and Turck, *Reparations*, 37–42. The overview is based on Patterson, *Slavery*.

8. The story appears in Salzberger and Turk, *Reparations*. It is taken from Jacobs, *Incidents*.

9. The story appears in Chenu, *Trouble*, 19–20. It is quoted from Blassingame, *Slave Testimony*, 372.

10. Rogers, *Delia's Tears*.

11. Ibid., 19.

12. Ibid., 226. Rogers draws from Fanon, *Black Skin*, 116 and DuBois, *Souls*, 3.

13. Salzberger and Turck, *Reparations*, 41; and Rogers, *Delia's Tears*, 244.

14. See Jewett, *Letter to Pilgrims*, 10–11; Sachs, *Hebrews*; Mackie, "Confession," 114–29.

15. Sachs, *Hebrews*, 9.

16. Jewett, *Letter to Pilgrims*, 11.

17. Chenu, *Trouble*, 122.

18. The entire contents of the spiritual are found in Lovell, *Black Song*, 323.

19. Versions of the spiritual appear in Johnson and Johnson, *American Negro Spirituals*, 1.25; and Chenu, *Trouble*, 238.

20. Johnson and Johnson, *American Negro Spirituals*, 1.126; Lovell, *Black Song*, 249, 333; Chenu, *Trouble*, 243.

21. Versions of the spiritual appear in Johnson and Johnson, *American Negro Spirituals*, 2.121; and Lovell, *Black Song*, 248.

22. A version of the spiritual appears in Johnson and Johnson, *American Negro Spirituals*, 1.54.

23. Versions of the spiritual appear in ibid., 1.145; and Lovell, *Black Song*, 295.

24. Versions of the spiritual appear in Johnson and Johnson, *American Negro Spirituals*, 1.134; and Lovell, *Black Song*, 232, 352.

25. Versions of the spiritual appear in Johnson and Johnson, *American Negro Spirituals*. 2.180; and Lovell, *Black Song*, 276.

26. Versions of the spiritual appear in Johnson and Johnson, *American Negro Spirituals*, 1.184-85 and Lovell, *Black Song*, 277.

27. Versions of the spiritual appear in Johnson and Johnson, *American Negro Spirituals*, 2.56–57 and Lovell, *Black Song*, 241.

28. Versions of the spiritual appear in Lovell, *Black Song*, 440, 441; and Chenu, *Trouble*, 280.

29. A version of the spiritual appears in Lovell, *Black Song*, 270, 309.

30. Roberts, *Liberation*, 70.

31. Chenu, *Trouble*, 122.

32. Jewett, *Letter to Pilgrims*, 2.

33. Ibid., 68.

34. See Guthrie, *Hebrews*, 116.

35. Lovell, *Black Song*, 270, 309.

36. Jewett, *Letter to Pilgrims*, 55.

37. The spiritual appears in Johnson and Johnson, *American Negro Spirituals*, 2.53–55.

38. A version of the spiritual is found in Chenu, *Trouble*, 251.

39. See Jewett, *Letter to Pilgrims*, 69–70; Guthrie, *Hebrews*, 117.

40. Guthrie, *Hebrews*, 58.

41. Johnson and Johnson, *American Negro Spirituals*, 2.56–57; Lovell, *Black Song*, 241.

42. A version of the spiritual is found in Chenu, *Trouble*, 281.

43. Jewett, *Letter to Pilgrims*, 216.

44. The spiritual, "Go Down, Moses," appears in Johnson and Johnson, *American Negro Spirituals*, 1.51–53. The spiritual, "Didn't My Lord Deliver Daniel," appears in ibid., 1.148–51.

45. Lovell, *Black Song*, 285.

46. Ibid.

47. A version of the spiritual is found in Carpenter, *Hymnal*, #131.

48. See Jewett, *Letter to Pilgrims*, 216–18.

49. These words of the spiritual are found in Lovell, *Black Song*, 320.

50. A version of the spiritual, "Bound for Canaan Land" is found in Chenu, *Trouble*, 234.

51. Ibid., 253–54.

52. The spiritual became one of the theme songs during the civil rights movement of the 1960s. The words are found in Lovell, *Black Song*, 277.

53. Cone, *Spirituals*, 50–52.

54. See Blassingame, *Slave Community*, 74–75; Cone, *Spirituals*, 46.

55. Cone, *Spirituals*, 46.

56. Chenu, *Trouble*, 174.

57. Versions of the spiritual are found in Lovell, *Black Song*, 231, and Chenu, *Trouble*, 248.

58. A version of the spiritual is found in Chenu, *Trouble*, 260.

59. Versions of the spiritual appear in Johnson and Johnson, *American Negro Spirituals*, 2.80–83; Lovell, *Black Song*, 230; Carpenter, *Hymnal*, #225; Jones, *Wade*, 18–19; Chenu, *Trouble*, 270–71.

60. A version of the spiritual is found in Chenu, *Trouble*, 274.

61. Ibid., 278–79.

62. Cone, *Spirituals*, 52–53.

63. Ibid., 54.

64. See: Jewett, *Letter to Pilgrims*, 77–82; Guthrie, *Hebrews*, 120–24.

65. A version of the spiritual appears in Chenu, *Trouble*, 236–37.

66. Ibid., 237.

67. The use of the term, "relational refugees" is analogous to its use in the book by Wimberly, *Relational Refugees*, 15, 22. See also Smith, *Navigating*, 36.

68. Versions of the spiritual appear in Johnson and Johnson, *American Negro Spirituals*, 2.80–83; Lovell, *Black Song*, 230; Carpenter, *Hymnal*, #225; Jones, *Wade*, 18–19; Chenu, *Trouble*, 270–71.

69. These words come from the earlier mentioned spiritual, "Ride On, King Jesus," versions of which are found in Chenu, *Trouble*, 270–71.

70. Ibid., 266.

71. A version of the spiritual, "Hold to God's Unchanging Hand" is found in Carpenter, *Hymnal*, #404.

72. Chenu, *Trouble*, 130.

73. Versions of the spiritual are found in Johnson and Johnson, *American Negro Spirituals*, 1.183–84; Lovell, *Black Song*, 334; Chenu, *Trouble*, 284.

74. Versions of the spiritual appear in; Johnson and Johnson, *American Negro Spirituals*, 1.94–95; Lovell, *Black Song*, 236; Chenu, *Trouble*, 276.

75. Chenu, *Trouble*, 196. Taken from Courlander, *Treasury*, 326.

76. Versions of the spiritual, "Lord, I Want to Be a Christian," are found in Johnson and Johnson, *American Negro Spirituals*, 2.72–73; Lovell, *Black Song*, 288–99; Chernu, *Trouble*, 262.

77. See Lovell, *Black Song*, 277.

78. Wimberly, *Relational Refugees*, 15–22.

79. Sachs, *Hebrews*, 2.

80. See Jewett, *Letter to Hebrews*, 50–51.

81. DuBois, *Souls*, 380.

82. Versions of the spiritual are found in Johnson and Johnson, *American Negro Spirituals*, 2.37–39; Lovell, *Black* Song, 237; Chenu, *Trouble*, 264–65.

83. Jewett, *Letter to Pilgrims*, 112–13.

84. This version of the spiritual, titled "Weary Traveler," appears in Johnson and Johnson, *American Negro Spirituals*, 1.184–187.

85. Jones, *Wade*, 46. Jones draws on Fisher, *Negro Slave Songs*, 29.

86. Hansen, "Coping Mechanisms," 13.

87. Ibid.

88. Ibid.

89. See Salzberger and Turck, *Reparations*, 47–49. These authors referred to the writing of Painter, "Soul Murder," 125–46.

90. Hansen, "Coping Mechanisms," 5.

91. Ibid.

92. The words are part of the spiritual, "All God's Chillun Got Wings." A version of the spiritual is found in Johnson and Johnson, *American Negro Spirituals*, 1.71–73.

6

Justification by Grace

Shame and Acceptance in a County Jail

DAVID M. RHOADS and SANDRA ROBERTS RHOADS

INTRODUCTION

THE PURPOSE OF THESE reflections is to explore the concept of justification by grace as a way to address human shame. Dave is a retired teacher of the New Testament and Sandy is a former pastor with experience as a jail chaplain. We have been working on a book together on the implications of justification by grace for the twenty-first century, so we are happy to have this opportunity to reflect on justification in relation to shame.

The reflections proceed with back-and-forth statements from each of us as Sandy describes her experiences with justification by grace in jail ministry and Dave presents an interpretation of justification by grace based largely on the letters of Paul.[1]

SANDY—*In 1995 I was called to be chaplain for the county jail in Kenosha, Wisconsin. As is true throughout the United States, anyone arrested for a crime who cannot post bail is housed in the county jail until the courts decide their fate. My "parish" was thus a rather diverse assemblage of around five hundred souls, ranging from poor folks who had not paid their tickets all the way to accused murderers and rapists.*

When I was called to serve at the jail, I went prepared to deal with guilt and forgiveness. After all, jail is the place where people's sins are public and writ large—sometimes on the front page of the local paper. And many of the inmates had reached a point where their lives were so out of control, their losses so great, and the threat of prison so dire that they were more than ready to get right with God.

So, during my five years at the jail, I offered a number of "courses" on forgiveness. Early on, I discovered that the inmates were, remarkably, able to confess, sometimes publicly, and seek forgiveness for multitudinous dark sins/crimes. Even more remarkable to me, they were able to forgive others, often for horrific abuses done to them, usually in their childhood. But, almost to a person they could not forgive themselves. They could not! I slowly came to understand that underneath all of the guilt for their sins were huge cesspools of shame. They could not forgive themselves because of their shame. And the ultra-powerful tool I was offering to them from our faith, the promise of forgiveness, was not the right tool to deal with shame. I also discovered that shame was much more complex and difficult to address than guilt. So what word other than forgiveness could I offer to address their underlying shame?

DAVE—Justification by grace is an apocalyptic concept that offers a broad vision for a new world. For Paul, justification by grace through faith was not a doctrine. It was a transforming reality that he himself had experienced. The term "justification" is little-used today. The Greek word, *dikaiosyne*, means both "justification" and "righteousness." The verb forms mean: "to set right" or "to be set right"; "to justify" or "to be justified"; "to become just/righteous" or "to be made just/righteous." As such, there is an intimate relationship between justification and justice, with the clear implication that the one entails the other. As a legal term, justification referred to "the status that someone has when the court has found in their favor." The person was therefore declared "'righteous,' that is, 'acquitted,' 'cleared,' 'vindicated,' 'justified.'"[2] Once the judgment came, it represented the person's standing, regardless of whether they were actually guilty. Paul borrowed the concept from the courts to describe how God, through Jesus, redeems humanity and indeed the whole creation. Paul was convinced that no one could be justified before God by doing works of the Law (the Judean Torah). For Paul, one is justified and one becomes just through the grace of God active in the death of Jesus and the life in the Holy Spirit.

Justification by grace has a long history. It has its roots in Jewish history and the Hebrew religion. Through the centuries, many Christian communities have embraced justification as an expression of the gospel. Justification by grace was "rediscovered" by Martin Luther as he studied Romans in his quest to find a gracious God. Lutherans sometimes identify it as "the doctrine upon which the church stands or falls." Methodists consider it foundational, with an emphasis on sanctification by the Holy Spirit. American Baptists have turned to it as the theology that undergirds their commitment to religious freedom. Many people of color and people living in colonized nations have embraced justification by grace as a way to affirm that God is no respecter-of-persons, that all are justified freely and equally.

Justification by grace is not the only, nor indeed the most common, view of redemption in Christian churches. The most common view of redemption among Christians is that Jesus died for people's sins to be forgiven. This is the abbreviated formula: All people have sinned and, as such, they deserve judgment and death. Through Jesus, God forgives their sins and saves them for eternal life. There is a tendency to collapse justification by grace into this popular formula of forgiveness, as if they were the same thing. After a recent lecture I gave on this subject, a former Lutheran bishop acknowledged that it had never occurred to him that justification and forgiveness were not the same.

Justification and forgiveness are, in some sense, quite different models of redemption.[3] One way to understand the difference between justification and forgiveness is to realize that forgiveness works *within a system*. Forgiveness leaves in place the legal/moral system that is used to make ourselves right with God and others. It affirms our successes in meeting the lawful standards and addresses only our sinful failings. So, we do our best to follow the laws and be good moral humans—and God forgives us when we fail to live up to that system. The system remains in place and also our efforts to justify ourselves before God remain in place. We make it in the system because we get help from God, who forgives the failings. The status of the legal/moral system is reinforced in the process of forgiveness. And the performance principle—our efforts to justify ourselves before God by our actions in living up to a system of law—is also reinforced.

By contrast, justification by grace is an action by *God* (not by us) that justifies (sets us right with God) by (God's) free choice to do so as a gift—based neither upon a system of standards nor upon human performance.

Justification does two things. First, grace obviates the legal system of standards. There are two ways to deal with sin. One is to forgive the sin. The other way is to get rid of the law. So in contrast to forgiving us when we fail to keep the law, God justifies us by getting rid of the system of law as a basis for justification (Gal 3:6—4:11). For Paul, the Law in itself is good. However, as a system of making ourselves right with God, it does not empower us to do goodness. In fact, in Paul's view, it is a system of enslavement that leads to sin and death (Rom 7:1–25). Paul declares that justification by grace is the end of the legal system as a basis for justification (Rom 10:4).

Second, justification by grace also obviates the works people do in an effort to live up to the law as a means to justify themselves before God. By grace, we are made right with God (accepted), no longer based on works of the law but on God's freely given favor. Hence, in contrast to forgiveness, justification by grace gets rid of the systemic requisites for redemption and eliminates human behavior as the basis for justification. Justification by grace is a free gift, no matter what we do or do not do, no matter what system of standards we may or may not live up to. We are accepted by God unconditionally apart from law and apart from our efforts to keep the law. Therefore, justification addresses sin in a way that is different from forgiveness.

Additionally, justification also addresses shame. Forgiveness focuses on the act committed, whereas justification addresses the whole person. When you say, "You are forgiven," you are dealing with the act, but not always with the shame that underlies the act. When you say "You are accepted"—accepted apart from the system of law and apart from your compliance with it—you address not only the sin but also the underlying shame for being the kind of person that would commit such a sin/crime. And you also liberate the person from the tyranny of the system that has caused the shame.

SANDY—*In my work in the jail, I discovered that the real roots of the profound shame that prevented these prisoners from forgiving themselves lay even deeper than the shame related to their crimes; these roots usually went back to their childhood. It is obvious, but nevertheless it is shocking, to realize that most of the perpetrators of crimes are also the victims of crimes. Most of those I met who had committed crimes had also had horrible things done to them. In no way does this excuse their actions, but it does explain a great deal. I was not at the jail for more than a few weeks before I began to say to myself and anyone else who would listen: "We could empty our jails if we could find a way to stop child abuse and neglect." I remember a man who told me a horrific story of being locked in closets for many hours at a time as punishment when he was a child; another was made to kneel on uncooked peas with his face to the wall; many were beaten with belts or fists by drunken fathers; they often grew up answering to degrading names like "stupid," and "asshole." There were huge numbers of women and men in the jail who had been sexually abused; it was not uncommon to find that every single woman in a given cycle of our women's treatment program had been sexually abused.*

The neglect the inmates had experienced in childhood was even more pervasive. They often came from homes where parents were addicted to drugs, overwhelmed by poverty, or had never been parented themselves. Many of the inmates were obviously unwanted by their parents, and they knew it. Some had become foster children, while others had raised them-selves on the streets.

No wonder, then, that there was shame—a feeling that they were unlovable, unacceptable, defective in some deep, rotten-to-the-core way—before they ever committed their first crimes. And then, tragically, "shame begot shame."[4] *Because of their early experiences, many inmates became vulnerable to addictions, toxic relationships, and all manner of other poor choices that eventually landed them in jail. Thus, they were dealing with the added shame from their crimes and the damaging effects of their crimes on their victims, their loved ones, and themselves.*

This was, I believe, the root cause of their inability to forgive them-selves. They were filled with shame. They believed that they were not wor-thy to be forgiven.

DAVE—Sandy said that the declaration of forgiveness did not adequately address the shame that the prisoners in the jail were experiencing. So what about the shame they had experienced as victims? Could forgive-ness address this shame?

Forgiveness is good news indeed for those who have sinned. But if forgiveness is the only message of redemption, then what is the good news for those who have been *sinned against*? These prisoners had not only sinned, they had also been sinned against. How do we address this? Some years ago, a South African wrote a book called *A Black Future? Jesus and Salvation in South Africa.* His argument was that black children in Soweto have done nothing of any significance to sin against anyone. So, if an offer of forgiveness is the only Christian gospel for them, then there is no future theology to address these children, children who had been relegated to extreme poverty and treated with such discrimination and oppression that they had lost hope.[5]

I once read a book on counseling rape victims. The book was based on the model of confession and forgiveness. The author had the audacity to argue that the offer of forgiveness to a rape victim was good news since they usually felt somehow responsible for their rape and this was a way to address their guilt! It may be true that everyone has committed some sin at some time, however small, but a challenge to victims to repent of their sins and be forgiven is really no good news at all!

Elsa Tamez of Mexico poses the same problem on behalf of the poor and oppressed in Central America. The English translation of Elsa Tamez's book is *The Amnesty of Grace.* Different from forgiveness, justification by grace declares *amnesty,* a pardon from God that releases the oppressed from the guilt and shame foisted upon them by their oppressors. It declares oppressed persons to be fully accepted, despite how the oppressors seek to define their identity and determine their existence. Justification by God's grace says that people are free to define themselves and to see themselves as human beings with dignity, even when others do not. Put another way, justification frees a victim from the story given to them by their victimizer: the story the oppressors give to the oppressed; the story the rich give to the poor they exploit; the story the predator gives to the victim; and so on. God gives the oppressed an open story to determine their existence in response to grace freely given so that they are able to face their oppression with new-found dignity and hope.[6]

The point is this: there is an underlying shame for those who have been sinned against because of the shame heaped on them by oppressors, even when there is no rational reason for them to feel shame. This shame prevents people from being able to forgive themselves or to accept forgiveness from God. Justification deals with the shame of being sinned against by declaring unconditional acceptance.

This does not mean that people who have committed crimes avoid the consequences of their own guilty actions in the legal system. Rather, it means that they can face the consequences of their actions because their identity as a person is placed on a different basis—not on the basis of the shame instilled by those who victimized them, but given as a gift by God. They are declared just or righteous as human beings before God, regardless of their status before the legal system.

SANDY—*Once a week we held worship services for the inmates. On Wednesday mornings, twenty men were escorted single-file into a room filled with plastic chairs, a desk, and a blackboard. The door was locked behind us, and we would commence to sing, preach, and pray. After the men's service was over, I would radio the guards, who would come and take the men back to their cells and usher in twenty women for their service.*

The worshipers were always an odd mix. Some of the inmates were born-and-brought-up Christians who knew the hymns and added their hearty "amens" to the sermon; others were desperately seeking God in this, their time of reckoning; and there were always a few who just wanted to escape the cell block for a brief hour. Thankfully, the guards only screened out known jail troublemakers; as a result, some of those with the more serious charges and the bleakest prospects for freedom were often in attendance.

I remember vividly the first time I preached on justification by grace through faith. It was early in my ministry there, and I was a little worried about preaching on Paul, as I was afraid his more abstract, theological points might be somewhat difficult for my listeners to comprehend—or perhaps I should say, for me to explain. But as I began to read the words from Romans—"For there is no distinction, since all have sinned and fall short of the glory of God; they are now justified by his grace as a gift, through the redemption that is in Christ Jesus . . . ," I began to be aware that the air in the room had changed. I looked up to see all eyes riveted on me, as if the worshipers literally were watching the words coming out of my mouth. Somewhere in the back of my mind it dawned on me: Paul's archaic legal metaphor of "justification" is not going to be obscure to this congregation!

I took heart and began the sermon, rewording Paul's incomparable words into more pedestrian twentieth-century vernacular. I remember using Philip Yancey's definition of grace: "Grace means there is nothing we can do to make God love us more—no amount of spiritual calisthenics and renunciations, no amount of knowledge gained from seminaries . . . no amount of crusading on behalf of righteous causes. And grace means

there is nothing we can do to make God love us less—no amount of racism
or pride or pornography or adultery or even murder. Grace means that
God already loves us as much as an infinite God can possibly love." So
then, I went on to say, we are made right with God, not because we have
been good but because God is good. It's a gift we didn't earn—none of us,
because we have all sinned and fallen short. It's given to us because God is
that gracious. I asked them, what if they went before their judge and the
judge said, "You're free. All charges have been dropped. You can walk out
of this court right now and go home to your family—not because you are
innocent, mind you. I am choosing to set you free because I love you."[7]

There were tears in quite a few eyes, perhaps because they were keenly
aware that they could not literally walk out of jail that day. But they got it!
Paul's archaic, juridical metaphor was as powerful for them as it must have
been for Paul's first-century congregations in Rome and Galatia.

DAVE—Justification by grace, the declaration of unconditional acceptance, is rather astounding when you place it against the expectations of
any given cultural context. The weight of those cultural expectations in
terms of law and public opinion can bear heavily on everyone, especially
criminals. It may have been even more difficult in antiquity. We tend
to understand justification individually, as if it is solely about my own
personal relationship with God. But the ancient Mediterranean cultures
were collectivist cultures in which people got their fundamental identity
from the community of which they were a part. So the system of law (the
works of the Law) of which Paul speaks was the Judean *community's* laws
and standards by which they determined guilt and innocence, honor and
shame. The weight of guilt and shame was especially heavy when one's
identity was embedded in the community.

In some sense, Paul's real concern was with these larger communities of which individuals were a part. As such, the issue of justification comes up in Paul's letters when there is a conflict between Judeans
and Gentiles. In Paul's view, no one culture has a right to be the basis
for bringing guilt and shame upon another culture, even if it be the
Judean culture. In Galatians, for example, Paul refuses to allow Judeans
to impose their Law upon the Gentile Galatians. When Paul says in
Romans that "all have sinned [guilt] and fall short of the glory of God
[shame]" (Rom 3:23), he was referring not just to individuals but also
to the failure of cultures to justify themselves—even in relation to their

own standards. Paul says that no system of prerequisites—even the Judean law of Moses—can serve as a basis for justifying a group. When he says that "there is now no condemnation" (Rom 5:1), he is claiming that justification by grace obviates both Judean and Gentile systems of justification.

Collectivist cultures were also strongly based on honor and shame.[8] In collectivist cultures, there was little introspection.[9] So "honor" came much more from the external favor of the community than from internal feelings of pride. The guilt and shame of which they spoke came much more from the attitudes and actions of the community toward that person than from internal feelings of guilt or shame. This public disapproval was especially harsh in light of the fact that the behavior of the individual brought honor or shame on the whole community. In the face of these cultural standards, the declaration that justification came freely by divine grace apart from those standards was rather astounding.

The offer of justification by grace, which was scandalously undeserved in the eyes of the community, mirrors the offer of justification to prisoners in the jail who face public guilt and public shame for their crimes. To declare them accepted in God's eyes does indeed obviate both the absolutism of the system of judgment of the community and the behavior of the criminal. This is precisely what Paul meant when he said, "God proves his love for us in that while still we were sinners, Christ died for us" (Rom 5:8). And he writes, "For while we were still weak . . . Christ died for the ungodly" (Rom 5:6). The label of "sinners" in the society bore the public weight of guilt, and the label of "weakness" in the society bore the public weight of shame. This was tremendous public pressure, because the culpable behavior of the individual also brought guilt and shame on the whole community.

Paul makes his statements even bolder when he declares: "There is therefore now no condemnation . . ." (Rom 8:1). He then asks, "If God is for us . . . who will bring any charges against God's elect?" (Rom 8:31–33). And he adds, "It is God who justifies. Who is to condemn?" (Rom 8:33–34). Paul refers to murder and adultery as charges that would incur public condemnation and shame by the community. Nevertheless, those who do these sins/crimes are justified by God's grace. Paul himself knew this dynamic first-hand based on his own life. Before his conversion, Paul's zeal for the Judean Law led him to destroy Christians, and to do so in this case to gain public honor. And he approved the stoning of Stephen. Although he was acting directly contrary to the will of God in Jesus, astoundingly, God called him "by grace" to be an apostle. Paul knows the unconditional acceptance of himself by grace—"while still we were sinners" (Rom 5:8).

"While still we were sinners" means that there are no preconditions to receiving grace, not even repentance. Paul did not repent *before* he received grace. In Paul's case, it was only *after* grace came to him that he recognized his sinfulness and the shame of it ("For I am the least of the apostles, unfit to be called an apostle, because I persecuted the church of God," 1 Cor 15:9). When grace precedes even repentance, you know it is grace! As he says elsewhere, "Do you not know that God's kindness is meant to lead you to repentance?" (Rom 2:4).

Before his conversion, Paul the zealot was devoted to the law and he lived it to the letter. When he was justified by grace, however, he saw that the Law itself and his efforts to keep the Law were null and void as a basis for acceptance by God. Justification by grace comes "apart from law" (Rom 3:21).

It is hard for the public to swallow the idea that justification by grace is the way God acts to bring about justice and righteousness. But that is precisely what Paul proclaims.

SANDY—*The best part of the sermon on justification did not come from me. As was often the case, my words were followed by some sharing—sometimes a testimonial, sometimes confession, or some words the men and women thought might help another inmate. After I talked on this particular day about justification by grace, one man spoke up: "I'm freer sitting right here in this jail than I've ever been in my life." A stunning statement coming from a man living twenty-four hours a day inside a cage! Then others began to share about how they also were actually free—free on the inside. Free of guilt and shame, free of hopelessness and aimlessness, free of loneliness and emptiness—because of a new (or renewed) relationship they had found with God inside the jail.*

One man who had not yet experienced this freedom talked about how he had been taught to be terrified of God, a God who was always keeping score of everything he did and making sure the fires of hell were being stoked good and hot just for him. I believe he spoke for others sitting there who had literally never heard about this God of grace. To hear that God could not only forgive them, but could accept them—defective, "rotten" as they thought themselves to be—this was something they had never experienced before.

DAVE—For Paul, freedom is the signal mark of those who have been justified by grace. When we say freedom, we mean radical freedom. Paul had difficulty explaining it. And his churches had trouble getting it. Paul declares in Corinthians: "All things are lawful [everything is permissible]" (1 Cor 10:23). No wonder they engaged in all kinds of outrageous behavior, one man sleeping with his stepmother, others going to prostitutes, and still others suing each other in court. By contrast, the danger for the Galatian community was just the opposite. They thought they needed to return to following the law as a means of justification—as a means of security and control of their destiny. Paul tells them not to return to the law, to what he calls "a yoke of slavery" (Gal 5:1). In fact, when Paul warns them that they have "fallen from grace" (Gal 5:4), it is not a plunge back into sins that is their risk, but a reversion to law! They are in danger of dropping out of the freedom of grace back into the enslavement of living by law (Gal 5:2–4). Paul means it when he writes, "For freedom Christ has set us free!" (Gal 5:1).

What are they freed from? In *Paul for a New Day*, Robin Scroggs describes it well in modern terms: "What are we freed from? All sorts of things: freed from the old world and that part of it which is our own past history; freed from what people think about us; freed from what we think about ourselves, either positively or negatively. Thus we are freed from the agony of failure and the tense striving for success . . . We are freed from the tyranny of someone else's claim about what is true and what is morally correct behavior. We are freed from the claim that some set of rules and regulations is ontologically true and eternally binding. We are even freed from the fear of going to hell unless we can subscribe to a given set of theological dogmas."[10]

What are we freed for? This freedom can be frightening, because with such radical freedom we are in the same dangers that Paul's communities faced. On the one hand, like the Corinthians, we might abuse the freedom and do anything that would ruin our lives and the lives of others. On the other hand, like the Galatians, we might revert to some moral standards of being good as a way to find security in knowing that "if we follow these moral laws, we will be accepted." The dilemma was stated well by the title that a congregation gave to a retreat we did on justification by grace. They called it: "What do you do when you don't have to do anything?"

SANDY—*There are many who dismiss "jailhouse conversions" because they may not be sincere—perhaps just another attempt to manipulate the system. So I watched with interest what happened to these men after this conversation about grace. What would they do now that they were free on the inside, now that they knew they didn't have to do anything at all to earn God's acceptance? Would this be license to sin all the more? Here and there, I noticed some of the inmates behaving more kindly, trying to resolve conflicts without fighting, not letting themselves be triggered by admittedly very difficult cellmates—and you can take my word for it, a jail pod is the acid test for living with other people! It was quite an impressive event to see people behave this way toward others who were apt to test them even more viciously when they tried to change.*

While I was at the jail, I was given permission to turn two dorms into program dorms for drug addicts. We called the program "Living Free." Although it was not a specifically Christian program, many of its participants were also involved in church and Bible studies. Unlike inmates in the cell blocks, these men and women did have a community to support their changes.

When the program began, there was quite a bit of harassment from some of the guards. But after a time, some of the guards began to notice the changes in these prisoners. Their job of guarding these two dorms became easier. Some of the guards even began to recommend other inmates who might be appropriate for treatment.

One day, after several months had passed, one of the sergeants asked if he could put a mentally ill man (who was not even an addict) into the men's Living Free dorm because he was being mistreated in other cell blocks. The men took him in and took care of him without incident for some months until he was transferred to prison.

DAVE—Paul's understanding is that justification by grace will be so liberating that it will engender a relationship of grace with others. Just as shame begets shame, so grace begets grace. In Paul's view, law is impotent to make us good (Gal 3:21). It might help to deter bad behavior but it does not generate goodness. In fact, it can provoke sinfulness (Rom 7:7–25). Goodness has to come freely, from within, from a *desire* to be good. And this goodness can happen in response to grace given.

How can people be made righteous without laws of some kind? In Paul's view, grace is precisely the way true righteousness/justice happens. Sin and injustice occur when people use some standard to justify themselves and others—resulting in arrogance for those who succeed and envy for those who do not. Sin also results from our need to use others in our project to justify ourselves (Gal 6:13). As long as I am seeking to justify myself or my group, I will use and manipulate others in my project to justify myself. Even when I seek to love, I will love others for *my* sake, so I can get love or so I can think of myself as a good person.

By contrast, justification by grace drives justice and goodness.[11] When honor is already bestowed freely, there is no need to prove anything. There is no need to compete and no need for arrogance or envy, since I am already accepted by grace. And, when I have already been justified, I am free from the need to use others to justify myself. I can love others for *their* sake rather than for mine.

Besides, grace is not just an "attitude" of God. It is fundamentally a relationship. Acceptance implies openness and accessibility. When God accepts us, God makes God's self freely available to us. For Paul, the event of Jesus' death and resurrection that establishes justification by grace leads to a relationship of grace whereby God gives the Holy Spirit, an ongoing gift of grace (Gal 5:16–18). This Spirit has a moral structure that generates goodness in persons and communities and engenders/empowers the desire for goodness. Its "fruit" is love, joy, peace, patience, kindness, goodness, faithfulness, humility, and self-control" (Gal 5:22–23). As Paul says, "there is no law against such things!" (Gal 5:23).

Paul established communities living out justification by grace. He preached to generate freedom that comes by grace and he wrote to reaffirm freedom from systems of enslavement—so that people could live by the Spirit in love for one another.

SANDY—*One of the most difficult parts of my ministry was seeing people leave the jail with great resolve, only to come back after committing another crime. We all know that this happens a lot; recidivism rates are very high. One reason for this, in addition to the internal shame that many carry, is the external environment to which they return. It is obviously difficult to return to one's old world and still live in God's new freedom. Almost always, the systems to which incarcerated people return are toxic and heavily shame-based. For example, they might return to families who* scapegoat them once again or who are themselves using drugs; to friends who are still stealing cars or dealing drugs; to an abusive boyfriend who is waiting to involve her in his drug dealing; to a gang that demands "eye for an eye" retribution rather than "this turn-the-other-cheek crap"; to a society that heaps shame upon shame by closing doors to way too many jobs and other opportunities.

It is hard enough for any of us to keep Paul's vision always before us. How much harder for someone who must create a new family and friends, find a grace-based church, and look for the places in the community that will welcome them back and help them get a new start. Of course, ex-offenders must stay crime-free and drug-free, for their own sakes and for ours! But the enormity of the task is very daunting.

Nevertheless, there were some who made it, not just by staying crime-free and drug-free, but by actually changing the systems that were stacked against them. One of these was a man named Tony, who had never stayed out of jail more than four months at a time in his adult life. While in the Living Free program, Tony began to talk about starting a group for ex-offender addicts when he got out. He would call it "Birds of a Feather." I had heard many people express good intentions before their release, and so I had hope for him without much expectation. However, when he got out, Tony got into a church, got his drug counselor certification, and started his group. He now has a master's degree and is director of a drug treatment agency. Birds of a Feather has been helping men and women for ten years and is still going strong.

Another inmate who heard the gospel of grace and who completed the Living Free program developed a ministry to other prisoners when he went on to complete his incarceration in a medium-security facility.

Dave—What about these other systems the prisoners faced when they returned to society—gangs, families, friends? Were they also not systems of honor and shame from which they needed to be liberated?

Paul himself never intended that justification by grace would address only the system of the law. His vision of justification is more expansive than that. For Paul, justification by grace addresses any system—cultural, familial, or whatever—by which we try to gain honor so as to justify our existence and we try to avoid the shame that comes from not living up to that system's expectations.

Such systems are writ large in Paul's letters. In Philippians, Paul includes a number of systemic, communal factors that he claims could justify him—his family pedigree, his tribal and national identity, his sectarian affiliation, along with his moral and ritual achievements under the legal system (Phil 3:3–6). In addition, in I Corinthians, Paul cites the standard of wisdom that was embraced by Greeks and the appearance of signs that Judeans sought (1 Cor 1:22–23). Any system that sets up expectations and justifies people by those expectations represents a system that justifies by works. In modern culture, for example, Protestants seek to justify their existence with the work ethic. Americans often consider people to be justified by their income or their financial status.

Paul seeks to obviate *any* identity/*any* justification that comes from such cultural, national, or religious systems. He declares that he himself has received a righteousness (justification from God) based not on his own honor—either honor that was attributed to him by dint of birth or honor that came to him by virtue of his achievements (Phil 3:9). Rather, honor is solely bestowed by grace from God outside of these systems. Grace subverts these systems and seeks to establish identity based on God's freely given favor rather than on human standards—even legal and moral standards that purport to be from God.

It is not incidental that, in Paul's theology of justification by grace, the cross is central. Justification comes by means of a *shameful* death on a cross. On the cross, Jesus is stripped of all that would give him honor. The cross is nothing but shame—foolishness, weakness, rejection (1 Cor 1:26–31). If God works through such a shame-filled event, then there is no confusing God's redemption with any culture or system claiming redemption, such as wisdom or wealth or honor or power or signs or law or any other system of standards. The cross does not present any of these as a basis for justification. Redemption through a cross obviates the systems of the world by which people gain honor and are treated with shame.

Hence, justification by grace addresses not only the shame of the sinner and the shame of the victim; it addresses shame that comes from any system that purports to justify people. Justification by grace offers freedom from the enslavement of such systems. In their place is a freedom freely bestowed by God. To sustain this freedom, Paul went around the ancient Mediterranean world establishing communities that would support converts in their efforts to live lives based on the freedom of grace. As his letters to these little communities make clear, he fervently admonished and cajoled and inspired them to hold fast to the freedom he had taught them.

CONCLUSION

For Paul, justification by grace was a vision for the redemption of the world. It was a vision for the people of Israel and all Gentile nations, in fact, for all creation. It was a vision that redeems us not just from works of the legal system, but from all systems—including economic systems that exploit, racial systems that discriminate, and ecclesial systems that condemn—by undermining the systems themselves with grace and freedom.

And Paul sees this vision of redemption also in terms of whole systems in relation to each other—nations at war, cultures in conflict, groups within a society vying for supremacy, one race dominating another. For Paul, justification by grace is a force that defeats the principalities and powers. It is a world vision of justice and peace in which the claim to absolutism of each group is undercut by grace so that all people and communities are put on equal footing. "In Christ, there is neither Judean nor Greek, neither slave nor free, no male and female" (Gal 3:28). These pairs that Paul cites were the core domination systems of the ancient world: Greek over Judean, free over slave, male over female.[12] Grace undercuts the systems that justify domination of one group over another. This is an ultimate liberation both for oppressed groups and for oppressor groups alike.

Paul's vision was apocalyptic. He believed that grace can "set us free from the present evil age" of injustice and conflict (Gal 1:4). He believed that the watershed event of the death and resurrection of Jesus had already begun to create a world of love, justice, and peace. He was convinced that, in Christ, systems that seek to justify us do not count for anything. The only thing that ultimately counts is the "new creation" (Gal 6:15), the new order based on the freely given grace of God that justifies all equally. This is Paul's apocalyptic vision of a new world.

ENDNOTES

1. Justification by grace is a complex and changing doctrine, both in terms of the interpretations of Paul, especially in light of the so-called "New Perspective" and in terms of interpretations of theological principles of the Reformation. We do not attempt to explain fully our views on it in this brief presentation, but simply to draw upon them to discuss various aspects that relate to shame.

    Paul's letters make a contrast between justification by grace and the works of the Jewish Law. Despite this polemic against some Jews (who perhaps shared the views Paul himself held before his call to apostleship), we know that many Jews believed in the priority of grace and that Paul considered the Law to be good in and of itself. We wish to explore the universal implications of Paul's understanding of justification by grace without in any way denigrating Judaism, then or now.

2. Wright, *Justification*, 90–91.

3. Paul talks about justification rather than forgiveness as a model of redemption. See Stendahl, *Paul among Jews and Gentiles*, 23–40.

4. Bradshaw, *Healing the Shame*, 15.

5. Nicolson, *A Black Future?*

6. Tamez, *Amnesty of Grace.*

7. Yancey, *What's So Amazing About Grace?*, 70.

8. See, for example, the treatment of honor and shame in Malina, *New Testament World.*

9. Stendahl, *Paul among Jews and Gentiles*, 78–96.

10. Scroggs, *Paul for a New Day*, 29.

11. For a discussion of the ethical life that flows from justification, see especially Scroggs, *Paul for A New Day*, 57–74.

12. Braxton, *No Longer Slaves*, 92–96.

7

No Shame in Wesley's Gospel

EDWARD P. WIMBERLY

INTRODUCTION

THROUGHOUT THE AGES THE concern for human happiness has been a major theme for both religion and philosophy. Pre-Enlightenment religious thinkers such as Augustine emphasized that happiness resulted from investing in a relationship with God. The Christian church was the major vehicle for facilitating and nurturing this investment. Enlightenment philosophical developments, particularly the rational thought of Rene Descartes, were highly suspicious about investing happiness in God or the church. They sought happiness through investing in rational and concrete human activities alone.

On the philosophical and religious stage in the eighteenth century was the same debate about whether to invest one's happiness in spiritual things in contrast to concrete things that could be confirmed by the senses. John Wesley publicly declared that it was perfectly rational to invest one's happiness in God's "present but not yet" future rule and reign. Through a variety of practical theological strategies, Wesley sought to persuade others that investing in the spiritual realm was not only rational, but was the source of happiness in the future as well as in the present.

In this essay, my aim is to demonstrate that Wesley's rhetorical method of persuading people to invest in the spiritual realm of God's "present but coming future" is the source of Wesley's gift to the twenty-first century. Again, the concern is about whether to invest one's happiness in the spiritual realm or in the concrete world of the here and now. In fact, more than at any other previous historical period, the enticements for confining our quest for happiness, identity, human worth, and dignity to material rewards and benefits are huge. Being wealthy, prosperous, possessing status, position, and power are marketed as the real source of happiness and well-being. For example, equating being loved with being wealthy and prosperous is an increasing possibility for large numbers of persons on most continents. Moreover, through the development of the Internet and large-scale media marketing, it is easier to persuade people to become preoccupied with the enticements of wealth, prestige, status, position, fame, and public recognition. It is not until events like death of movie stars and popular singers, the failure of athletes like Tiger Woods and Michael Vick, the Enron scandal, the beginning of the economic meltdown in 2007, the earthquake in Haiti, and the BP oil fiasco in the Gulf of Mexico that we begin to recognize that there is more to life than just material things and a false sense of honor and bogus fame. The pursuit of happiness through material well-being has its limitations.

THE SHAME FACTOR

There is a major connection between Wesley's interest in the topic of happiness and the topic of this lecture series. Because eighteenth-century England was well into the Industrial Revolution, Wesley saw very clearly that seeking one's identity and worth through wealth, prestige, position, status, fame, and what society deemed honorable and worthwhile led to a false sense of happiness, and in fact, led to unhappiness on a grand scale and to a false sense of identity. More precisely, blind commitment to the pursuit of wealth and honor defined as material possession, would eventually lead to personal and spiritual bankruptcy. Wesley believed that the only true source of happiness was our relationship with Jesus Christ. In relationship with Jesus Christ we had dignity, worth, value, identity, and true happiness despite our status or position in culture.

Wesley's practical theology grew out of his effort to convince people that wealth, honor, prestige, status, position, and power were not the source of happiness, identity, worth, and love. His method of practical theology also makes rational sense today. What makes sense is investing our lives in a relationship with God through Jesus Christ and the promise of God's "present but not yet" rule and reign as the source of our happiness, identity, worth, and dignity.

WESLEY AND THE SHAME FACTOR
FOR THE TWENTY-FIRST CENTURY

Given this brief background, this essay will present Wesley's rhetorical strategies as a major way to demonstrate Wesley's practical theology for the twenty-first century. This essay will draw on a case study of a successful African-American businessman who was obsessed with achieving wealth and prosperity. His early adulthood and life leading up to age forty was preoccupied with grasping for the lure and attraction of this world's honor, fame, and prestige. This preoccupation continually failed. It was only when he learned the lesson of divesting from this world's enticing lures, and reinvesting his life in seeking a relationship with God through Jesus Christ and God's "present but not yet" rule and reign, that he discovered happiness, his identity, his worth, his dignity, and his calling.

In terms of the conference title, "The Shame Factor," it was not until this man experienced at the spiritual level the loss of honor in the marketplace and was a business failure that he discovered that there is no shame in the Gospel of Jesus Christ. Shame in this lecture is defined as experiencing the loss of what society defines as worthy and valuable, and without possessing these symbols of worth and value, one is not loved and has no worth. In short, shame is the anxiety felt from living without wealth, material prosperity, position, status, and power, and the feeling that one is unlovable and worthless. It was only when our main characters in our case study lost everything that they found they had invested their lives in the wrong thing. It was only when they discovered God's prevenient, justifying, and sanctifying grace in Jesus Christ did they actually find happiness. God's love in Jesus Christ wipes out all shame.

Crucial in the discussion of happiness is how shame is a major factor in the twenty-first century. Shame is a feeling of being unloved and unlovable. During Wesley's time, guilt was a number one experience in the eighteenth-century context. The critical question guiding this lecture is whether Wesley's rhetoric of guilt is suited for our contemporary shame-based culture. The lecture will begin, first, to explore how the world is experienced by many in contemporary North American society, and the effort is to show that shame is a different experience than the guilt experienced by Wesley's contemporaries in the eighteenth century. Second, despite this difference between the experience of guilt and shame, Wesley's therapeutic practical theology will be examined for its potential use in the twenty-first century. Third, narrative rhetoric is introduced as one way to update Wesley's therapeutic rhetorical method in order to speak to the twenty-first century. Fourth and finally, an illustration of how Wesley's therapeutic rhetoric in a narrative frame can speak to this century will be presented.

THE CONTEMPORARY EXPERIENCE OF SHAME

This lecture takes seriously Wesley's use of rhetoric to persuade people that investing their identity, worth, value, and happiness in a relationship with God in Jesus Christ was worthwhile and beneficial. He believed that this relationship was the source of all happiness in the present as well as in the future. Present happiness was in having a meaningful relationship with God through Jesus Christ, but happiness also depended on participating in God's "present but not yet" rule and reign.

Wesley believed that it was reasonable for human beings to respond to his persuasive logic and arguments. The critical concern today, however, is whether eighteenth-century reasoning is suited to our twenty-first-century experience. My answer is yes and no. The eighteenth-century experience was one of feeling guilt over wrong behavior. Wesley's juridical model focused on justice and guilt as well as repentance and forgiveness for sin and bad behavior. Such a model would not be foreign to many of us today. It would be dismissed as irrelevant by many, however.

Wesley's therapeutic model was different from his juridical model in that his therapeutic model would speak forcefully to the twenty-first-century experience of shame. Wesley's therapeutic rhetoric focused more on the relationship with God and the beneficial consequences of that relationship for happiness and healing of guilt and shame. In the contemporary sense of this century, relationships are the major source of all healing and fostering of happiness. Chief among the relationships is the relationship with God through Jesus Christ. More than the juridical model, the therapeutic relationship healed guilt through relationships with God and with others. Not only did it heal guilt, it addresses the contemporary experience of shame, and here shame is understood as the overwhelming feeling of being unloved and unlovable.

As indicated previously, the experience of guilt is not the experience in our contemporary society. The experience of sham far the most prevalent experience. This lecture takes seriously that contemporary experience is not primarily the need for forgiveness for wrong behavior. Rather, "our contemporary experience is one of disconnection, of being unloved, of being overwhelmed by information, of experiencing nihilism or the loss of meaning, and of being inept and clumsy in human interaction and interpersonal relationships."[1] The age of shame is the loss of love. It is the loss of meaningful community. It is the feeling that one is unlovable and will never be loved. The point is that a juridical model of guilt over sin and wrong behavior makes no sense when the dominant experience is being unloved. The guilt model presupposes an intact community where one's sense of connection is not threatened unless one commits a heinous crime. Shame, however, is based on disconnection and a breakdown in community. Moreover, shame is a fundamental experience and is prior to guilt in the developmental cycle. Guilt, however, comes later in the developmental cycle when relationships are better formed.

Three Dimensions of Contemporary Shame

Three primary experiences exist today. Contemporary psychotherapy fosters one view of the self as commoditized. The self is defined as a commodity to be bought and sold.[2] The contemporary self is pictured as "an isolated and self-contained individual completely oriented to consumer and marketing values."

A second view emphasizes the shift from self-actualization of the self, which was connected to community. Rather than being connected to community, the self's need for community is replaced by a deadly form of self-admiration. Community has been replaced by a narcissism epidemic, which is as dangerous as a vile disease. The following quote defines narcissism and its manifestation in self-admiration:

> American culture's focus on self-admiration has caused a flight
> from reality to the land of grandiose fantasy. We have phony
> rich people (with interest-only mortgages and piles of debt),
> phony beauty (with plastic surgery and cosmetic procedures),
> phony athletes (with performance-enhancing drugs), phony
> celebrities (via reality TV and YouTube), phony genius stu
> dents (with grade inflation), a phony national economy (with

iment debt), phony feelings of being special
/ith parenting and education focused on self-
fantasy might feel good, but, unfortunately,
s. The mortgage meltdown and the resulting
ire just one demonstration of how inflated de-
dy crash to earth.[3]

of the Internet has contributed greatly to the disconnect from community and reliance on phony community as a substitute for real community. There is a third view, however, which goes to the heart of the meaning of shame. This view is called *status anxiety*. Undergirding the disconnection from community and the narcissistic craze for self-admiration is the phenomenon known as status anxiety. Status anxiety is all about shame defined as the absence of a sense of being loved and unlovable. It is the equating of love with wealth and high status as opposed to being grounded and rooted in relationships. For example, Alain de Botton in the book *Status Anxiety* says the following about the nature of status anxiety:

"The predominant impulses behind our desire to rise in the social hierarchy may be rooted not so much in the material goods we can accrue or the power we can wield as in the amount of love we stand to receive as a consequence of high status. Money, fame and influence may be valued more as tokens of—and means to—love rather than ends in themselves."[4]

Love is no longer defined relationally. Rather, it is defined as the pursuit of things, and such a pursuit starves the soul and makes people shallow.

Wesley's emphasis on a relationship with God through Jesus Christ as well as being connected with others in a faith community is the primary practical and strategic source of his theology. Laying treasures on earth as opposed to in relationship with God and Jesus Christ leads to bankruptcy. Investing in this world's status craze, its self-deceptive self-admiration, and becoming a commodity are not the source of happiness. Wesley understood this, and it was exemplified in this therapeutic use of rhetoric to convince people to invest their lives in a relationship with Jesus Christ and God's coming rule and reign in the world.

WESLEY'S THERAPEUTIC AND NARRATIVE RHETORIC

For Wesley, the starting point for true happiness was the person's relationship with God through Jesus Christ, and following this, the soul was made alive and vigorous through the Holy Spirit, which suggested a movement toward sanctification or continued growth in love.

Wesley's therapeutic rhetoric was based on his belief that happiness and healing of earthly spiritual, emotional, and interpersonal ills rested on a significant relationship with God through Jesus Christ as well as significant relationships with the faith community. It is this emphasis on relationship that makes Wesley's ideas and rhetoric significant for dealing with twenty-first-century shame. Of course, a relationship with God through Jesus Christ was central to dealing with sin and the behaviors associated with sin for Wesley. The key element in Wesley's practical theology for this century is the fact that shame can only be healed through relationships. These relationships include the primary relationship with God as well as relationships with others.

It is my contention that contemporary shame has its roots primarily with our culture's narrative myth that identity, worth, meaning, and happiness are rooted in our total investment in this world's honor and shame system of evaluation. Alain de Botton is correct in his insightful analysis of status anxiety. Wealth became a substitute for love and the relationships that produce love. I am not so naïve in believing that our marketing strategies are driven by an effort to convince the buying and consumer-oriented public that material things are good substitutes for human relationships. After all, relationships are more painful and expensive to maintain than what we possess materially. Of course, marketing strategies are not geared spiritually to look at the ultimate costs of how we spend and invest our money.

Wesley's rhetoric, however, was clearly not market or consumer driven. In the eighteenth century he saw very well the "dangers of riches" and how investing in them could destroy our spiritual well-being and our souls. It is important then, to explore just how Wesley's therapeutic or relational healing rhetoric laid the foundation for our addressing twenty-first-century shame.

To understand Wesley's therapeutic and healing rhetoric, it is important to understand his narrative rhetoric. For me, narrative rhetoric is the method of persuasion where reality is understood in terms of story plots or story direction.[5] It is clear to me that it is possible to analyze Wesley's sermons in light of the narrative rhetoric. It is possible to envisage narrative story plots existing in his work.

One example is Wesley's sermon, "The More Excellent Way." In this sermon Wesley used a narrative rhetoric that contrasted two story plots. One story plot represented a tragic vision of reality. This tragic story plot was detrimental to the human soul and led to complete destruction of the self and the soul. In this sermon, however, there was another plot line with a hopeful end, and it would ultimately lead to happiness on earth and in heaven. Wesley tried to persuade those in his reading and listening audiences that choosing the wrong story plot led to complete unhappiness.

A closer examination of Wesley's narrative rhetoric in his sermon "The More Excellent Way" will help identify how he saw these two story plots working in the lives of human beings. In this sermon he used the financial metaphor of "lay up." Wesley made an analogy between investing in the banks of this world or "earthly bank" and investing in the coming rule and reign of God or the heavenly bank. In this sermon he tried to convince his hearers and readers based on the following reasoning:

> Suppose it were not forbidden, how can you on principles of reason, spend your money in a way which God may possibly forgive, instead of spending it in a manner which he will certainly reward? You will have no reward in heaven for what you lay up; you will, for what you lay out. Every pound you put into the early bank is sunk: It brings no interest above. But every pound you give to the poor is into the bank of heaven. And it will bring glorious interest; yea, and, as such, will be accumulating to all eternity.[6]

In this brief passage Wesley identified two narrative plot lines. They had different endings.[7] Investing in the earthly bank resulted in a tragic ending. Investing in the heavenly bank, however, was an eternal investment of happiness in God's future. In contrast, investing in the earthly realm alone ended in bankruptcy with no future. "Earthly investing flirted with disaster and deficits in meaningful living."[8] Our task was to invest in that which was enduring rather than to invest in that which was perishable.

In the twenty-first century there are still two plot lines in which we can invest. As in Wesley's century, there is this world's attractions and lures, and there are the heavenly investing opportunities of God's "present, not yet, but coming" future world of God's rule and reign. This worldly happiness is short-lived. God's present relationship with us and the coming and not yet rule and reign of God provide happiness on earth as well as in the future.

What is different in this century from Wesley's century is the dominance of shame as we talked about earlier in this lecture. Shame is defined as the feeling of being unloved and unlovable, and the fear that one might never be loved. The source of this feeling is the loss of community and the breakdown in village life. The industrial and technological revolutions were just beginning to impact the feudal system and economy in the eighteenth century, but the sources of love within community were sufficient for most people to feel a sense of belonging. This is not the case in the twenty-first century.

Status anxiety is so strong, as indicated earlier, that the dominant reality is that we equate wealth, status, prestige, position, and power with being loved. Our whole economic, consumer-oriented culture rests on the assumption of shame. The assumption is that material things will provide the happiness that human relationships cannot give. Modern addiction to substances and sex is all about the pursuit of being loved by the standards of this world. As a result, people invest their need for love in this world's economy and its possibilities for providing worth, dignity, hope, and identity.

The value of Wesley's rhetoric is that his sermons helped people to distinguish between investing their lives, identity, worth, and happiness in the here and now as opposed to that which is in the future. In the final section I will illustrate Wesley's rhetoric updated with narrative rhetorical methods relevant for today.

A CASE ILLUSTRATION

To illustrate the significance of John Wesley's rhetoric for the twenty-first century, I use the autobiography of Glenn S. Henderson. He is an African-American who is a much-sought-after Christian speaker and successful entrepreneur. He is founder and CEO of AFC Worldwide Express, a very successful global transportation and logistics company headquartered in Atlanta. His endeavor in business is "to offer a glimmer of the synergy of what a Christ inspired corporation could be."[9] His example is of a person who developed his business rooted and grounded in being faithful to the "present but not yet" unfolding rule and reign of

God showing how he struggled successfully to invest his life and business practices constantly in the coming reality.

To take narrative rhetoric seriously in the Wesleyan spirit, we must look for evidence of the two opposing plots. To be effective, Wesley's rhetoric for the twenty-first century has to address the way contemporary culture entices people into its image of what it takes to be happy. Even as a pre-adolescent Henderson was very aware of how hard his parents worked to make ends meet, and he immediately saw the contrast between his parents' work ethic and the view of happiness existing in wider culture. For him, work had no value unless it had a profit motive associated with it. In fact, he indicated that he did not associate work with strengthening character, family teamwork and relationships, or benefiting the soul.

His view of work and profit relating to happiness influenced his attitude toward his parents as well as the black church. As an adult Christian, however, Henderson learned to value his past through spiritual eyes based on the "present but not yet" world that was coming. About his growing-up years and his relationship to his father, he wrote:

> I didn't recognize his dedication until he passed away. As I was preparing his eulogy in 2000, the Lord took me back to the very years where I felt I had experienced some of my greatest pain and revealed to me the greatness of my father and mother. I was reminded that they raised four boys and, later on, two girls, basically on one income. We grew up during a time when they were challenged almost daily with some form of prejudice either racially, economically or socially. He opened my eyes that they, too, once had dreams that they put aside for their children and, in some cases, they sacrificed time together as a couple and they did all of this so seamlessly.[10]

As an adult in middle age, Henderson realized that he was raised with the appropriate relational and spiritual value system for life, but the attractiveness of a life of wealth, prosperity, fame, fortune, and admiration was far stronger than honoring his parents.

Henderson testifies in his memoirs that his initial business effort was not Christ-centered in the sense that he and his future wife did not invest their entrepreneurial effort in the leadership of the Holy Spirit nor in the "present but not yet" coming and unfolding salvation narrative of God. In fact, he said they were controlled more by the demands of the marketplace and its reward and punishment system of merit and financial gain. He said: "We had what was probably an unhealthy and ungodly fear of failure that later caused us to make choices that lacked integrity."[11] Henderson concluded that he was building his "house on sand."[12] His use of the sand metaphor was grounded in what was his later faith conversion, and he used the words of Ps 127:1: "Unless the Lord builds the house, its builders labor in vain."[13]

It is clear to me that Henderson's primary motivation was his investment in this world's honor and shame system of merit and seeking worth, dignity, identity, and happiness through economic wealth, success, prestige, and status. He and his soon-to-be wife sought happiness and love through investing in economic success. In short, they invested in the enticements of this world, and as a result they developed what I have identified as status anxiety or the fear that only love, respect, worth, value, dignity, hope, and happiness could come by "investing in the bank" of worldly success. He admitted that "cheating, lying, and deception were no problem for me, especially if it would keep my image intact and get me to where I thought we needed to be."[14]

Of significance to me is the reality that Henderson was recruited early in his life to invest in the bank of this world. It began with his being very critical of his family of origin, believing that it did not provide him with what he needed to be successful in life. In a real sense he evaluated his family life in light of what the world held up as the norm for instrumental success. He was recruited early into being ashamed of his origins. He lifted instrumental values of making it in the world of wealth, value, and prestige over (against) the relational values that his parents and church were teaching him.

Henderson admitted at that time he had no idea about the plans God had for his life. He quoted Jer 29:11, saying that God knew the plans God had for him, "plans for his welfare and not for harm."[15] God was about to use the Internal Revenue Service to bring lasting changes in Henderson's life and in the life of his future wife. God would use Glenn's and his future wife's business misfortune to edit and re-author their investment in this world's honor and shame system. They were about to learn that happiness was not in the investment in this world but in the "present and not yet" coming world of God. They had to go through hell, however, before they could make the new investment.

The story of Glenn Henderson and his future wife illustrates the contemporary dilemma of investing in this world, and it also gives us a clue into how this kind of status anxiety and desire for identity and worth can lead to bankruptcy. This problem is an earthwide concern. So far in their unfolding story as a couple, they were on the verge of losing everything, but God stepped in and led them through the "dangers of riches" in the Wesleyan sense.

Up to this point, their desire for this world's riches had led to nothing but trouble. Their experiences resembled the evangelical and orthodox theological pattern of sin. Investing in the idols of this world led to the awareness of the need for redemption and renewal. Finally, their experience led them to the need to revise their investment in this worldly story or this earthly story. It was time for a new investment, but what were the steps to take to make this new investment?

The first step in their renewal was realizing that God was using their business losses and problems with the IRS to sensitize them—"God was active in getting" their attention.[16] They realized they needed to begin to go to worship, and they needed to get married and stop living together without the benefits of being married. They realized that God was fostering within them the primacy of investing relationships with God and with each other. They began to see that they were using their relationship to gain what they needed to advance in status, but they were not investing in their relationships with God and others in ways that would advance the happiness of others.

The key lesson that Glenn and Regina, his partner in ministry, learned was to trust God to be the faithful guide who, through the Holy Spirit, leads people to happiness. The most difficult thing for modern and postmodern people to do is to trust that God is a trustworthy God who will lead and guide us through all of our Job-like difficulties, whether they are created by our own faulty investments in this world or as the result of problems that just come because of living.

In our culture the grand narrative of honor and shame functions on the plot that investing in God is foolish and lacks wisdom. The grand narrative of the "present and not yet" investing in God's future rests on trusting God to lead us from one scene to the next scene and from one chapter to the next chapter, trusting his direction. As Glenn and Regina put it: "God causes all things to work together for the good of those who love him and who are called to his purposes." Glenn said: "The missing link to this passage, though, is that, at the time, I did not love him (God)." God taught them both through God's incarnational participation in their lives that God was righteous and would keep his promises to be present. God helped them to trust what God was doing in their lives, and they learned to depend on what God was doing. Listen to Glenn's testimony:

> Regina, my gift from God, was not my problem. The IRS was not my problem. Vendors and cash flow were not my problem. My problem was threefold: me, myself and I. God intervened as no others could, using the things for which I cared most. It was not my friend, Regina, who I managed to ignore, but rather the source of my being—pride, driven by wanting to be something, to be someone. My past hurt, pain and desires fueled everything I did to satisfy what I believed I needed. What I needed most was acceptance, support and appreciation, but only God could fulfill my needs. He (God) would call into account my misplaced actions.[17]

CONCLUSIONS

Glenn's and Regina's experiences of learning to trust God demonstrate how Wesley's eighteenth-century rhetorical methods are well suited for the contemporary human pursuit of happiness. It must be emphasized also that Wesley's rhetoric was holistic. It was more than just personal, seeking to bring individuals into a significant relationship with God. His whole effort was relational, and involved the entire ministry of the church. It involved caring and nurturing/educational ministries, small group and communal worship practices, public theology, and public policy efforts. His goal was to demonstrate the pre-Enlightenment theme that happiness and virtue rested in God, and this understanding (of happiness rested in God and in) what God was doing to bring about God's "present and not yet" rule and reign. This understanding of happiness and virtue rested in orthodoxy or right doctrine, orthopathy or right feeling, orthopraxis or right practice, and orthonarrative or right story. The case illustrates that personal, relational, and private and public ethical concerns of the twenty-first century are interrelated. Contemporary twenty-first-century ministry must use a narrative rhetoric in every aspect of ministry. This rhetoric must serve the end of helping people invest in the "present but not yet" unfolding rule and reign of God.

ENDNOTES

1. Wimberly, *Wesleyan Spirit*.
2. Cushman, *Constructing the Self*, 290.
3. Twenge and Campbell, *Narcissism Epidemic*, 4.
4. Botton, *Status Anxiety*, 6.
5. Wimberly, *Wesleyan Spirit*.
6. *The Works of John Wesley*, vol. 7, 37.
7. Wimberly, *Practical Theology in the Wesleyan Spirit*.
8. Ibid.
9. Henderson, *Treasures*, back cover.
10. Ibid., 49.
11. Ibid., 106.
12. Ibid.
13. Ibid., 109.
14. Ibid., 107.
15. Ibid., 106.
16. Ibid., 108.
17. Ibid., 112.

8

Avoiding Shame in Ancient Israel

Victor H. Matthews

THERE CAN BE NO honor in a society that cannot grasp the concept of shame.[1] These two polar opposites function as the foundation of a social control mechanism designed to value honorable behavior and speech and to avoid whatever may result in shame. Realistically, if a person is certain that their bad behavior cannot be detected or found out, and then the likelihood that they will engage in dishonorable behavior is increased. However, even without the possibility of others knowing about their actions feeling guilt or shame can still cause us to "interrupt any action that violates either internally or externally derived standards or rules." Society internalizes mental commands that cause the conscious mind to say, "Stop. You are about to violate a rule or custom." If the person is capable of listening to this inner voice, then incorrect or inappropriate action is prevented.[2] In fact, it is shame that "helps to expose us to ourselves for what we are and what we might become.[3]

As Thomas Scheff has pointed out, in instances of social interaction "signals of normal shame serve to regulate social distance and as a compass for moral behavior."[4] Gershen Kaufman recognizes shame as a type of "social barometer" that gauges the "distance and amounts of honour and respect that are exchanged between individuals in social relationships."[5] When there is a clear sense of shame present and functioning within a society, it is susceptible to abuse by individuals, the community, and those in authority who wish to regulate behavior. Conformity is not always personally beneficial and there are some actions such as charging into battle that do not protect the self or one's life. But feelings of shame can be enforced on persons who are convinced that it is better to conform to authority than to face charges of cowardice, treason, or some other negative label.[6]

Still, it is necessary for the community to define what is honorable in order to determine what is dishonorable. That, in turn, suggests that cross-cultural conceptions of shame between Western and Eastern societies are problematic because cultural variables differ quite widely between individualized and collectivized communities. Cultures that emphasize the identity and worth of the individual and the priority of personal goals differ widely from collectivized communities such as those of ancient Israel or in Asia, which are "characterized by the interdependence between members of the group."[7] Since ancient Israel also has been identified as a "shame culture," it is necessary to add the determination that "public esteem is the greatest good, and to be ill spoken of the greatest evil."[8] As Stephen Pattison puts it, "The things that are protected by the dynamics of honour and shame will differ according to the culture, society, or reference group within which a person is brought up and lives."[9]

Zeba Crook has recently made the case that Mediterranean culture is collectivistic and therefore a "shame culture."[10] As such, ancient Israel would "tend to be governed less by individual desires than by communal expectations." The ethics of a collectivized community that include feelings of loyalty, honor, respect, and duty are focused on protecting the household's status and the community rather than on preserving the self or on maintaining personal liberty.[11] In that context, Crook points to the "public court of reputation" (PCR) as the "first, last, and only arbiter of honorable and shameful behavior."[12] Scheff[13] refers to the experience of shame in terms of the "reflected appraisals he or she receives from audiences in the course of social interaction."[14] It should be noted, however, that consciousness of shame can and does occur in a private setting and is not solely dependent on an audience being present. In other words, it is not necessary for a household to be publicly exposed to shaming to feel shame. The potential for a status change, whether in a public or private setting, functions as a means of social control over behavior and may well lead to an equal measure of collective anxiety.[15]

As an honor-based, collectivistic society, the ancient Israelites made a point in their wisdom literature, their legal pronouncements, and in their extended narratives of extolling the community benefits derived from right behavior, cool-headed thinking, and appropriate and timely speech. Conversely, it is made clear what kind of damage can be caused by the "fool" who "takes no pleasure in understanding" (Prov 18:2) and to whom "doing wrong is like sport" (Prov 10:23). For instance, an unbridled tongue that takes advantage of the opportunity to belittle someone of lesser status or power simply because it is possible to do so injures both the target of the verbal attack and also the speaker since the latter will be judged a "fool" in the eyes of the community (Prov 11:12; 25:23).

As a result, it advantages the community and its leaders to inculcate social control methods and accompanying social values that inhibit petty or malicious self-indulgence and promote conformity to social expectation.[16] The degree to which they are successful in internalizing cultural moral standards will determine the effectiveness of shame as a social control mechanism.[17] For that reason, Michael Lewis is quite correct in saying that "the function of guilt and shame is to interrupt any action that violates either internally or externally derived standards or rules."[18] In examining the manner in which honor and shame function within ancient Israelite society, particular attention will be given to evidence of social standards and the ways in which households are portrayed in the biblical text as they strive to avoid shame and attempt to acquire or add to their store of honor.

Preserving the Honor of a Household: David and Michal

Shame status may result from physical defects, failure to perform as desired or expected, or outside forces beyond the household's control. Attempts can also be made to impose shame on a household. That effort can be based on anger, rivalry, class or race hatred, or political affiliation. Donald Nathanson's Compass of Shame model is one way to analyze how households might cope with shame.[19] According to this clinically developed model, there are four "shame-coping" scripts[20]: Attack Self, Withdrawal, Attack Other, and Avoidance. Note that this set of four poles of behavior and thought do not directly address the cause of the shame, only how the person chooses to cope with that feeling.[21] For the purposes of this study, both ascribed cause and reaction will be addressed.

Narrative tends to be more vibrant in addressing violent or aggressive reaction to shame or shaming than withdrawal or avoidance. As a result this point of the shame compass will be the focus of the examples provided here. The Attack Other pole of the compass "is [part of] the

family of scripts, where the shame message may not be recognized, typically is not accepted, and attempts are made to make someone else feel worse."[22] This point of the compass appears in the story of David's triumphant entrance into Jerusalem with the Ark of the Covenant (2 Sam 6:16–23). The touch point for a mixed reaction will be David's decision to remove his garments and lead the dancing celebrants as they pass through the gate (2 Sam 6:14, 20).[23]

Why David is portrayed in this scene without his robes of office and only wearing a linen ephod that is typically worn by priests is uncertain. It is possible that he is taking on the temporary role of priest-king leading the joyous celebration welcoming Yahweh's presence into the capital city.[24] There is also the possibility that this is a political ploy intended to demonstrate his affinity with his subjects and perhaps do penance for his failure to follow proper procedures while transporting of the ark from its storage place in Kiriath Jearim (2 Sam 6:3–9).[25]

Regardless of the motive, David's actions created a positive impression with the people. David's delight is infectious. His gesture of egalitarianism, accompanied by the evidence of Yahweh's favor in the form of the ark, helps to fulfill his royal ambitions. When David joins the revelers gathered around the ark and dances into the city, he shows his mastery over the public will and joins them in celebrating the end of years of disunity and conflict.[26]

While the political context in this narrative is important, it is David's effort to combine a show of authority with shared joy with his audience that conveys and confirms the message of support for his regime. David's actions are designed to shape consensus, but there is always some uncertainty in any political event since it is dependent upon the reaction of the people to the words and actions of the political agent. When they spontaneously join David in the celebration at the sound of pealing horns, his authority is confirmed.[27] Furthermore, their participation in a covenant meal provided by the new king acknowledges their acceptance of David's role as their royal patron and the distributor of Yahweh's bounty to the people (2 Sam 6:19a). Finally, when the proceedings are completed the text says that "all the people went back to their homes" (2 Sam 6:19b). That peaceful dispersal signals that this is a well-ordered society, one that recognizes political authority by showing they are content with their ruler.[28]

While there seems to be a mutual consensus for David's right to the kingship, the narrator adds some spice to the story by recounting the reaction to the scene by Michal, Saul's daughter and David's first wife. The passion that she had once felt for David (1 Sam 18:20, 28) has waned over the years and now has been replaced in this story with an equal passion for a nostalgic and idealized view of the Saulide regime. To indicate to the audience that there is a confrontation ahead, the narrator makes it clear that Michal had witnessed David's dancing before the people (2 Sam 6:16). Her reaction when David arrives at the palace suggests that she is experiencing deep shame as a result of his public display. In fact, we are told she is so consumed with anger that "she despised him in her heart."[29] Her mortification at his behavior is couched in terms of the disgrace he has cast on the role of the king. To cope with her shame, she now employs an Attack Other script.

To better understand the strain that had grown between David and Michal, it is important to note that she had originally been infatuated with him (1 Sam 18:20, 28).[30] However, afterward Michal is exiled from the royal court and their marriage is annulled, Saul gives Michal to Palti ben Laish and their marriage lasts until David's return to power (1 Sam 25:44). Realizing her political worth as a tie to Saul's household, David re-acquires Michal by ruthlessly taking her away from her husband (2 Sam 3:13–16).[31] Political expedience may serve David's purposes, but it shames Michal and her father's household. The result is that her loyalty for David is transformed into pure hatred and a desire for revenge.[32] The narrator signals to the audience that Michal's loyalties remain with her father by referring to her as "the daughter of Saul" (2 Sam 6:20). As a result, her verbal attack on David will be better understood in the context of the political rivalry between David and Saul.

With the stage set, the confrontation begins as David prepares to enter his own house. Naturally, he would expect the members of his household to greet him with the respect due the "father of the household." However, what he receives is a political diatribe from Michal, who steps out of the ordinary routine expected of her and "comes out to meet David." Her anger and indignation spew out as she publicly separates herself from him and his political position.[33] By speaking to the king in a manner that is in no way submissive and is in fact quite demanding, she attempts to shame him before the public.

In fact, Michal attempts to usurp David's authority at the threshold of his house (a parallel with Jerusalem's city gate). In a shocking example of vituperative speech, Michal sets aside the normal standards of social decorum and chooses to violate the established social routines of public interaction between husband and wife and between king and subject.[34] Rather than allow David to take charge and bestow a blessing on the household, she violates the standard "turn-taking" rules of discourse by speaking first and thus gaining through surprise a temporary victory as she attempts to cast off her shame.[35]

The charge she makes against David is an obvious ploy to shame him and to raise the political stock of the Saulides: "How the king of Israel honored himself today, uncovering himself today before the eyes of his servants' maids, as any vulgar fellow might shamelessly uncover himself! (2 Sam 6:20)." She couples this sarcastic remark with a comparison to her father's much more dignified manner, asserting that he would never engage in such a vulgar display that shames her and diminishes the status of the king before his subjects.[36] Her clearly hostile attitude questions David's role as king and head of household.[37] What is interesting is to see how David reacts.

David is not about to allow Michal to deflate the growing sentiment for his kingship, and he manages to easily deflect her attempt to shame him by refusing to acknowledge her right to reprove him.[38] David matches Michal's caustic rhetoric with his own authoritative speech to strip her of all credibility and privilege: "I will make myself yet more contemptible than this, and I will be abased in my own eyes; but by the maids of whom you have spoken, by them I shall be held in honor (2 Sam 6:21–22)."

By employing overstatement David transforms her charge of impropriety and turns his actions into a way of honoring Yahweh, "who chose me in place of your father" (6:21).[39] With the aid of divine protection and guidance, he makes it clear that the people have already judged his actions as honorable. He rejects her attempts to shame him, deflecting her charges and her claim to a higher form of honor. Instead, his submission to Yahweh and his efforts to demonstrate that he is free to worship and celebrate Yahweh's role for him is an honor he will cherish and share with all of the people of his kingdom.

Unsuccessful in busting David's political frame or in championing the political rights of the Saulides, Michal is silenced and left to conform to the shameful role of barren wife.[40] She will spend the remainder of her life isolated within David's harem, unloved and forgotten (2 Sam 6:23). The biblical narrator can now point to the shame of her barren state as just punishment for her failure to honor her husband. The political book is now closed on the Saulide dynasty. Its bloodline will have no connection to the House of David. Michal's attempt to use the Attack Other script to shame David has backfired and she is forced into the "Withdrawal" script of the exiled, forgotten person.[41]

Shame and Law

Every regulated society draws a line between honorable and shameful behavior. Although legal codes and judicial interpretations function as one fairly straightforward method of defining legal and illegal actions and providing incentives and disincentives, they are seldom the only methods employed. Oftentimes a culture chooses to explain the value of right action and the consequences of wrong action in storytelling or in wisdom sayings, and these popular means of social shaping in ancient Israel were based on the concepts of honor and shame.

If the premise is to seek honor and avoid shame, then certain societal guidelines must exist that assist each household in right behavior, speech, and thought. There is also a built-in incentive found in the ability to acquire honor through proper performance of social obligations for both the host and the guest(s). Although it appears that

there is a limitless ability to add to one's store of honor and thereby
contribute to elevated status, moderation is also demanded. Seeking
honor for its own sake rather than to contribute to the well-being of
the community demonstrates a lack of self-control and is to be avoided
(Prov 25:27–28). Conversely, failure to meet social expectations or to
actively reject what a society deems to be honorable behavior results in
being labeled as anti-social, criminal, and shameful to oneself and to
the community in general.

The Psalmist ties honorable behavior and the avoidance of shame
to keeping Yahweh's statutes. By clinging to these decrees and speaking
of them before kings (presumably in defense of justice) "I shall not be
put to shame" (Ps 119:1–6, 31, 46, 80). A litany of right action such as
this that celebrates a society governed by divine law can expect not only
Yahweh's blessing, but true harmony. Of course, human societies have
seldom been as introspective and law-abiding as the Psalmist would like.
That plus the desire of rulers to portray themselves as "just kings" explains at least in part why the cultures of the ancient Near East produced
extensive law codes. The most famous of these codes in ancient Israel is
the Ten Commandments, but they are apodictic formulas—command
law without extensive explanations. Communities usually need more
than commands, no matter how fundamental they are, and in ancient
Israel that resulted in both extensive lists of legal pronouncements
(Covenant Code, Deuteronomic Code, Holiness Code) as well as the
inclusion of a number of legal scenarios in wisdom literature and the
biblical narratives.

Israelite wisdom literature contains several instances in which a
particular item in the Decalogue is referenced as the basis for a judgment of foolishness or disrespect. For example, the axiom, found in Prov
19:26, serves as a negative echo of the Fifth Commandment to "honor
your father and your mother." It declares that "those who do violence to
their father and chase away their mother are children who cause shame
and bring reproach." Such dishonorable behavior, while not entirely specific, suggests that the son has been or intends to despoil his father's
estate and has thrust his mother away from the comfort and care she
deserves in her old age.[42] One could also point to Prov 28:24, which describes a person robbing his father or mother while declaring that "no
crime" has occurred. In both instances the son has put his household at
economic risk. The second proverb, however, is an indication that some

individuals believe that they can fool the community and themselves with false claims. And, perhaps as Zeph 3:5 suggests, "the unjust know no shame," being able to set what are considered normal emotions aside to indulge their own self-interests.[43] Proverbs 29:15 even suggests the origin of such an anti-social attitude when it concludes that "a child that gets his own way brings shame to his mother."

In these extreme cases, the parents and the elders are obligated to step in to provide justice and to restore the honor of every member of the community. That may be the origin of the story of the incorrigible son in Deut 21:18–21.[44] The young man is apparently so out of control that no amount of parental discipline has any effect on him and his disobedient nature.[45] His failure to respond to parental admonition and punishment has brought shame on his household, diminishing it in the eyes of the community. Now, however, his actions have become so serious that they are a public matter that has been identified as a real and present danger. If left unchecked, they threaten to undermine the stability and harmony of the entire community.[46]

The collective nature of traditional Israelite society now comes into play. The social and legal expectation is that the parents will bring their son before the elders at the city gate.[47] In that significant place they are to publicly testify that he is "stubborn and rebellious" and has become "a glutton and a drunkard." These compound charges may relate back to the Prov 19:26 passage, suggesting intemperate misuse of his father's property that endangers/shames the household, and to Prov 23:19–21 that warns against drunkenness and gluttonous eating of meat. Given the original judgment of "stubborn and rebellious," the second and related charge takes the son's violations to a new level. They go beyond the problems of a single household to the community as a whole since both drunkenness and gluttony drain public resources and leave the city open to violence and destruction by persons who have no control over their actions.[48]

In these circumstances and to prevent this wayward son from infecting others in the village with his shameless attitudes, he is stoned to death right there in his place of judgment in the city gate.[49] What originally touched primarily the honor of a single household has become a problem for the entire community. As a public issue the unruly son's behavior "undermines social peace, and thus the relationship to Yahweh, since it is the duty of the parents to educate their children in the faith

of God."⁵⁰ It is therefore appropriate that the elders be involved and that
a collective form of capital punishment be imposed to purge the shame
that had attached to them all.⁵¹ Only in this way can the honor and the
respectability of the community be restored.⁵²

Another example from the Deuteronomic Code once again makes
the connection between shame and law while discussing the rules of
warfare. The Case of the Beautiful Captive (Deut 21:10–14) reflects on
the fact that warfare was a common occurrence for the ancient Israelites
and the other peoples of the ancient Near East. They were continually
engaged in defending their territory from the incursions of their neighbors or attempting to extend their own holdings at the expense of other
nations and tribes.⁵³ During the course of these military engagements
there was ample opportunity to gain land, various personal goods, and
slaves (Deut 20:10–15). However, an orderly distribution of the loot was
required to prevent disputes and to ensure that when the call to arms
was again raised, the men would be willing to come and fight.⁵⁴

For those who are taken captive, it can be expected that in addition to their wounds they would experience dismay and confusion
(2 Kgs 19:26). They may even be stripped of their clothing to remove
their sense of honor and identity and to shame them before their fellows
and their captors.⁵⁵ Isaiah plays on this shameful circumstance in his
"naked circuit," an enacted prophecy in which he portrays himself as a
captive and walks about naked to indicate the fate of the people of Judah
if they rebel against the Assyrians (Isa 20:2–6). Prisoners of war would
be doubly shamed in the sense that their hometown or village has been
defeated and destroyed in battle and they have been enslaved. Not only is
their freedom taken away, but they also are denied the benefits of a civil
society that would never under normal circumstances force persons to
display their naked bodies.⁵⁶

The enslavement of prisoners of war also differs from debt slavery,
which has a time limit of six years of servitude (Exod 21:2–11; Deut
15:12–18). There is no provision for the release of prisoners of war from
servitude under normal circumstances. However, there is one option
open to women who are taken captive that may result in their becoming
free members of the Israelite society. That possibility is spelled out in
Deut 21:10–14 in the case in which an Israelite sees a beautiful woman
and wishes to make her his wife.

Particularly interesting is the required transformation ritual that
she must undergo to modify her cultural identity, set aside past associa-

tions, and prepare her to join the Israelite community. She is required to "shave her head, pare her nails, discard her captive's garb," and spend a month "mourning for her father and mother" as if they were dead. Taken in turn, shaving the head is associated with the mourning process (Job 1:20; Jer 16:6) as well as efforts to transform the character or status of an individual (shaving the Nazarite's head when he completes his term of consecration in Num 6:13–20; partially shaving David's ambassadors in 2 Sam 10:4). Paring the nails, like cutting the hair, addresses those two bodily items that continue to grow throughout a person's life.[57] The ritual represents a symbolic drama that represents the woman's death to her old life.[58]

One way of looking at this ritual is that cutting hair and paring nails symbolically puts an end to a past life and as they grow out in the coming month of mourning could represent the person's re-emergence and acceptance into a new social situation.[59] Also, in several ancient cultures there is a connection between hair and nail clippings and fertility.[60] If the object here is marriage, then ritual transformation of a past social identity and the promotion of fertility would be important facets of the process.

The woman is also required to remove her prisoner's garment. That most likely means the clothing she has been wearing since her capture or those distinctive garments given to her by her captor that indicate to all who see her that she is a slave.[61] As is the case in a number of biblical narratives (see Gen 38:12–19), removing garments in this instance is clearly a social act. The purpose is to replace her former garments with clothing more appropriate for an Israelite wife. In this way she takes on the outward appearance of her new social status.

Once her period of mourning for her parents is complete,[62] the Israelite male is allowed to "go into her" and they are joined as husband and wife. However, as is so often the case in legal narratives, an escape clause is included that focuses on the consequences of the man being dissatisfied with the former prisoner of war.[63] In that instance, she is allowed to leave his household as a free woman and she cannot be treated as a slave. The legal justification for this judgment is tied to two things. First, she has been transformed by the ritual described above and then by the shame mechanism implicit in the sexual act. The text in Deut 21:14 uses the expression "violated her," *'initah* in Hebrew, from the root *'anah*. Given her circumstances throughout this process, the woman has been powerless to resist the decision made by the Israelite. Although "sexual violence is conveyed in all the quoted instances where '*anah* is used" in the biblical text, "there is no specific mention of rape in Deuteronomy 21:14." Therefore the use of the word '*initah* in this case "implies that the woman's consent (if any) to intercourse was due to her circumstances."[64] Regardless of whether she is forced to accede to intercourse or welcomed the opportunity for a better life, what matters now are the Israelite legal and social guarantees of justice and proper treatment under the law. Her status has been transformed from a prisoner of war into a free member of society and that cannot be rescinded. To do so would result in a shaming pronouncement, like Tamar's to her half-brother Amnon. She labels his attempt to take her by force as "vile," something that "is not done in Israel" (2 Sam 13:12).

Once she has been released from any further obligation to her former husband's household, it may be presumed that the now unattached woman can marry again (compare the Code of Hammurabi #177). However, her only consolation for being dishonored is her freedom. Like the woman who is divorced by a dissatisfied husband in Deut 24:1–4, she probably has the right to marry again, but the very fact that she has been married and experienced intercourse would narrow her choices and could possibly serve as a social stigma for the remainder of her life.

To conclude this section on shame and the law, I want to examine two laws dealing with the fair treatment of poor day laborers (Deut 24:12–15). The first case addresses the acceptance of a garment in pledge, either for a loan or as noted in Amos 2:8, as surety for a full day's labor. The premise is that the peasant involved is so poor that his only piece of property is his outer robe. It is hard to imagine such poverty, but the robe also had symbolic value since it represented the difference between a free man and a slave in their society. As long has he owned a robe, he was not dependent on a master to provide him with clothing, but clearly he is on the very margin and could easily slip into such financial exigency that he must sell himself or members of his family into debt slavery (see Exod 21:2–11).[65] The plight of the poor in such circumstances is at least partially protected in this legal statement since it guarantees the return of the robe at sunset each day so the man may sleep in comfort as a free man through the night. The reward for extending care to destitute debtors or day laborers is the blessing offered up to Yahweh by the poor man.[66] In a sense, the poor man's blessing can be symbolically worn as a badge of honor by the more fortunate Israelite landowner (see Lev 25:36–38).[67]

It should be understood however, that it is very likely that a law such as this is framed in response to a real situation or because of the potential for abuse. Day laborers were at the mercy of large landowners and in many cases the only way to protect their rights was through a process of public shaming. That becomes clear in a seventh-century BCE Israelite inscription found at Yavneh Yam on a piece of broken pottery (see inset).[68] Written to support a claim of unjust treatment, this document demonstrates that there was an appeals process and that even a poor day laborer could call on the local administrator to hear his case.[69] The very fact that the document exists also points to the effort to indict and shame the harvest foreman by making his unlawful actions public.

YAVNEH YAM OSTRACON[70]

Several days ago, your servant was harvesting in Hasar-asam. The work went as usual and your servant completed the harvesting and storing of my quota of grain. . . . Despite the fact that your servant had completed his assigned work, Hoshaiahu, son of Shobai, kept your servant's cloak. He has held my cloak for days. All my fellow workers will testify—all those who work in the heat of the day will certify—that I am not guilty of any breach of contract. Please order my supervisor to return my cloak either in fulfillment of the law or as an act of mercy. Please do not remain silent and leave your servant without his cloak.

The second case requires that field workers receive their wages at the end of the day for "their livelihood depends upon them" (Deut 24:15a). These workers have no other means of feeding their families and paying their debts except the small payment they receive for their work each day.[71] A similar version of the law appears in Lev 19:13, but it refers to the rights of all workers, not just those on the edge financially. Apparently, the potential abuses that are contained in this legal stipulation are long-standing since the prophet Malachi, in the period after the exile (post-500 BCE) condemns those "who oppress the hired workers in their wages." Failure to adhere to these humanitarian statutes that are designed to support the needs of the poor in their society (98 percent of the population) could result in the oppressed workers crying "out to the Lord against you, and you would incur guilt" (24:15b). The presumption being that the one who violates the law would be publicly shamed before the community.[72]

The possibility for bringing a case of injustice to Yahweh as well as to the community at large brings us back to the Psalmist. In Ps 25:1–3, a supplicant calls on Yahweh to prevent his household from being "put to shame" or to "let my enemies exult over me," especially those "are wantonly treacherous," and who should therefore be shamed for their evil deeds. Since the assumption in these laws and supplications is that Yahweh is to be considered the "ultimate patron of the powerless," a petition addressed to the deity, like the Yavneh Yam letter addressed to the administrator, will bring both justice and retribution.[73] Shame can be avoided by both parties if they each adhere to their contractual obligations. In that way they both benefit and obtain the honor due a diligent worker and a humanitarian employer.

Shame and Stigma (2 Kgs 7:3–15)

As Martha Hollander has noted, "shame is profoundly visual, operating across an interface involving seeing and being seen."[74] We wish to be seen when we are engaged in honorable behavior or when we can display enhanced status in the context of public ceremonies.[75] Conversely, we want to hide our shame from public view to save face or at least partially preserve a semblance of family honor. One visual way that we demonstrate shame is blushing. It is the body's way of signaling heightened emotions and has some face-saving properties.[76] There is also an inherent sense of self-consciousness when caught performing a mishap or a social transgression, which signals that the person realizes that he or she is engaged in improper behavior and therefore feels the sting of embarrassment and shame.[77] Interestingly, studies have shown that the ability to blush and therefore signal social understanding and a possible desire to appease those who witness a shameful act has a mitigating influence on public opinion and observers' judgments.[78]

It is public interest that constitutes the connection between persons, a kind of social investment we have in others. If, for whatever reason, interpersonal interest is interrupted, we tend to feel deprived and that is when we are susceptible to feelings of shame. "Shame marks the break in connection. We have to care about something or someone to feel ashamed when that care and connection— our interest—is not reciprocated."[79] If for some reason someone does not wish to commune with other individuals or a group, then the likelihood of shame becomes more remote. One can only feel shame or blush involuntarily if there is both the desire to interact and a sense of damaging a desired relationship. As Leon Wurmser has written, "shame is triggered when there is a danger of 'contemptuous rejection' by another person."[80]

Therefore, when social connections or social understandings are severed and no shame is felt, then the expectation is that no blushing or other negative emotion will occur. There are a number of passages in the Bible, primarily in the prophetic materials, that describe persons or nations who have no shame in the face of their various religious and moral infractions and therefore do not blush in shame. For instance, Jeremiah charges the Israelites with brazen adulteries and prostitution as a metaphor for their idolatry. He says that they ignore the signs of Yahweh's displeasure (rains have been withheld) and "yet you have the forehead of a whore, you refuse to be ashamed" (Jer 3:3). The NIV translates *kālam* and the passage as "yet you have the brazen look of a prostitute; you refuse to blush with shame."[81] The humiliation that should result from their idolatry has been transformed into the obduracy of the hardened prostitute who feels no shame while engaging in her profession.[82]

While a lack of shame may be the result of a difference of opinion over which divine patron to serve, it is also possible for persons to become inured to what would be considered a shameful condition. That may be the case with persons who are reduced to a permanent form of servitude or imprisonment, are disabled, or who have a physical defect that cannot be hidden. For them, shame is not "episodic" and the social mechanisms that can be employed to deflect or remove shame as part of normal social interaction are either less effective or totally ineffective.[83] For them, shame is felt acutely as a manifestation of what they are or have become rather than what they do.[84]

Very likely for permanently stigmatized persons, "shame is triggered when there is a danger of 'contemptuous rejection' by another person" or by the community at large.[85] What is particularly interesting are the methods employed by various societies over time to identity persons who may be part of their community, but are pushed, for whatever reason, to its fringes and are stigmatized by having to wear a badge or a style of clothing as a signal of their shameful condition. Modern examples include the "pauper badges" worn by debtors in eighteenth-century England, and the yellow Star of David that Jews were forced to wear under the Nazi regime.[86]

When lepers in ancient Israelite society are publicly labeled as "unclean" or defiled (Lev 13; Num 5:1–4) they are faced with both the physical effects of the disease as well as the metaphorical repercussions of potential pollution to others. Pattison notes that in cases like this, "Shame, like pollution, has elements of social dislocation and exclusion. The shamed person feels they stand outside the social order and social relationships."[87] Their shame-based reaction leads to maladaptive behavior if they accept this view by others of their condition.[88] Although the biblical text does not discuss directly how their condition affects their family, a collectivist culture always extends the self to include the household.[89] It may therefore be surmised that given other examples of actions or conditions that elicit shame for the household, the person's family collectively would be shamed by having one of its members stricken with leprosy, but for the lepers, shame may eventually become a badge but not necessarily a further social burden in comparison to their disease.[90]

Excluded from the normal course of social interaction and family relations, lepers are shunned and forced to adopt a distinctive clothing style, cover their mouth, and signal their approach with the cry "unclean" (Lev 13:45).[91] Their institutionalized shame leaves them stigmatized by society because their body has become the locus for their shame.[92] The only recourse they have is to be periodically examined by a priest to determine whether their physical state has returned to normal (Lev 13:9–17). If that never occurs, then the leper's only associations will be from a "safe" distance as a beggar or with others who have been similarly afflicted. Once shame has become institutionalized it seems likely that the person(s) involved can fall into despair or can become hardened to their condition and adapt to being a social pariah, even to the extent of using their disability to obtain help or to shame others into doing things for them.[93]

That brings to mind the group of four lepers who live on the fringes of Samaria (2 Kgs 7:3–15). While the people had fled within the walls of the city during a siege by the Aramaean army, the lepers were left outside. In their desperation the lepers consider two alternative actions: (1) attempt to enter the city, but face the fate of its starving population; and (2) defect to the enemy and see if they will feed them. There is great uncertainty in both instances since it is unlikely they would be welcomed into the city because of their diseased condition and because they would represent four additional mouths to feed. Furthermore, there is no guarantee that the Aramaeans would treat them kindly, but the lepers fatalistically say "if they kill us, we shall but die" (2 Kgs 7:4).

They have little to lose and they choose to go to the enemy camp as, perhaps, the better of two bad choices (2 Kgs 7:5). What they find there is a deserted encampment that provides them with temporary relief from their hunger. However, it does not take them long to realize that their long-term interests lie with the people of Samaria. By withholding the news of the empty camp, their institutionalized shame would be compounded with charges of treason (7:9). What is interesting is that when they do report the situation to the gatekeepers and that message is transmitted to the king, he thinks it is part of a trap to lure his soldiers out of the city (2 Kgs 7:10–12). Not only are the lepers stigmatized because of their unclean state, but their credibility and loyalty to the city is also in doubt. As a result, scouts are sent to the Aramean encampment to check out the report of the lepers and when it proves to be true, a general rush takes place to loot its contents and end the famine that had plagued the city (2 Kgs 7:16). The lepers do not receive a reward from the king and there is no expression of thanks by the people. Instead the lepers must be content with a resumption of their liminal existence, living on the charity of the citizens of Samaria. They cannot be shamed to any greater degree than they already are, but at least their social shunning does not include permanent exile.

Becoming Shameless (2 Kgs 6:24—7:20)

Sometimes social situations become so stressful that the normal forms of social interaction and social restraint are compromised. Warfare has always been one of these social disruptors since it contributes to acceptance of heightened levels of violence against person and property and civil disorder.[94] Military activities can also disrupt normal market activities, travel, and create shortages that in turn cause a ripple effect on how people interact. In the story below, the city of Samaria is under siege and has been for some time. The population of the city has grown as people from the countryside seek shelter from the invaders and that puts a strain on the food and water supply within the city. In the midst of their crisis, two women make a deal that sets aside their normal role as mothers as they strive to find a way to survive.

Like other stories that portray cases brought before the king, the episode of the "cannibal mothers" serves as a test of the ruler's ability to make a wise decision and dispense justice to the people (2 Kgs 6:24–7:20). In each case in which this scene appears in the biblical narrative, there is a possibility for public shame if the monarch fails to perform as a "just king." Of course, shame already exists in the sense that a crime or an injustice has already occurred and the king is shown to have failed, at least to some extent, in fostering a cohesive and law-abiding community. He may not be directly responsible for the crime himself, but as the leader of the people he is obligated to find a just solution or punishment. Otherwise, the cry can be raised, as Absalom does against David, that there is no justice in the land and the people need to direct their support to a new leader who will serve them and their interests (2 Sam 15:1–6).

ELEMENTS OF SHAME IN THE NARRATIVE

1. Inability of the king of Israel to prevent the invasion of his country or the siege of Samaria.

2. Abandonment of social norms of behavior as evidenced by the contract between two starving women driven by their own desire for survival to sacrifice the lives of their sons.

3. Israel's king faced with the breakdown of his community and civic virtue during the siege.

4. Israel's king reduced to wearing sackcloth while doubting Yahweh's willingness or ability to end the siege.

Since the city of Samaria is besieged by the Aramaeans and the inhabitants are reduced to starvation, the warning to serve the Lord on pain of divine wrath in Deut 28:47–57 might be considered as theological backdrop to the scene. That would mean that it is covenantal disobedience that has brought Samaria to this desperate state and its people to the edge of dishonor. The question arises whether the siege of Samaria and this report of cannibalism is an exemplar for the Deuteronomist to make his point or whether the Deuteronomy passage is based on the actual events of Samaria's siege in Jehoram's time.[95]

In their attempt to define what constitutes community, Samuel Bowles and Herbert Gintis note that "connection, not affection, is the defining characteristic."[96] However, the only association between these two women is their residency in the city of Samaria during the siege. Otherwise, the only things they have in common are extreme hunger and sons. Their contract transcends normal behavior and affection for one's children[97] and their desperation removes their sense of shame for making this compact and performing this cannibalistic act.[98] Such behavior is certainly not unheard of during warfare or famine. Additional biblical references to cannibalism are found in Jer 19:9 and Ezek 5:10. The seventh-century BCE Assyrian Annals of Ashurbanipal proclaim that during one campaign against Babylon the inhabitants "ate each other's flesh in their ravenous hunger" (*ANET*, 298).

Ironically, after one child has been eaten the mother of the other child refuses to give him up to be consumed. The lack of reciprocity triggers anger against the noncompliant mother and the desire for punishment, at least in the form of intervention by the king to ensure the child is given up.[99] The noncompliant mother's action may imply a sense of shame or regret or even remorse on her part when she hides the child, but that emotion is clearly not present in the mind of the other woman. She does not feel that the current situation is her fault. After all she did not bring on the siege of the city. Instead, she and the other woman had contracted a survival pact and she had carried out her part of the bargain. Furthermore, she takes no responsibility for the other woman's covenant-breaking actions. There is no sense of moral outrage at the death and consumption of her child, only outrage that the other child is not being made available for consumption.[100] Furthermore, she is willing to publicly make known their plan without embarrassment. Her desire is to fulfill the stipulations of the contract and her passion reflects the idea that both the king and the audience should support her in this aim.

The degree of indignation expressed against the other woman is another particularly interesting aspect of this story. The two cannibal women are rivals for the life of the remaining child. Given the patriarchal nature of ancient Israelite society, it is possible that there is a male bias here rendering these women as fractious and uncaring creatures who are only interested in serving their own needs. However, that implies that women never choose to abuse each other. Certainly, gender does not restrict human nature in terms of self-interest.[101]

There are several interesting parallels to this woman's cry for justice. For instance, Solomon is confronted by two prostitutes, who are also arguing over the life of a child after another child has died (1 Kgs

3:16–28).[102] However, that story simply begins with the statement that the two "came to the king and stood before him" (1 Kgs 3:16). Mordechai Cogan is correct to note that this is a direct link to Absalom's promise to hear the cases of all who came to him if he were king (2 Sam 15:3–4).[103] It is important that Solomon, from the outset of his reign, demonstrates his openness and skill as a "Just King." In this way he obtains honor and avoids the shameful charges that Absalom had made about a neglectful and unjust David (2 Sam 15:3).

There also is a marked contrast between Solomon's expressed wisdom and the inability of the king in 2 Kgs 6:27 to find a solution.[104] That, of course, may be the Deuteronomist at work contrasting non-Davidic kings with Davidic monarchs. In the case of the cannibal mothers, it is the singular lack of wisdom on the part of the king in the face of extreme emotion and crisis that provides a stark comparison with "good kings" like Hezekiah and Josiah. Furthermore, when the "injured" mother of the dead child seeks out the king for justice she does not find him in his throne room. Instead, the king is wandering the city's parapets and is clearly distracted by the military catastrophe enveloping his capital. When brought out of his revelry he discovers that his macro concerns also have micro repercussions for his subjects when without any sense of shame or decorum a woman asks him for the life of another woman's child.[105] In form, the woman's initial address to the king is reminiscent of the plea of the Wise Woman of Tekoa to David in 2 Sam 14:4–20),[106] but in that case the mother asks for the life of her surviving son rather than his death.

The two prostitutes who address Solomon serve as the initial test of the new king's wisdom and judgment. What ties their story to the cannibal mothers is the loss of a child and the potential threat to the other. There is also a similar callousness expressed by one of the mothers in each scene. In both instances the accusing woman claims to have been injured or deprived of her rights. There is an argument between the prostitutes as Solomon stands there, and that contrasts with the fact that the other cannibal woman never speaks in the interview with the king.[107]

In making her case to the king, the "cannibal mother's" shifting of blame is matched by the statement by the king.[108] In many ways, the woman's plea for aid and justice matches the king's despairing statement in 2 Kgs 6:33 where he shifts the blame for the disaster on Yahweh.[109]

His response to the woman's plea shows his sense of powerlessness: "No! Let the Lord help you. How can I help you? From the threshing floor or from the wine press?" (2 Kgs 6:27).[110] In his frustration he demonstrates his shamed condition by sarcastically stating that she might as well turn to Yahweh for relief since he is incapable of doing anything for her.[111]

Both the cannibal woman and the king refuse to take responsibility for their own actions. Gina Hens-Piazza suggests her plea may be designed "to confront the highest authority with how very serious circumstances have become for citizens. Her plea to him for help seems more likely a very desperate cry to do something about the dire conditions of starvation."[112] However, there is also a clear disconnect between the thinking of the woman and the king. She is unembarrassed and in fact shameless over the matter of her cannibalism. He is outraged, but more on a global scale. Certainly, he expresses a sense of outrage, tearing his mourning garments.[113] But at the same time he once again shifts the blame for the current state of affairs by condemning Yahweh's prophet Elisha for their circumstances (2 Kgs 6:30–31).

Keep in mind that the king of Israel already is shamed by his inability to raise the siege. Now that shame is further aggravated when he learns that his people have sunken so far that cannibalism is occurring.[114] Still, he manages to come out of his depression and acts like a king by giving her permission to express her grievance (2 Kgs 6:28). But when she does, his rage is not directed at her. Instead he focuses his anger at Elisha, as his shame compass shifts in the direction of Nathanson's Attack Other script.[115] In his frustration, the king blames Elisha for the siege because the prophet had counseled him not to kill the Aramaeans when he had the chance (2 Kgs 6:21–23). In his unthinking anger he takes an oath (2 Kgs 6:31) to have Elisha executed that day and sends a man[116] to carry out his orders. However, Elisha, who is sitting with the elders (2 Kgs 6:32) remains calm, although he gives instructions to shut and hold the door against the messenger to give time for the king to arrive.

Unable to maintain his anger, the king has second thoughts and goes to Elisha's house himself, but once again he speaks in a despairing voice: "This trouble is from the Lord! Why should I hope in the Lord any longer?" (2 Kgs 6:33)This question, of course, is the narrative cue for Elisha to predict that Yahweh would lift the siege and the economic straits that the people have been in will be relieved (2 Kgs 7:1–2).[117] The king and the city will receive relief and the shame associated with his failure to accomplish these goals on his own will be lessened. However, it seems likely that the king will find it difficult to forget his feelings of helplessness, guilt, and shame.

CONCLUSIONS

The collectivistic, honor-shame culture of ancient Israel made good use of the two ends of the spectrum as a social control mechanism. In the marginal ecological environment in which they lived, their society recognized the need for cooperation and respect of all persons, at least as an ideal. By framing achieved and ascribed honor within the context of right speech, right thought, and right behavior, they created an interactive social vehicle to protect the weak, promote the intrinsic values of each generation to the community, and establish a system of justice that was understandable to all. At the same time, they used story, law, and prophecy to reinforce their social value system and make it clear that those who did not obey the covenant, who flaunted the law, and who lacked concern for their fellows would be publicly shamed or punished in some other way. While their literature makes it clear that some persons lived without shame, uncaring what the public might think about them, the expectation was that all should strive to obtain honor and avoid shame.

ENDNOTES

1. Pattison, *Shame*, 80.
2. M. Lewis, *Shame*, 35.
3. Lynd, *On Shame*, 20.
4. Scheff, "Shame and Related Emotions," 1056.
5. Kaufman, *Psychology of Shame*, 21.
6. Nathanson, *Shame and Pride*, 449.
7. Dost and Yagmurlu, "Constructiveness and Destructiveness," 118. See Kitayama, et al., "Culture, Self," 439–64.
8. Taylor, *Pride, Shame, and Guilt*, 54.
9. Pattison, *Shame*, 85.
10. Giordano, "Mediterranean Honour," 39–44, cautions against ethnocentric tendencies.
11. Shweder, "Toward a Deep," 1120. See Matthews and Benjamin, *Social World of Ancient Israel*, (1993), 142–54.

12. Crook, "Honor, Shame," 598–99.

13. Scheff, "Looking-Glass Self," 147–66.

14. Gardner and Gronfein, "Reflections on Varieties," 175.

15. Tangney and Dearing, *Shame and Guilt*, 14–15.

16. Nathanson, *Shame and Pride*, 449, indicates shame is "elicited deliberately and offensively as a tool of social control."

17. Bedford and Hwang, "Guilt and Shame," 127–43.

18. M. Lewis, *Shame*, 35.

19. Nathanson, *Shame and Pride*, 303–77. Graphic is based on Nathanson, 312.

20. Tomkins, *Affect/Imagery/Consciousness*, 84.

21. Elison, Lennon, and Pulos, "Investigating the Compass," 222.

22. Elison, Pulos, and Lennon, "Shame-Focused Coping," 162.

23. Dancers are usually young women (Exod 15:19–21; Judg 11:34; 1 Sam 18:7), but that does not preclude male celebrants.

24. Wright, "Music and Dance in 1 Sam 6," 201.

25. See Matthews, *Old Testament Turning Points*, 89–95.

26. Compare dancers in Jer 31:10–14.

27. See Scheff, "Sociological Model," 35.

28. See E. Goffman, *Presentation of Self*, 53.

29. See Lakoff, *Women, Fire*, 380–96.

30. See Exum, *Fragmented Women*, 43.

31. Sakenfeld, *Just Wives*, 79–81.

32. H. Lewis, *Shame and Guilt*, 82–91.

33. Alter, *Art of Biblical Narrative*, 124.

34. Asma Afsaruddin, "Hermeneutics of Gendered Space," 9.

35. Goffman, *Relations in Public*, 34–38.

36. See Clines, "Michal Observed," 59–60.

37. Steinsaltz, *Biblical Images*, 149–51.

38. Scheff, "*Deciphering Frame Analysis*," 375. See Scheff and Retzinger, *Emotions and Violence*, 125–26.

39. Leggitt and Gibbs, "Emotional Reactions to Verbal Irony," 21.

40. Scheff, "Shame and Conformity," 401.

41. Pattison, *Shame*, 41–43. Michal's guilt arises from her failure to shame David and her shame results from her inability to rehabilitate the House of Saul. See H. Lewis, *Shame and Guilt*, 11.

42. Miller, *The Ten Commandments*, 182–83.

43. Broucek, *Shame and the Self*, 135–39.

44. Fleishman, "Legal Innovation in Deuteronomy XXI 18–20," 312.

45. Fleishman, 314, n. 18 concludes the son is mentally sane, not a pathological psychopath, because he is capable of understanding his parents reproofs.

46. Hagedorn, "Guarding the Parents' Honour," 104.

47. See Matthews, "Entrance Ways and Threshing Floors," 25–40.

48. See Fleishman, "Legal Innovation in Deuteronomy XXI 18–20," 322–24, on addictive behavior.

49. See Marcus, "Juvenile Delinquency," 47–48, on capital punishment.

50. Hagedorn, "Guarding the Parents' Honour," 106.

51. Willis, *Elders of the City*, 164–69.

52. The parents are not condemned for their failure to control their son (see Deut 24:16).

53. See 1 Sam 11 and 1 Kgs 22.

54. See Jer 50:11–13.

55. Bleibtreu, "Grisly Assyrian Record of Torture and Death," 53–61, 75.

56. See Isa 47:3; Jer 13:26; and Nah 3:5 for lifting up "your skirts" to shame Judah or their defeated enemies.

57. See Galpaz-Feller, "Hair in the Bible," 75–94.

58. See Staubli and Schroer, *Body Symbolism in the Bible*, 96–102.

59. Joseph must shave and change his clothes before being presented to pharaoh (Gen 41:14). Compare the Egyptian story of the exile Sinuhe (*ANET*, p. 22).

60. Lincoln, "Treatment of Fingernails and Hair," 357.

61. See Matthews, "The Anthropology of Clothing," 25–36.

62. See Num 20:29 and Deut 34:8.

63. Compare Deut 22:13–21 and the law of divorcement in Deut 24:1–4.

64. Elman, "Deuteronomy 21:10–14," online at www.utoronto.ca/wjudaism/journal/vol1n1/v1n1elma.htm

65. See Lang, "Social Organization," 91–93.

66. Sonsino, *Motive Clauses*, 115–16.

67. Hoppe, *There Shall Be No Poor Among You*, 26–27.

68. This site is a coastal town located about 7 miles south of Joppa.

69. Westbrook and Wells, *Everyday Law*, 115.

70. Matthews and Benjamin, *Old Testament Parallels*, 355–56.

71. Wages in ancient Israel consisted of a portion of the harvest or the right to certain services.

72. See Job 31:38–39.

73. Tigay, *Deuteronomy*, 226.

74. M. Hollander, "Losses of Face," 1327.

75. See 1 Kgs 1:33–35; 2 Kgs 11:12.

76. De Jong and Peters, "Remedial Value," 287.

77. Crozier, *Blushing and the Social Emotions*.

78. Cutlip and Leary, "Anatomic and Physiological," 289.

79. Probyn, *Blush*, 13.

80. Wurmser, *Mask of Shame*, 53–54.

81. See J. Hollander, "Honour Dishonorable," 1062.

82. Holladay, *Jeremiah 1*, 115.

83. Gardner and Gronfein, "Reflections," 176–79.

84. Wharton, "The Hidden Face," 279–90.

85. Wurmser, *Mask of Shame*, 53–54.

86. Hindle, "Dependency," 6–35.

87. Pattison, *Shame*, 89.

88. Dost and Yagmurlu, "Constructiveness and Destructiveness," 113.

89. Bedford and Hwang, "Guilt and Shame," 130.

90. See Li, et al., "Impacts of HIV/AIDS Stigma," 432–42.

91. Retzinger, "Identifying Shame and Anger," 1104–13.

92. Goffman, *Stigma*.

93. Brown, "*Shame* Resilience Theory," 43–52.

94. Braithwaite, "Rape, Shame, and Pride," 3–4.

95. Hobbs, *2 Kings*, 78–79. Compare Josephus *J.W.* 6.3.4.

96. Bowles and Gintis, "Social Capital," 420.

97. Camp, "1 and 2 Kings," 108.

98. Hens-Piazza, *Nameless, Blameless*, 80. Lanner, "Cannibal Mothers," 107–16.

99. Bowles and Gintis, "Social Capital," 427.

100. See Taylor, *Pride, Shame, and Guilt*, 104–7.

101. See Spelman, "The Virtue of Feeling," 213–32.

102. Lasine, "Riddle," 1989, 69–70.

103. Cogan, *1 Kings* (2001), 194.

104. Rendsburg, "The Guilty Party," 535.

105. See Lasine, "Riddle," 66, and "Cannibal Mothers," 26.

106. The woman says, "Help, O King!" and David responses, "What is your trouble" in 2 Sam 14:5.

107. See Garsiel, "Revealing and Concealing," 229–47.

108. See Cogan and Tadmor, *II Kings*, 79.

109. Cogan and Tadmor, *II Kings*, 79–80.

110. Lasine, "Riddle," 66.

111. Taylor, *Pride, Shame, and Guilt*, 92.

112. Hens-Piazza, "Forms of Violence," 91.

113. Compare Jonah 3:6–9.

114. LaBarbera, "The Man of War," 646.

115. Nathanson, *Shame and Pride*, 364–65.

116. Cogan and Tadmor, *II Kings*, 80.

117. Bergen, "The Prophetic Alternative," 132.

9

Anachronism, Ethnocentrism, and Shame

The Envy of the Chief Priests

Bruce J. Malina

M Y CONCERN IS WITH the writers of New Testament documents and the people whom they describe and with whom they communicate. To get in contact with those people, I believe one has to leave the twenty-first-century U.S. for the first-century eastern Mediterranean. That trip in time covers two thousand years and passes through significant periods of our history. We must pass through the development of science and technology, of the Industrial Revolution, of economies of abundance and superabundance, of Romanticism with the rise of psychology, life as a story, individual subjectivism, of the Enlightenment and the separation of church and state, and of economics and government, of the Renaissance and the separation of pope and state, of the Christianizing of European Germanic and Slavic peoples, of the rise of universities due to heavy Arabic influences, of the rise of state Christianity with Emperor Constantine (Christianity as political religion), of the formation of Rabbinic Judaism (and Jewish religion), of Jesus groups and their domestic religion, and finally to the time of Jesus and his contemporaries. This passage through historical periods often entails navigating a range of social systems. Even today, Mediterranean peoples are culturally quite different from U.S. peoples. Now when people ask, "What would Jesus do?" they mean "What would a twenty-first-century American Jesus do?" The fact is there never was a twenty-first-century American Jesus. With a sense of anachronism and ethnocentrism, the question means

. would a first-century eastern Mediterranean, Israelite Jesus do. For most Bible readers, this is an insuperably unanswerable question. The only Jesus they know is one in their own U.S. image and likeness. In this essay I propose to leave our time and culture for that alien time and culture presumed by the New Testament writers. Relative to our theme of shame shaping society, I begin with the following observations.

Humans are born with a wide range of possibilities. Humans have some 450 sounds available to them for sounding out language, but most languages use less than 250 of these. Similarly, children go through three dimensions of human distress experience that parents around the planet have used and continue to use in the social control of their children. The three social control sanctions are called anxiety, shame, and guilt. They emerge in children in some sort of developmental fashion. While all persons can and do experience all three distress feelings, cultures around the world have chosen to emphasize one or another of these as central. Since the work of anthropologist Ruth Benedict (1934), writers have come to speak of shame cultures and guilt cultures.[1] And for a number of reasons, anthropologists have considered the Mediterranean culture area as typically focused on the sanction of shame (and honor).

Awareness of anachronism and ethnocentrism would have historically sensitive persons question whether these terms mean the same thing today as they did in the past. Did they mean the same thing in the ancient Mediterranean as they do in the U.S. today? The way to overcome anachronism and ethnocentrism, of course, is to learn about or "enter" the culture of the people depicted in biblical writings. Readers (or hearers) must jump back in time to that early period so as to avoid the range of new features that emerged over the past two thousand years. What is required is a type of historical anthropology.

In this presentation and in a context of how shame shapes society, I broach the question of why was Jesus killed. The writers of Mark and Matthew tell us explicitly why they believe Jesus was killed. They articulate their position in terms of Pilate's viewpoint as follows: Pilate "perceived that it was out of envy that the chief priests had delivered him (Jesus) to death" (Mark 15:10; Matt 27:18 repeats Pilate's assessment). Ancient writers thought of envy as a kind of pain at the sight of another's good fortune. Aristotle (*Rhetorica* 2.10.1) defined envy as a value that directed a person to begrudge another the possession of some limited and singular quality, object, or relationship that gave or expressed honor.[2]

The chief priests and their apparatus were envious of Jesus! This statement is clear enough, yet most commentators simply pass over it in their writings. It seems envy is not interesting enough to require a paragraph or two of explanation. Perhaps theological perspectives block out concern for envy. It is more interesting to deal with the death of Jesus for the salvation of the world, on behalf of sinners, for the redemption of humankind. None of these explanations crop up in the trial scene interactions dealing with Jesus' death. But envy does stand out quite clearly.

The task I have chosen, then, is to explain this motive of the chief priests' envy and Pilate's understanding of envy as taken for granted by the gospel writers. For what other reason would the temple political religious establishment want Jesus killed if not envy?

Of course, all biblical documents are ethnocentric. And if the documents of the New Testament are anti anything, they are anti-outsiders. The gospels' assessment of Pilate is expectedly ethnocentric. His judgment of the chief priests is typically ethnocentric as well. How could he know the chief priests were envious? A deeper look at envy in the perspective of first-century Mediterranean informants will tell us.

This is all the more necessary, given the general linguistic presupposition that meanings in language and behavior come from the social system of speakers and writers. Language consists of three levels: markings or soundings, wordings (patterns), and meanings that come from the social system in question. Communication involves letting the patterned sounds or markings evoke images that are shared by those communicating. Learning a foreign language for the most part entails learning the patterns of the sounds and markings of that language. But without an understanding of the social system of native speakers, language learners can only insert meanings from their own society, not of the writers of foreign documents, whether it is the Bible or any other non-U.S. writing. To take ancient social systems seriously in order to understand biblical writers is a type of historical anthropology, at times called social scientific criticism of the Bible.[3]

According to historically oriented anthropologists, culture areas are rather stable around the world. Scholars learn ancient social systems in the same way scholars have pieced together ancient languages. They begin with modern descendants in a specific culture area. They then go back through the ages and stages of development that led to the various forms found in history until they get to the period they search for. Biblical

writings come from the eastern Mediterranean culture area. A study of
the social system of native peoples of those regions, traced through the
various, significant historical stages up to the period one searches for
yields a useful approximation of what ancient social systems were like.
For example, the main social institutions were family and government.
There was domestic religion and political religion; domestic economy
and political economy—but no freestanding religion or economics.[4] The
separation of church and state or government and economics took place
in the eighteenth century BCE. To talk about religion one necessarily
talked of family and government; the roles, statuses, and values of family
and government were used to express religion. God was king and father,
of a people consisting of brothers and sisters or children.

Along with different institutional arrangements, social systems
have various clusters of values. Value in this context means a general
quality and direction of behavior. Values always inhere in value objects.[5]
For example, the value goodness always inheres in some good persons,
good foods, good housing, and the like. Goodness is a value, a general
quality. In the world of the Bible, the focal value was honor, some quality
and direction of behavior that is judged to be of social worth. Honor is
ascribed or acquired when people judge another person's standing or
behavior as of social worth. God is honorable, that is judged by those
who worship God as of eminent social worth—"our God, God of power
and might." Values inhere in value objects which include: selves, others,
nature, time, space and God (or gods). Next to honor, the main value in-
hering in persons is their gender: selves are always males or females (no
middle ground) and are honorable if they express their gender according to social norms. Males represent the family and group to the outside
of the group, females represent the family and group on the inside. The
lineage tracing through the father has entitlements—this is patriarchy.

The value object called "others" (or outsiders) deals with the worth
attached to ingroup over outgroup. Ingroup includes one's immediate
household, wider kin group, neighborhood or village (city) section, one's
village, region or tribe, people. The boundary around the ingroup shifts
according to one's interacting partner. An Arab proverb says: "I against
my brother; I and my brother against our cousin; I and my brother and
my cousin against our village," and so forth, in ever expanding circles.
The outgroup is always secondary, and often without entitlements at all
when some limited good is at issue.

Nature refers to every entity in one's social environment aside from people. Nonhuman personlike beings included the denizens of the sky (stars; spirits, demons, angels; storms, winds, rainfall), animate beings, trees and plants and special stones (meteorites) and everything else. Many of these entities were believed to behave just like humans. The people who populated the Bible believed humans were subject to nature, unlike God. Hence they had behavior forms that attempted to protect them from the impact of nature. Along with demon-caused drought and windstorms, there were various illnesses and social calamities.

Time as value object was concerned with assessing change: seasonal change that was circular and repetitive, and biological change that was linear from birth to old age. People in the Bible were concerned mostly with the present and the past insofar as it had shaped the present. They planned for the forthcoming: the birth of a baby, a new crop after planting. They had little or no concern for any abstract future. Biblical people had no eschatology, although they did believe the social environment was running down: crops were fewer, children were smaller, and the like. Hence they believed in a sort of devolution and a "worseology." Israelites expected the God of Israel to intervene and stop the trend with a renewed world and a revived people.

Space, both sky space and earth space, was marked off as territory belonging to someone. A sky segment and the land below were in the control of nonhuman celestial entities such as constellated stars. People born in some divinely owned territory believed that their ancestors, they, and their households were part of that land, although more powerful elites sought to steal their birthright, either by extorted purchase or simply theft. The purpose of the elite annual activity called "war" was to divert peoples and their lands to elite purposes and enrichment.

Along with value objects, social systems likewise consisted of person types.[6]

After gender and kin group, the sense of who one was derived from a social-psychological perspective that ranked social groups on a spectrum from individualistic self to collectivistic self. Individualistic cultures expect children to learn how to stand on their own two feet, to think for themselves and their own well-being first, to distance themselves from family in the pursuit of success. Collectivistic cultures expect children to live for the well-being of their ingroup, to support and maintain the group and its members at all costs, with success being defined as group rather than individual well-being. Most cultures in the world today are collectivistic (80%) and so were the people whom we confront in the Bible.

Along with situating biblical people and their communications in proper institutional, value, and person-type frameworks, there are a number of presuppositions common to people of the period.

First-century Mediterranean people lived in preindustrial societies. These people as a rule believed all goods in life were limited.[7] Every rich person was a thief or the heir of a thief. For them, wealth and well-being attached to the land. In the ancient Mediterranean version of preindustrial society, honor and shame were considered pivotal values. *It seems that the configuration of the perception of limited good, concern for honor and shame, coupled with life in ruralized society produces preoccupation with envy and with significant importance ascribed to it.*

Further, there was the belief that every effect that counted in a person's life was caused by some person, visible or nonvisible. The proper question to ask in the case of some negative event was "Who did it?" not "What did it?"[8]

In the Israelite tradition, for example, envy was the cause of that paramount and inescapable negative feature of human existence: death. And the personal agent was the devil. "Through the devil's envy, death entered the world" (Wis 2:24). Philo, an émigré Israelite who lived in Alexandria, insisted that envy was "the most grievous of all evils" (*Special Laws* 3.1.2). Once we learn how first-century Mediterraneans perceived envy, it will become apparent that envy was indeed a significant characteristic of ancient Mediterranean living.

Envy, as previously noted, is a feeling of begrudging that emerges in face of the good fortune of others relative to some restricted good that is equally of interest to us.[9] A person's envy focused on social equals in similar social circles. You will notice that Mark's report of Pilate's appraisal of the reason for Jesus' being put to death pits an individual against a group, Jesus against the high priests, who are envious of Jesus. When groups envy others, either single individuals or other groups, it is a good indication that we are dealing with a collectivistic, group-oriented society rather than an individualistic society. In collectivistic societies, people stay in the status in which they were born. Social standing is determined by birth, one's ethnic group in general, and one's status within that ethnic group. There is little, if any, social mobility upward or downward. Even when elites are dispossessed and defamed by their elite peers, they remain elites at the lowest levels of elite statuses.

Furthermore, just as honor and shame work differently in individualistic societies and in collectivistic ones, so too envy. You will recall that shame in the ancient Mediterranean (and in collectivistic societies) is a publicly rejected claim to worth. A person asserts some value or feature as honorable, such as to be a holy man, like Elijah and Elisha (Luke 4:24–27), and the public refuses to acknowledge the person's worth or even rejects him or her. This is shame marked by socially perceived disgrace. To be shamed by others inflicts a profound wound on the persons who are disgraced together with those associated with them, particularly family members. Whether it is a bumper sticker on a car or a sign on a Roman cross, it becomes humiliation for everyone in the ingroup. The ordinary reaction of collectivistic persons is to inform the group in which they are embedded of the refusal of acknowledgment with a view to planning revenge on the new or traditional enemy responsible for the dishonor.

In collectivistic societies, shame works only for individuals who feel an allegiance to others and to the social system in general, with a capacity to care about their social standing. There were alienated, unallied persons such as beggars, the dispossessed elites, or the conquered and exiled. If people are alienated, the effort to shame them is irrelevant and may only be a badge of honor among their status equals. Thus to be crucified by conquering Romans who likewise crucified many of one's fellow Israelites would not be shameful to fellow ethnics. But to be handed over by one's fellow Israelites for crucifixion by outgroup Roman authorities would be public shame, indeed.

In individualistic societies, where honor and shame are highly psychologized and bear deeply introspective resonance, shame is a denial of personal worth by some significant person (mother, father, teacher, relative, sibling). The person who is shamed believes he or she is simply not worthy to be alive, to be a person, to exist. This introspective sense of being shamed diminishes a person's self-worth and often activates urges of self-destruction as the only proper answer to one's lack of self-worth. This sort of reaction would rarely be found in the Mediterranean, past or present. Mediterraneans are anti-introspective and not psychologically minded. As I was recently told by a Mediterranean informant after we both witnessed an incident of public shaming, "If I was shamed and felt the urge to commit suicide, I would kill somebody." This, in a nutshell, is a typical anti-introspective, collectivistic reaction to being shamed.

In that response we find another Mediterranean presupposition, namely that there is no internal state without a corresponding external manifestation. For example, the honor that other people cannot see, perceive, and experience is simply no honor. It does not exist. Hence the need to do something to show one's honorable status is imperative. "Glory" for example, refers to the external items people have that reveal their status, their honor. "The heavens are telling the glory of God" (Ps 19:1); the devil took Jesus "to a very high mountain, and showed him all the kingdoms of the world and the glory of them" (Matt 4:8; see Luke 4:6); "In a multitude of people is the glory of a king, but without people a prince is ruined" (Prov 14:28); "For a man ought not to cover his head, since he is the image and glory of God; but woman is the glory of man" (1 Cor 11:7). These are so many instances of glory, of the external and visible showing the nonvisible social standing of the persons involved.

Honor is intimately connected with envy. Ancient Mediterraneans were absorbed with envy concerns, much as modern U.S. persons are taken by the preservation and increase of wealth in its many forms. Aristotle attempted to explain "for what reason, and of whom, and in what frame of mind, men are envious" in his very Mediterranean experience (*Rhetorica* 2.10.1). The motive, he states, is "love of honor," i.e., a drive to prominence through attention-getting and eye-catching behavior:

> It is equally clear for what reason, and of whom, and in what frame of mind, men are envious, if envy is a kind of pain at the sight of good fortune in regard to the goods mentioned; in the case of those like themselves; and not for the sake of a man getting anything, but because of others possessing it. For those men will be envious of others who are or seem to be like them. I mean like in birth-status, family relationship, age, moral habit, reputation, and possessions. And those will be envious who possess all but one of these features. That is why those who attempt great things and succeed are envious, because they think that everyone is trying to deprive them of their acquisitions. The same is true for those who are honored for some special reason, especially for wisdom or happiness. And those driven to prominence are more envious than the unambitious. And so too, those who are excessively appreciative of their own wisdom. for they are driven to

prominence in wisdom; and, in general, those who wish to be prominent in anything are envious in regard to it. And the small-minded, because everything appears great to them. (*Rhetorica* 2.10.1–3)

Aristotle presumed that we know what he and his world meant by "love of honor," a common term found throughout Greek literature. "Love of honor" was a frequently mentioned and highly prized quality from Homer to Augustine. Xenophon, for example, described the Athenians as passionate for praise: "Athenians excel all others not so much in singing or in stature or in strength, as in love of honor, which is the strongest incentive to deeds of honour and renown" (*Memorabilia* 3.3.13). Similarly, Augustine looks back on Rome and describes what seems to him the pivotal value that drove Romans in all their endeavors, the love of praise: "For the glory that the Romans burned to possess, be it noted, is the favourable judgment of men who think well of other men" (*City of God* 5.12). For love of praise, the Romans overcame vices common to other peoples: "He (God) granted supremacy to men who for the sake of honor, praise and glory served the country in which they were seeking their own glory, and did not hesitate to prefer her safety to their own. Thus for one vice, that is, love of praise, they overcame the love of money and many other vices" (*City of God* 5.13). Xenophon valued "love of honor" so highly that he identified it as one of the chief things that distinguish not only humans from animals, but noble humans from ordinary folk.

"Honor" for the ancients meant primarily prominence from renown and reputation. This "love of honor" produces envy. Since the ancients were intensely desirous of fame and honor and thought that all things existed in limited supply, envy naturally follows love of honor. Envy, in collectivistic cultures, clearly presupposes the perception of *limited good*.

Without the perception of limited good and the use of goods to express one's good fortune, envy does not emerge. The perception of limited good seems to be a necessary condition for envy to come forth in ruralized societies concerned with honor and shame. In other words, in a society where the perception of limited good is a common social perception, envy will be institutionalized. Mediterranean envy concerns acquire institutional shape because honor and shame are pivotal values that need to be concretized and externalized, and this in a subsistence-based rural society. Under such conditions, patterns of envy will be well-known, commented on, and frequently observed in ways that do not happen in guilt-oriented, urban societies with perceptions of limitless good.

Envy was a value that directed a person to begrudge another the possession of some singular quality, object, or relationship that gave or expressed honor. It is the limited nature of the honor-bearing quality, object, or relationship in question and the social status of the possessor that trigger envy. If Israel's high priests delivered Jesus to death out of envy, it means that in Pilate's outsider observation, Jesus was a social equal of the high priests. This, of course, may simply be derived from the Roman sense of superiority to all outgroup members. The "natives" are all the same status to the foreigner authorities.

Why would people think it is quite right to envy another? The reason is that persons who are envied stand out from the rest of the community. They stand above their fellows. The social deviance involved in possessing something perceived as singular is that the one possessing the unique item stands out or stands above his or her proper social status and/or the group in general. The one who is envious becomes negatively disposed toward the person with the singular possession and is often seized by the desire to deprive the other person of that possession—often in the name of the group. It is right to cut down anyone standing above his or her status.

It might to good to recall, once more, that ancient Mediterraneans were anti-introspective and not psychologically minded at all. That means that terms for internal states invariably entail corresponding external actions. It is only from the actions that one can actually know the internal states of another (and oneself). Although Aristotle calls envy a *lype* (distress, grief, pain) (*Rhetorica.* 2.10.1), it is a very dangerous phenomenon because it rarely stays at the level of an emotion, but emerges in observable behavior. What sort of behaviors, then, point to the presence of envy? As we might assume, envious people reveal their internal feelings in a number of ways. Among these, scholars have noted ostracism, gossip and slander, feuding, litigation, the evil eye, and homicide. All would agree that the prevalence of envy in ancient Mediterranean society was rather strongly underscored by belief in the evil eye. [10]

Further, an envious person might resort to physical violence and even *homicide* to reduce the status of the person envied. Israelite tradition ascribed Cain's murder of Abel to envy; the same was true of Saul's attempts to slay David. In Luke's special tradition, Jesus' own town mates seek to put him to death after an interaction that demonstrates their envy toward him (Luke 4:16–30). The same is true in Pilate's assessment of the high priests who want Jesus killed (Mark 15:10). Thus, envy is no empty emotion, but a galvanizing impetus to action.

Envy proceeds from the heart through the eyes. The usual suspects thought to harbor evil eye abilities were family enemies, strangers, outsiders, deviants as well as the physically deformed, disabled, and the blind. Strangers and outsiders were presumed to be envious of the good things locals and insiders enjoyed, the socially deviant (criminals, traitors) were envious of those not caught and labeled as deviants, while the crippled and the blind were envious of those enjoying good health. Resident outgroups were stereotypically believed to be afflicted with the evil eye. Philo stereotypes the Egyptians as an envious and evil-eyed people in his writing against Flaccus: "But the Egyptian," he states, "is by nature an evil-eyed person, and the citizens burst with envy and considered that any good fortune to others was misfortune to themselves" (*Flaccus* 29).

Scholars have listed various types of behavior undertaken by people who fear the envy of others and seek to reduce their own visibility and vulnerability. These include *concealment, denial,* a conciliatory *bribe, true sharing,* and an assortment of *amulets* and actions.

We begin with *concealment* or secrecy.[11] In a society like that in which Jesus lived, a personal self-disclosure may result in ridicule, hostility, gossip, envy and conformity pressures to change. As we know, in ancient Mediterranean society interpersonal relations are characterized by competition, rivalries, and conflicts of opinion. In this limited good world, where anything gained, whether new wealth, position, honor, or whatever, was always believed to come at someone else's expense, one could never appear grasping or self-aggrandizing in public without raising immediate suspicion. The much-discussed "messianic secret" motif so prominent in Mark (1:25, 34, 44; 3:12; 5:43; 7:24, 36; 8:30; 9:9, 30; 14:61; 15:32) can be seen in this light. Having been born to the low social status of a village artisan, claims by Jesus that he is anything more than a village artisan would have been viewed as grasping in the extreme. The gospel writers allow their hearers/readers to know what the true social standing of Jesus is right at the outset (Mark 1:1: a son of God; Matt 1:1: Jesus Messiah; Luke 1:32: son of the Most High; John 1:1: the Word of

God). But Jesus prefers concealment to ward off envy. He further shows himself to be an honorable person by trying to keep any talk of his being an extraordinary personage out of public notice. Note especially his silencing of demons who, given their higher position in the cosmic hierarchy, are readily able to identify this unexpected status for Jesus (see Mark 1:25, 34; 3:12). Boasting, the opposite of concealment, openly invites envy. "It is the glory of God to conceal things, but the glory of kings is to search things out" (Prov 25:2).

Denial might be the simple rejection of a compliment. Thus Jesus simply avoids envy by refusing the compliment when called: "Good Teacher." He properly responds: "Why do you call me 'good?'" No one is good but God alone" (Mark 10:18).

A *conciliatory bribe* is a gift bestowed on others to ward off or reduce sentiments of envy. It is takes little imagination to realize that the stories of the feeding of the crowds in the Synoptic Gospels work as conciliatory bribes (Mark 6:32–44; 8:1–10; Matt 14:13–21; 15:32–39; Luke 9:10–17; John 6:1–15). Instead of being envious of Jesus and thwarting him in his task of proclaiming the forthcoming theocracy, the crowds are duly astonished and enable him to continue his work.

True sharing was a way of leveling wealth and thus reducing envy. In the gospels, instances of such true sharing took the form of almsgiving and temple tithing. In the stories in Acts, we learn of Jesus' group members who, being "possessors of lands or houses, sold them and brought the proceeds of what was sold and laid it at the apostles' feet; and distribution was made to each as any had need" (Acts 4:34–35). But spectacular instances of such sharing in the Roman Empire involved wealthy aristocrats who funded projects in their cities, just as monarchs who did the same in the lands they controlled (e.g., King Herod rebuilt the Jerusalem temple as well as a number of "cities" in his kingdom). Such public works on behalf of the people were called "liturgy."

Amulets and actions were ways of warding off the evil eye. Author John Elliott observes that a common protective device was a staring eye worn as amulet or carved into a wall or put into mosaic flooring. The eye served as a mirror to reflect the evil eye back on its possessor. Equally effective was a phallus worn around the neck, inscribed in stone, or hanging from the wall. An unexpected meeting with an epileptic, a lame man, or a stranger, sources of evil-eye effects, could be protected against by spitting. Other personal protective measures included avoiding eye contact altogether, concealing prized possessions, covering one's women and children, denying any improvement in one's economic situation, and wearing a variety of protective devices (strings of knots, red or blue cloth, sacks of herbs such as rue or garlic, amulet jewelry inscribed with anti-evil eye symbols such as an eye under attack or miniature phalluses, phylacteries, horns, crescent moons, or bells).[12]

People rarely admit to being envious because it is an admission of inadequacy, hence shameful. One who hates others readily admits the fact, but not so people who envy.

SUMMARY

Envy is an emotion that makes a person feel aggrieved at the good fortune of another person, normally of the same social ranking. Good fortune meant honor, and honor sought expression through mediating goods. Envy sought expression in concrete actions that would reduce the envied person to a state of disgrace and misfortune. Envy differs from jealousy or zeal as well as from hate. It was of central concern in the ancient Mediterranean because all goods were considered limited, and the person expressing honor as well as the honor itself deprived others. It took away something, invariably at some other person's expense. Envious people demonstrated their envy by ostracism, gossip, negative challenges, litigation, homicide. The most common indicator of envy was the evil eye. To avoid envy and the evil eye, people used a number of objects and gestures. They likewise concealed or denied their good fortune, offered conciliatory bribes and practiced true sharing. During the time of Jesus, envy was regularly counted among the prohibitions given by the God of Israel in the Ten Commandments. The following chart summarizes the main features presumed in this essay.

Envy in U.S. Experience and Ancient Mediterranean Experience

U.S. Experience	Ancient Mediterranean Experience
Envy occurs between single persons, replicating individualistic culture.	Envy occurs between groups, replicating collectivistic culture, and within groups (e.g., mothers setting male children against each other to motivate).
Envy is not confined to persons in the same economic status because individuals aspire to ever higher statuses.	Envy is confined to status equals, determined by genealogy, gender, and geography because individuals remain in the same status for life.
The person envied is seen as fortunate and elated in his or her new possession or relationship.	The person envied is seen as rising above the social level to which he or she is entitled by birth and ethnicity.
The person who envies begrudges his or her rival's good fortune but can find other fields in which to find good fortune and happiness.	The person who envies begrudges his or her rival's good fortune because it marks a deprivation of good for the envier and his or her group.
Honor and shame are internalized and introspective experiences, and can serve as motives to action.	Honor and shame are externalized, social experiences.
Shame is the rejection of an individual's personhood.	Shame is the rejection of an individual's and group's claim to honor.
Shame provokes feelings of unworthiness, even suicide in the individual.	Shame provokes plans of retaliation and vengeance in the group.
Honor is an internalized feeling of social success.	Honor is an externalized expression of social success.

U.S. Experience	Ancient Mediterranean Experience
People need goods and awards to gauge their success in an achievement-oriented society.	People need goods and awards to proclaim their honor-standing, that is, their social glory in a content-ment-oriented society.
Since people need goods to mean, individualistic societies with individuals expected to express individualistic opinions require a far larger amount of goods than collectivistic societies.	Since people need goods to mean, collectivistic societies with central personages expected to express group opinions require a far fewer goods than individualistic societies.
All goods exist in endless, unlimited quantity and are usually always in abundant supply.	All goods exist in finite, limited quantity and are always in short supply.
An economy of superabundance: a short supply of goods indicates monopolistic practices and market control.	A subsistence economy: a short supply of goods indicates the normal condition of human society.
Social and economic improvements are beneficial to individuals and society as a whole.	Social and economic improvements are always at the expense of others.
Social and economic improvements are perceived as outcome of hard work and initiative.	Social and economic improvements are perceived as a threat to the well-being of one's ingroup (family, neighborhood).
Economic stagnation points to social dysfunction.	Economic stagnation points to community harmony and stability.
Envy is an internal state, best analyzed by introspection and psychological methods.	Envy is an internal state with a corresponding external manifestation—the evil eye.
No awareness, much less concern, for the evil eye.	Much awareness and great concern for the evil eye.

ENDNOTES

1. See Augsburger, *Pastoral Counseling*, 111–43.
2. See Malina, *New Testament World*, 108–33.
3. See Halliday, *Language as a Social Semiotic*.
4. See Smith, *The Meaning and End of Religion*.
5. See Houlden, *Ethics and the New Testament*.
6. See Triandis, "Cross-Cultural Studies," 41–133.
7. See Foster, "Anatomy of Envy," 165–202; Malina, "Limited Good," 162–76.
8. See Malina, *New Testament World*, 100–104.
9. See Hagedorn and Neyrey, "Out of Envy."
10. See Elliott, "Evil Eye and the Sermon on the Mount," 51–84. Elliott has a large range of studies on the evil eye and envy in the Bible.
11. See Pilch, "Secrecy," 151–57.
12. See Elliott, "Paul, Galatians and the Evil Eye," 262–73.

10

Turning Shame into Honor

The Pastoral Strategy of 1 Peter

DAVID A. DESILVA

INTRODUCTION

WHEN WE READ THROUGH 1 Peter for clues about the situation of the addressees, and particularly those features of their situation that most concern the author, we find repeated emphasis on the addressees' experience of socially imposed shame.

> In this [hope] you rejoice, though for a little while it is necessary for you *to be grieved by a variety of trials.* (1 Pet 1:6)

> Keep living honorably among the Gentiles in order that, *although they slander you as though you were evildoers,* they may observe your honorable deeds and glorify God in the day of God's visitation. (1 Pet 2:12)

> This is a gift—*if for the sake of his or her mindfulness of God a person endures affliction, suffering unjustly.* (1 Pet 2:19)

> Even if you should *suffer on account of what is just,* you are privileged . . . Keep your conscience clean in order that, *when you are slandered, those who keep on abusing your good conduct in Christ* may themselves be put to shame. (1 Pet 3:14, 16)

> They are put off because you no longer run along with them into the same flood of disgraceful behavior, *and so they slander* [you]. (1 Pet 4:4)

159

> Beloved, *do not be put off by the fiery trial taking place among you* as a test . . . Instead, rejoice to the extent that *you are sharing Christ's sufferings . . . If you are reproached in Christ's name*, you are privileged . . . *If any one among you [suffers] as a Christian, don't be ashamed*, but give God honor because you bear this name. (1 Pet 4:12–16)

> Let *those who are suffering* in alignment with God's will entrust their lives to a faithful creator as they continue to do good. (1 Pet 4:19)

> *After you have suffered for a short while*, the God of all favor . . . will himself restore, raise up, strength, and establish [you]. (1 Pet 5:10)[1]

The frequency and pervasiveness of these references to the painful, disconfirming experiences of slander, reproach, and even physical affront—and the effects these experiences have on the addressees' ability to persevere in the direction they have chosen—establishes this aspect of their situation as central to the author's concern and pastoral agenda.[2]

This essay explores the social dynamics of shaming at work in this situation and the rationale behind the non-Christian neighbors' responses to the Christians in their midst. It then focuses on several strategies by means of which the author seeks to insulate the addressees against the experience of shame, with the result that the hearers can find sufficient grounds for self-respect and sufficient affirmation of worth within the Christian group to persevere in the beliefs, associations, and trajectory to which they chose to commit themselves in response to hearing the message about deliverance in Jesus Christ. It concludes with reflections on how the Christian community can become more sensitive to, and effective in addressing, the presence and effects of social shame upon the alternative global community known as the church.

SHAME ON YOU!

The first-century Mediterranean world was a complex, multicultural environment. We can speak broadly of a dominant culture—the culture of those with power and resources—composed of deeply Hellenized and increasingly Romanized elites throughout the Eastern Mediterranean. In this regard, Herod Antipas had far more in common with Pontius Pilate than with his fellow Jews, Jesus of Nazareth or James of Jerusalem.

We may also speak broadly of majority cultures in various regions that tended to accept rather than challenge dominant-cultural values and the traditional values and practices of their particular region and ethnic background. We could also identify numerous minority cultures throughout the Roman Empire. The Jewish subculture was itself such a minority culture, the pressures upon it being the more keenly felt in the Diaspora. Philosophical groups like Stoics and Cynics, Jewish sects like the community at Qumran and the various branches of the early Christian movement, are all minority cultures insofar as their adherents are numerically far fewer than adherents of the majority culture and their resources and access to power far inferior to that of representatives of the dominant culture. Often, these cultures held to conflicting values and promoted practices that would be variously viewed by members of other groups, and groups would use whatever resources they had at their disposal to defend the values and enforce the practices that *they* held dear or deemed important for the ordering of their lives.

The author of 1 Peter presents Christians living throughout five Roman provinces in what is today the western half of Turkey—Pontus, Bithynia, Asia, Galatia, and Cappadocia (1 Pet 1:1)—as persons subjected to their neighbors' verbal and physical abuse. They are insulted, slandered, and, at the very least in the case of Christian slaves in the houses on non-Christian masters, beaten or otherwise physically affronted. All of these actions have a common goal—to shame the Christians, even more specifically, to make these people ashamed of being Christian, saying the things that Christians say, doing the things that Christians do, avoiding the things that Christians avoid. They represent social sanctions aimed as "correcting" those whom the more powerful group regards as deviating from acceptable ways of living in their midst. This was a common experience of Christians from the very inception of the movement.[3] Notably, insults, reproach, getting beaten up, suffering financial ruin, even being thrown into prison are frequently mentioned as part of this shared experience, but lynching or execution only rarely. The Christians' neighbors were trying to reclaim, not destroy, these wayward members of their society.[4] Their words and actions conveyed a simple message with a simple agenda—"Shame on you! Shape up!"

Shaming is an essential tool of social control within groups. As a subjective experience, shame has its roots in external factors that press themselves upon and into the consciousness of an individual, negating

the individual's worth, warping the individual's self-image into something that the individual himself or herself comes to reject as worthless,
as something either to be changed to conform to what the external voices
celebrate or, if that is impossible for one reason or another, to be hidden
and covered up. Shame is imposed within a social system in an attempt
to rehabilitate some member or members within that system who have
transgressed what is valued, expected, or required within that system. If
rehabilitation is not possible, shame becomes significantly *de*bilitating.

Shame was a particularly potent mechanism of social control in
the Greco-Roman world, where, as one native informant put it, "the one
firm conviction from which we move to the proof of other points is this:
that which is honorable is held dear for no other reason than because it
is honorable" (Seneca *De beneficiis* 4.16.2). "Bottom line" reasoning—the
basis for the ancient "cost/benefit analysis," if you will—proceeded in this
environment by inquiring whether a course of action would lead to the
securing or loss of honor, esteem, face.[5] Their neighbors had been seeking to convince the addressees of 1 Peter that adherence to the Christian
group and perseverance in its practices was disadvantageous, to make
them feel deeply the loss of face that came as a consequence of their
altered allegiances and behaviors. There was a way to escape this shame:
rehabilitation.

The non-Christian majority and dominant culture's complaint
against the Christian movement was far from trivial. To the majority
of people in the cities through which Christianity spread, the effects of
the "proclamation of the good news" looked something like this. Some
wandering preacher blows into town and talks about a crucified revolutionary from the sticks who came to life again and is about to return
to crash the present world order and set up a new empire in which his
followers will come out on top. This is not good news to the elites, who
are very comfortable with the Roman peace, and neither is it good news
to many of the non-elites, who are generally the most vulnerable during
times of social and political upheaval.

Some people are attracted to this message and begin to meet together at night in one another's houses to hear more, to sing hymns to
this crucified criminal as if to a god, and to engage in some new kinds
of rituals. They stop participating in traditional rites and refuse categori-
cally to give honor to any of the gods they used to honor, upon whose
favor and gifts the majority think the well-being and secure ordering

of their families, cities, indeed empire depend.[6] They go so far as to say that those gods are *no* gods at all, which makes them not monotheists so much as atheists in the public eye, for they do not believe in the gods. Honorable people were *pious* people,[7] and those neighbors who were getting mixed up in this Christian movement were fast becoming the most *impious* people in town.

Their strict avoidance of anything that smelled of an idol meant that the Christians withdrew their presence from most every civic gathering and even private social event or dinner, for some acknowledgment of the gods accompanied every such event, and the social life of the city was organized in large measure around public sacrifices and festivals.[8] Roman historian Ramsey MacMullen correctly observes that "there existed . . . no form of social life . . . that was entirely secular. Small wonder, then, that Jews and Christians, holding themselves aloof from anything the gods touched, suffered under the reputation of misanthropy."[9] The non-Christian neighbors of Christian converts are indeed "surprised," "estranged," even "alienated" (*xenizontai*) by the anti-social behavior of former friends, associates, and otherwise reliable citizens (1 Pet 4:3–4).[10] *? Christian Bubble*

The converts' change in behavior and way of thinking aroused feelings of rejection and even indignation among their neighbors, who also no doubt felt their own world view and ethos threatened by the converts' withdrawal from supporting the same and their promotion of an alternate and incompatible world view (polytheism and exclusivist monotheism do not make good neighbors). Those who are not won over to this new group (i.e., the vast majority of the population) respond predictably. They express their disapproval for their neighbors' abandonment of the cherished values of piety and civic solidarity under the umbrella of the gods and the *pax Romana*, and apply all the pressure they can to get them to shape up and return to an acceptable way of thinking and living.[11]

The Christians were forced into a position to conduct a new "cost/benefit analysis" of their options. They could yield to the social pressures of shame and re-engage those practices that their neighbors required of them to regard them as worthwhile and supportive members of the larger system. This would have the benefit of relieving them of the experience of "slander" and "various [other] trials," but it did carry a cost. At the very least, they would need to relinquish their insights into, and moral choice concerning, the life that they had lived within the majority culture (or, in the case of Jewish Christians, within the Jewish ethnic subculture), and to betray that moral and spiritual faculty within them that led them to move out from that way of life and into a new direction. If, on the other hand, they chose against *rehabilitation*, they would need to find ways in which to come to grips with their experience of shame so that the latter should not become *debilitating*, quenching the fire of their new life in Christ.

It is to this complex of considerations that we find the author of 1 Peter speaking, giving us a window into how a leader within a minority culture deflects the majority culture's attempts to impose shame as a "corrective" measure, thus nurturing the continued life and witness of the minority culture. He insulates his audience against their neighbors' attempts to shame them by explaining why the judgment of outsiders is fundamentally flawed and not a reliable indicator of a person's true worth. He further insulates them by reinterpreting their experiences of shaming and rejection in such a way that continued resistance and endurance emerges as the noble response. He contributes positively to their identity formation by speaking at some length about the basis for and affirming the group members' genuine (if popularly unrecognized) honor, as well as by directing their focus to those "others" whose opinion truly matters when it comes to assessing honor or disgrace.[12] By means of such strategies, the author of 1 Peter equips the converts to withstand the social pressures of shame inveighed against them so as to empower them to continue in the Christian associations, convictions, and practices which they have chosen as their new life matrix.

CONSIDER THE SOURCE

The author of 1 Peter reminds the hearers that they made a conscious decision to disassociate themselves from their former way of life, the ongoing lifestyle of the people around them. They had rejected "doing what [their fellow] Gentiles like" for what they considered to be a better, more honorable way—"doing what God wants" (4:2–3)—which they understood to involve pursuing the personal and community formation nurtured in the environment of the early Christian movement. If they left their old life behind for good reasons, why should they so value their neighbors' evaluation of them as to desist from their new commitments when those neighbors are still mired in the less honorable life the Christian converts left behind?

It was a commonplace that not everyone could form reliable judgments concerning what was honorable or disgraceful, so that a person ought not to feel shame in regard to the opinion of just anyone.[13] Some people are ignorant of what is truly virtuous and valuable, and their own conduct shows them to be shameless. Whether such people heap praise or abuse on an individual says nothing meaningful about that individual's worth, and the latter would be led astray from what is truly honorable if he or she were to conform to the social pressures of the shameless. The author of 1 Peter uses this insulating strategy in a number of ways.

First, he speaks of the converts' neighbors as people who live dishonorably. Those outside the Christian movement are still indulging in "impure acts, desires, drunken spells, feasts, revels, and unseemly idolatries" (1 Pet 4:3). Their lives can be described as "a flood of debased living" (4:4). The source of their neighbors' hostility and shaming speech is their feeling of alienation (*xenizontai*, 4:4) from the Christian converts, who have withdrawn from joining them in these practices. Unlike the converts who, while treated like deviants by their neighbors, have now fallen into alignment with God through obedience to God's word (1:2, 14), the converts' detractors are headed for a fall on account of their "disobeying the word" (2:8), refusing to respond to God's summons. The latter are the ones who are ultimately deviant and "out of line."

This strategy is further reinforced wherever the author characterizes the converts' former way of life as one of ignorance and degrading behaviors. By responding to the "good news" as they have, the converts have moved out of "darkness," a standard image for ignorance, into the "marvelous light" of acquaintance with the One God (1 Pet 2:9). This leaves the converts' neighbors in the dark, and therefore without the necessary illumination to see clearly to make an informed evaluation concerning what is honorable and what censurable. The converts have left behind "the empty way of life inherited from their ancestors" (1:18), the way of life that still holds their non-Christian neighbors in its grasp. That way of life involved being conformed to one's passions and desires (rather than mastery of the same, conforming the passions and desires to one's reason), passions and desires aroused, moreover, in ignorance rather than on the basis of reliable knowledge of what was truly valuable, desirable, or good (1:14). Their neighbors, then, are attempting to shame them back into a less honorable, more limited way of life. Their censure is mere "slander" (4:4); it is the "ignorance of foolish people" (2:15) that the nobility of the converts' lives shows up.

Minority cultures, by definition, had to face the problem that sheer numbers were on the side of the majority culture. The positions taken and evaluations imposed by the latter would weigh upon members of the former by simple virtue of the fact that so many people were in agreement about the majority cultural values. How could so many people be wrong about the nature of the divine, the expectations of honorable people, and the identification of what was acceptable and what was deviant behavior? The author of 1 Peter subtly touches upon this topic in reference to the precedent of the Flood. Then, only "a few, that is, eight persons" (1 Pet 3:20) were rightly aligned with what is ultimately honorable and disgraceful, and the overwhelming majority of humanity mired in ignorance and vice apart from any knowledge of God's perspective on, and evaluation of, their way of life. Since God's judgment did not depend on majority opinion, but only upon God's opinion and will, it proved in the end to be far more expedient to be among the few than to allow the opinion of the majority to weigh upon one's mind and commitments, so as to be swayed thereby.

WHO'S ON TRIAL HERE?

In a manner reminiscent of contemporary Cynic-Stoic philosophers, the author helps the converts turn the tables, as it were, on their neighbors, such that the non-Christians' responses to the Christians says more about the non-Christians themselves than the converts. Epictetus provides a fine example of how the esteem in which the nonphilosopher holds the sage reveals the wisdom or ignorance of the nonphilosopher, and not the honor or shame of the sage:

> If the one who has power over you says, "I hold you to be impious and profane." What has happened to you? You have been pronounced "impious and profane," and nothing more. If this person had passed judgment upon some syllogism and had declared, "I judge the statement, 'If it is day, there is light,' to be false," what has happened to the syllogism? Who is being judged in this case? Who has been condemned? The syllogism, or the person who has formed a false judgment about it? . . . Should the sage, then, pay attention to an uninstructed person when the latter passes judgment on what is holy and unholy, and on what is just and unjust? (*Dissertationes* 1.29.50–54)

If the noninitiate evaluates the sage—or the Christian—to be worthless or to be acting shamefully, when in fact the sage or the Christian is showing proper piety to God and living in accordance with what divine knowledge has revealed to be honorable and advantageous, who is really being judged by that display of contempt?

The example of Jesus provides definitive proof that the evaluation human beings form about a person can be dead wrong in God's sight. The story at the center of the church's faith is one that forces a decision about the reliability of the world's estimation of honor and shame. Jesus suffered crucifixion, nailed up naked at a crossroads like a human billboard advertising the consequences of serious deviation from the dominant culture's values.[14] Coming to faith in Jesus and joining the Christian movement necessitated first and foremost accepting that God's perspective on what kind of behavior merits honor can differ substantially from the perspective of human beings.

The author of 1 Peter describes Jesus as the "living stone, rejected as worthless by human beings but choice and precious in God's sight" (1 Pet 2:4). The author brings together two authoritative texts from the Scriptures using the interpretive method *of gezera shawa*, the linking word between the two texts being "stone" (*lithos*): "the stone (*lithos*) which the builders rejected—this stone has become the head of the corner" (LXX Ps 117:22); "Look! I set in Zion a stone (*lithon*)—a choice, precious cornerstone, and the person who depends on it will never be put to shame" (Isa 28:16). The first text provides an authoritative statement that the estimation of human beings (the "builders") is not the last word on a person or thing's worth. The second text expressly identifies the prevailing estimation of this stone as God's estimation (the "I" of the prophetic oracle") and God as the agent of the stone's move from toss-off reject to cornerstone. When God raised Jesus from the dead, God vindicated Jesus' honor over against the evaluations of Jesus imposed by his detractors. Blended together thus, these texts pit the estimation of humans against the estimation of God, affirming the triumph, and therefore the greater importance, of God's approval. If human beings regard as worthless the person who is "choice" and "precious" in God's estimation, this shows the inability of those human beings to form a reliable judgment about what is honorable and valuable.

The author addresses the converts as people who know right from wrong, and who know that there are substantial areas of overlap between what the Christian community affirms as noble and avoids as vicious and what the non-Christian majority culture should be able to recognize as noble or vicious as well. So the author calls the hearers to counter feelings of shame by developing a healthy self-respect based on the embodiment of ideals and virtues they *know* to be held in esteem both within the Christian subculture and the dominant culture, the culture of their primary upbringing.

He draws, for example, on the familiar ethical topic of mastering one's desires and cravings, rather than being mastered by the same, so that one could live a consistently virtuous life: "I exhort you to abstain from the fleshly desires that wage war against your soul, keeping your conduct among the Gentiles honorable" (1 Pet 2:11–12).[15] Self-controlled, just, beneficent conduct is honorable in the sight of all people. If the outsiders shame the converts now over "disputed" matters, like whether or not to worship one God or many, whether to affirm the kingdom of the Caesars or await the kingdom of the one God's Son, the converts will be better able to resist both the rehabilitating and debilitating power of shame to the extent that they cultivate—and affirm in one another—this solid basis for self-respect *in terms outsiders should be able to understand*. If the outsiders continue to degrade and reject the Christians, the latter will be in a position to consider this to be a reflection of their neighbors' ignorance, and so nullify the social pressure of shame rather than internalize and act upon it.

The author's instructions to Christian slaves of non-Christian masters provide a radical case in point. Such slaves were completely under their masters' authority. The latter were not reticent to demean and physically punish slaves of whose behavior they disapproved. Christian slaves were to act as the guardians of their own conduct, making sure that they did not behave in such a way as offered any unnecessary (or even genuine) cause for punishment. The author would encourage Christian slaves, however, to continue to resist the significant pressures that their masters could put upon them to compel them to participate in domestic rites or to perform services that would compromise their commitment to obey God's commandments. In such cases, "submission" does not preclude resistance. If a slave endures some form of degradation as a result of his or her commitment to maintain a pure conscience before God, God recognizes their pious loyalty and they continue in God's "favor" (1 Pet 2:20).

The slave is empowered hereby to formulate an evaluation of the human master: to the extent that the latter abstains from degrading the Christian slave for his or her commitment to Christian values and practices, the master is "good and gentle," but to the extent that the master seeks to inflict shame and pain upon the Christian slave for the same, the master is "crooked" or "perverse" (1 Pet 2:20). The disgrace the master inflicts in that instance becomes a measure *not* of what is wrong in the slave and needs to be rehabilitated, but what is wrong with the *master*, for which the master himself or herself stand under God's judgment. Since the slave suffers "unjustly" (2:19), the inflicting of disgrace should cause not the slave, but the master, to blush—and this knowledge is put in the hands of the slave, to empower him or her to resist internalizing the externally imposed shaming.

Several paragraphs later, addressing all converts, the author poses the rhetorical question: "Who is the person who will hurt you if you are an enthusiast for the good?" (1 Pet 3:13). The common-sense answer is obvious. No one in his or her right mind would wish to abuse such a person. The author poses this rhetorical question knowing full well the reality of the hearers' situation. He thereby makes a bold statement: the non-Christian neighbors are acting out of line with any rational expectation for human behavior. There may be many of them, but that does not make them any less the truly "deviant" ones. He follows this with a conditional sentence—one of a very rare class in the Greek New Testament called the "future less vivid," reserved for improbable future conditions: "Even if you should happen to suffer on account of justice, you would be privileged" (*makarioi*, 3:14). But again, against all rational expectations, the Christians *are* suffering disgrace and abuse for righteousness's sake. This does not signal that something is wrong with the converts, but rather that something is defective in their neighbors who respond thus to their change of lifestyle. Because of this, the believers should not "harbor fear of, nor be troubled by, their intimidation" (3:14), their attempts to derail the converts' progress in virtue and piety.

The author positions the hearers to regard their neighbors' slander as unjust, since the converts do, in fact, live in line even with Greco-Roman society's highest ideals, such as mastery of the passions (1 Pet 2:11–12; 4:2), and assiduously avoid the vices and foibles common to so many (2:16, 20a; 4:15). Nevertheless, the converts are being reproached and disgraced as if they were "evil-doers." But, as even Plato would

affirm, committing injustice is far more dishonorable than suffering injustice (thus explicitly in 3:17: "It is better to suffer for doing good, if God
should thus will it, than for doing evil"). The author puts the hearers in
a position to determine whether shame, reproach, or any other social
sanction is being justly imposed upon them. If they know they have
not committed any act that is truly censurable—for example, murder,
theft, evil-doing in general, or meddling (4:15)—then they know that
the shame imposed upon them is wrongly imposed, for it is imposed as
a result of their obedient response to God's Son (4:15–16), and therefore
is no cause for shame at all. A similar strategy appears in Seneca's treatise
De Constantia:

> Both schools [i.e., Stoic and Epicurean] urge you to scorn inju-
> ries and, what I may call the shadows and suggestions of injuries,
> insults. And one does not need to be a wise person to despise
> these, but merely a person of sense—one who can say to him-
> self or herself: "Do I, or do I not, deserve that these things befall
> me? If I do deserve them, there is no insult—it is justice; if I do
> not deserve them, he who does the injustice is the one to blush."
> (*De Constantia* 16.3)

Similarly, the author of 1 Peter assures his hearers that their neighbors
will eventually blush at how they have treated the virtuous Christians in
their midst (1 Pet 3:16). Their rejection and abuse may constitute hardships for the Christians, but there is no cause for them to provoke shame
within the Christians.

REINTERPRETING EXPERIENCES OF SHAME

As is also common in minority cultural literature from the Greco-
Roman world, the author of 1 Peter offers alternative interpretations of,
and perspectives upon, the addressees' experiences of shame and rejection that are more conducive to promoting perseverance *through* those

experiences rather than backing down in the face of those experiences.
Successful continued endurance, rather than yielding, becomes the honorable path and the path to an honorable end.

First, at the outset of his letter, the author interprets the "various trials" that beset the addressees (their varied experiences of being
shamed) as the proving ground of the genuineness of the believers'
trust and commitment to God (1 Pet 1:6–7). He returns to this topic
toward the conclusion of his letter, speaking of the "fiery trial" that

they face "coming upon you as a test" (4:12). The author draws on the well-established philosophical tradition of the "probative" value of suffering, according to which God uses hardships to prove the worth of the righteous or the wise person and test the reality of their virtue.[16] Their neighbors' censure and rejection no longer constitute an actual assault upon their honor, but an opportunity for them to attain greater "praise and glory and honor" when Christ returns in glory (1:7, 14) to the extent that they maintain their public identification with God and the way of life into which God has called them. This is a stunning re-orientation—resistance to the pressures around them becomes the path to honor, whereas society would have them regard yielding to those pressures as the road to recovering honor.

Second, the author defines liminality as the "new normal." The people outside the Christian group were shaming the Christians in an attempt to make them feel abnormal, deviant, out of place, and out of line. By pushing them, socially speaking, into a place of uncomfortable abnormality, the converts' neighbors hoped that the converts would cross back into the place of "normality" by returning to their former way of life, falling back in line. The author of 1 Peter, however, turns the experience of being despised and rejected into something "normal" for the experience of believers as long as they are in the world. He seeks to protect the converts from experiencing alienation from their new way of life ("do not be surprised," "do not be put off," 1 Pet 4:12) on account of the resistance and disapproval with which they have met, lest their mental and social discomfort shake their resolve and detach them from their new commitments.

The example of Jesus once again plays an important part. He is the new norm that renders the trials Christians experience "normal," and not "something strange" (1 Pet 4:12). The pattern of Jesus is a pattern of attaining honor through rejection, scorn, and suffering: the foreordained plan of God foretold through the prophets involved "the sufferings that would befall Christ and the glories that would follow" (1:11). His experience both "normalizes" the disciples' experience of society's deviancy-control techniques as well as provides an historical precedent for the positive, honorable consequences of persevering in the face of shame.

Throughout the letter, then, the author will invite the addressees to fall in line with the pattern of Jesus. "It is better to suffer for doing what is right, if God so wills, than for doing what is wrong" explicitly "because

Christ also suffered once for all on account of sins, the just person for unjust people" (1 Pet 3:17–18). Slaves in particular are urged to regard being punished for doing what is right in God's sight as giving them "a place of favor before God" specifically because "Christ also suffered on your behalf, leaving behind an example for you, in order that you would follow in his footsteps" (2:20–21).[17] Following Christ's example, the converts would steel their minds and wills to embrace the experience of their neighbors' rejection as the crystallization of their commitment to separate themselves from ignoble vice, that is, from all that is *truly* dishonorable: "since Christ, then, suffered in the flesh, arm yourselves as well with the same mindset. The person who has suffered in the flesh has ceased from sin, in order to live for the remainder of his or her time in the flesh no longer for what people crave but for what God wants" (4:1–2).

The converts are urged to keep their focus fixed on Christ's norm and paradigm, assured that, as they share now in Christ's experience of enduring shame and rejection for the sake of God, they would come to share also in his honor and vindication before God: "Rejoice insofar as you share in Christ's sufferings, in order that, when his glory is manifested, you may exult exceedingly" (1 Pet 4:13).[18] Because the pattern of Christ is the God-ordained path for bringing the disciples through this upside-down world to a place of honor in God's presence, those who are "reproached" or "shamed on account of Christ's name" are actually the "privileged" ones (*makarioi*, 4:14).[19] The same God who "raised Jesus from the dead and gave him glory" (1:21) is "the one calling [the converts] into glory, after suffering for a short while" (5:10). Slipping away from the group and back into the embrace of their neighbors would mean *losing* this significant privilege, not restoring face.

The author does not hereby dismiss the real difficulties and sense of displacement that the converts potentially face. He knows that they are now living as people who are no longer at home in their communities, who no longer "belong." He speaks of them as "resident aliens" and as people who are "sojourning" or "living as foreigners" now in their home cities (1 Pet 1:1–2, 17; 2:11).[20] But they are not merely "resident aliens": they are "*chosen* resident aliens," "resident aliens chosen according to God's foreknowledge" (1:1–2; see also 5:13). Though now pushed to the margins in disgrace in their social networks, they stand at the center of God's focal concern.

There was a prominent figure in sacred history who identified himself as a "resident alien" and a "foreigner" as well—Abraham (see Gen 23:4; 24:37). In response to God's choice of him as the recipient of a special promise and inheritance, Abraham left behind the comfortable places of his homeland and embraced the liminal status of a resident alien and foreigner for the remainder of his life. Abraham is subtly recalled here as a prototype for the believers, further "normalizing" their experience. The identity of "resident alien" within the "Diaspora," the scattering of the historic people of God from their native land beginning in the Assyrian and Babylonian conquests, and the author's identification of his location as "Babylon," holds up yet another normalizing lens to the addressees' experience. The people of Israel, God's elect, are scattered resident aliens in this world (irrespective of the fact that some, at least, became fully enfranchised citizens in their locales). Displacement in this world is *normal* for the people of God, who look to a future gathering by God into their true home. The converts' displacement within their host society, therefore, is appropriate for people who have been gathered into the elect people of God (cf. 1 Pet 2:4–5, 9–10).

Third, it was important to help the believers understand that the resistance they encountered and losses they endured were *not* a sign that they were out of favor with God, but rather assured them that they were moving in precisely the direction that God was leading. As people who "are suffering according to the will of God," they are invited to entrust their lives to the faithful creator as they continue in doing what is good (1 Pet 4:19). This is a potentially difficult verse. That these believers are "suffering in accordance with God's will" means that their obedience to God's will and alignment with God's cause has resulted in suffering, not that God delights in abusing God's faithful ones nor that God seeks to make life difficult for those who are trying to leave behind death-dealing and inauthentic ways of life. The author is trying to tell people who might all too easily interpret the experience of loss, pain, and suffering as a sign of divine displeasure that God is not in the reproaches and abuse of the unbelievers punishing the sufferers, but *with* the believers in the midst of their experiences of hostility and resistance. It was God who provided for their redemption from a futile way of life, dissociation from which is the cause of their present suffering (1:19). Their suffering "in accordance with God's will" means they are moving in the direction that God wants for them, even though their neighbors are responding to them with hostility (as they had responded to Jesus).

Further, in the midst of the censure and insult they endure, God associates God's Self with the converts by means of God's own Spirit: "If you are insulted on account of the name of Christ, you are privileged, because the spirit of glory, which is the Spirit of God, rests upon you" (1 Pet 4:14). Far from separating them from God, their endurance of trials confirms their intimate connection with God, for they experience precisely what God's own Son experienced. This strategy appears · throughout the letter, as first slaves and then the whole community are assured that their experience of shame, pain, and marginalization does not mean the loss of God's favor, but is, on the contrary, a *proof* that "you stand in favor with God" (2:19–20; 3:14a).

The convert enjoys God's favor because the hardships he or she experiences are endured on account of association with Jesus and the Jesus movement (i.e., "as a 'Christian,'" 1 Pet 4:16). In embracing the cost of loyalty to Jesus and obedience to the One God, the convert is actually giving God his proper honor (4:16), for he or she is bearing witness to the value of God's friendship and promises before the eyes of his or her neighbors. The convert is therefore encouraged not even to *feel* shame (*mē aischynesthō*, 4:16), not to internalize the social pressure from outside so as to reject that aspect of himself or herself that the disapproving members of the system find objectionable.

Finally, the author also sets the hearers' struggle with the experience of being shamed against another interpretative backdrop—the cosmic framework of the spiritual war over their lives: "Be sober; watch out! Your enemy, the Devil, is walking about like a roaring lion looking for someone to devour. Resist him, remaining firm in your trust, knowing that your sisters and brothers throughout the world face the same kinds of suffering" (1 Pet 5:8–9). The enemy of God, Satan himself, stands ultimately behind the experiences of shame, suffering, and "correction" faced by the disciples and by their brothers and sisters in Christ throughout the inhabited world. The addressees should see not merely their neighbors' faces in these assaults, but Satan's face: he is the one attempting to trip them up—indeed, to swallow them up—by subverting their commitment to Jesus, thus depriving them of experiencing the "praise and glory and honor" that shall crown those who persevere through these trials (1:7). This interpretative frame orients the Christians quite differently to shame. Their neighbors' attempts to "rehabilitate" them become their cosmic enemy's attempts to disqualify them. They are thereby repositioned to see resistance to these social pressures as the honorable path to victory, and acquiescence ("rehabilitation") as suffering a disgraceful defeat at the hands of God's enemy.

DEFENDING YOUR HONOR

Cultural anthropologists working in Mediterranean villages have observed a social interaction that they have termed a "challenge and riposte."[21] If an honorable person is subjected to insult or to some other challenge to honor, that person is culturally conditioned to retaliate, offering a "riposte" that will counter the challenge and preserve honor in the public eye intact. It falls to the bystanders to decide whether the challenged person has successfully defended his (and, indeed, usually "his") own honor.[22] Christians confronted with such attacks on their honor as verbal challenges, reproachful speech, or even physical affronts might be sorely tempted to respond in kind, playing out the challenge-riposte game before the onlookers. Beginning with Jesus, however, Christian leaders sought to cultivate a specifically Christian riposte. The follower of Jesus will meet challenges to his or her honor, but not by using the same currency of insult or violence that the outside world throws at them.

Once more, the example of Jesus is the starting point for the author's reflection. Specifically in his trial and passion, Jesus did not allow his honor to be engaged by the assaults of his detractors. "When he was reviled, he did not riposte with more reviling in kind," but instead "committed himself to the One who judges justly," that is, to God (1 Pet 2:22–23). The author calls *all* Christians, and not just the slaves who would lack the power to respond in kind anyway, to respond to their detractors following Christ's example, "not returning injury for injury or insult for insult, but, on the contrary, extending blessing—for to this you were called, in order that you might inherit a blessing" (3:9).[23] The Christian is challenged to answer the hostile challenge with generosity, the violent challenge with the courageous refusal to use violence, the challenge in the form of a curse with a blessing from God's inexhaustible resources of goodness and kindness.

The author maintains the hope that, eventually, the converts' ongoing commitment to "do what is good" and to live as respectful, respectable citizens, "keeping [their] conduct noble among the Gentiles," will overturn the reproach that their neighbors attach to the name of "Christian" and thus "silence the ignorant slander of foolish people" (1 Pet 2:13–15). Their neighbors may yet come to acknowledge the virtue and nobility of the Christian way of life and, therefore, give honor to the God whom the Christians proclaim,[24] even if this indeed takes until "the day of visitation" (2:12).

Rather than *either* yield to the feelings of shame *or* riposte in a manner that would antagonize, the Christians are called to be ready to give a gentle but committed verbal defense (an *apologia*, 1 Pet 3:15) for their new commitments and practices. The author wants them to know why they themselves have made their choices (and thus why they are not going to give up continuing in the same direction) and to use this, moreover, as an opportunity to bear witness to their hope as Christians. In this context the author returns again to the conviction that, sooner or later, the virtuous conduct of the Christian group will win over their neighbors to their witness and make those who now shame the Christians ashamed themselves (3:16).

Honored in God's Sight

While giving extensive attention to the addressees' experience of being shamed by their neighbors, the author also approaches the issue of their identity—and the challenges to their worth—from a completely different angle. Moving out from their former way of life into the fellowship of the Christian movement may have brought them shame in the eyes of those who remain "in the dark," but it has also brought them greater honor than they could ever have hoped to attain in their old way of life. Their neighbors do not recognize this honor, but it is recognized in the most important court of opinion—the court of God and those who have been illumined by God's light, namely one's fellow believers.[25] This is the court whose judgment about the honorable and the shameful is truly reliable, for it is derived from God's superior knowledge of what is truly and lastingly valuable, and it is a value judgment that lasts for eternity rather than the short span of this mortal life.

Those who currently heap shame upon the Christians "will give an account to the One who stands prepared to judge the living and the dead" (1 Pet 4:5). God, who stands at the center of the "court of opinion" whose verdict matters ultimately, will hold all people accountable for their commitment or their failure to give God his due. The converts are not, therefore, ultimately accountable to their neighbors, nor to their neighbors' evaluations of honor and shame. Indeed, if they were to act as people accountable to their neighbors' attempts to shame them into "rehabilitation," they would move themselves into a place of danger and disgrace in regard to God's judgment. They would forsake obedience to "the will of God" for them (4:2) in favor of returning to chasing after "what the Gentiles want" (4:3).

As they continue to live as members of God's household, the converts enjoy an immensely privileged position vis-à-vis the outsiders to the Christian group, who overtly disobey the One God (1 Pet 4:17–18). The testing that they now endure, in which they are called to prove their faith toward God genuine, may be difficult, but the sifting that awaits those outside the Christian group is far more severe and its outcome far more dire. Honor, and the clear manifestation of their worth in the eyes of all, lies ahead of the converts: the genuineness of their faith, manifested through their tests, will redound "unto praise and glory and honor at the revelation of Jesus Christ" (1:7). This is the divine gift that awaits them at Christ's coming (1:13), for the sake of which they are to persevere (5:12).

The author cites an authoritative oracle of God—"whoever believes in him will not be put to shame" (Isa 28:16)—as proof of the certainty of the converts' ultimate vindication: "Honor, then, is for you who believe" (1 Pet 2:7)[26] just as honor came to the One who had been "rejected by mortals" but was "chosen and precious" in God's estimation (2:4). Even though their neighbors seek through reproach and abuse to imprint feelings of shame upon the converts, the converts' trajectory is ultimately one of honor and vindication, as all the psalmists who put their trust in God and prayed not to be put to shame eventually discovered on the far side of their trials.

Honor, however, is not merely a future promise for the converts. The author of 1 Peter devotes significant attention to the honor and privilege into which they have already entered by virtue of their obedient response to the call of God in Christ. He counters the socially constructed identity of shame that their neighbors seek to impose upon them by reminding them of their identity in Christ and of the ground for self-respect and mutual esteem within the group that this provides.

"God ... gave us a new birth to a living hope" (1 Pet 1:3). This new birth is superior in every way to their physical birth and its legacy: they have joined a new, more honorable family, God's own family. They are reborn to an unending life, rather than a life subject to death and decay (1:23). The legacy of this new birth is "an inheritance that is imperishable and undefiled and unfading, kept in heaven for you who are being guarded by God's power through trust for a deliverance that is ready to be revealed in the last season" (1:4–5). If their neighbors set little value on them now because of their changed practices and commitments, they are reminded of their value in God's sight, a value demonstrated in the price God paid ("the precious blood of Christ, as of a spotless, unblemished lamb," 1:18–19) to buy back the disciples from their former life with its "futile ways." As people who have "purified their souls by their obedient response to the truth (1:22), they enjoy a better standing before God now than prior to their conversion, even if they now have a lower standing in the eyes of their non-Christian peers.

As they gather like "living stones" (*lithoi zōntes*, 1 Pet 2:5) around Jesus, the "living stone" (*lithon zōnta*, 2:4), they share in the honor of the "choice, precious cornerstone" as they continue to be fitted together around him into "a spiritual house." They are invested with the high dignity of being named a "holy priesthood," a company set apart for special service and access to the Almighty God. Priests were held in honor in both Jewish and Greco-Roman environments. In the former, the honor came through genealogy; in the latter it often came as a reward for beneficence or extraordinary civic service. In both, "priesthood" was a recognized claim to honor. The "sacrifices" they are offering in connection with Jesus, they are assured, are well pleasing to God (2:5). God looks approvingly on the changes they have made and continue to make in their lives to conform themselves to a new way of living in obedience to the teachings of and message about Jesus. God accepts and esteems as suitable gifts to himself their acts of loyalty, brotherly or sisterly love, and hospitality, as well as the "sacrifices" that they are making in terms of their commitment to virtuous conduct even in the face of mistreatment, insult, and slander.

The author lets loose an avalanche of honorific titles as he closes the opening section of his letter: "You are a chosen race, a royal priesthood, a holy nation, a people of God's special possession" (1 Pet 2:9). They have moved from a shameful place ("darkness" [2:10], nonidentity as "no people" [2:10], a "futile way of life" [1:18], a life "conformed to the desires [1 Peter entertains] in ignorance" [1:14], running along with their neighbors "in a flood of dissipation" [4:4]) to a new frontier of nobility, a basis for self-esteem and moral courage rooted in their relationship with God and one another ("God's marvelous light" [2:10], identity as "God's people" [2:10], a life of "purification" through "obedient response" to God [1:2, 22], abstaining from the "carnal passions" [2:11], running after "the will of God" rather than "human cravings" [4:2]). In every way, their new identity and the honor it affords them is worth being preserved intact rather than being relinquished for the sake of a return to the esteem of people who continue in the mind set and way of life that the converts weighed in the balance and found wanting.

The Social Matrix of Perseverance

If shame was a socially imposed phenomenon, honor ("worth") was also a socially maintained phenomenon. Rejection by friends, family, and society, and the subsequent loss of personal, emotional, and material support from those connections, left a dark vacuum that powered the shame that led either to rehabilitation or debilitation. Members of a minority culture like the early church had to make up for these losses, providing the social support and personal affirmation that could keep individuals from crossing back into their former way of life and its networks of support.[27] Thus the author urges the hearers to show one another "an unfeigned brotherly and sisterly love . . . constantly from the heart" (1 Pet 1:22; see 3:8), shaping their relationships within the church according to the ethical ideal of family at its best.[28] They were to seek harmony and unity (3:8), to display ungrudging mutual support and hospitality (4:8–11), and to bear themselves with that gentle humility that nurtures solidarity and harmony (5:3, 6)—much needed qualities in the midst of a hostile environment.

This latter attitude is rather countercultural, as, for example, the church in Corinth shows. There, Christians engaged in competition for honor within the congregation, and sought to display their honor in ways that violated the spirit of unity within the group. In so doing, they had brought the majority culture's ethos into the church. The author of 1 Peter proscribes this, supporting his exhortation with a citation of Prov 3:34: "God opposes the arrogant, but gives favor to the humble." Their humility in their interactions, perhaps together with their acceptance of humiliation in the eyes of their non-Christian neighbors, becomes the for hope of exaltation: "Humble yourselves under the powerful God, so that in due time he may exalt you" (1 Pet 5:6).

e relationships of Christian husbands and wives receive special attention in regard to the affirmation of believers' honor. Speaking to the husbands, the author writes: "in your living together, give consideration to your wives as to the weaker gender, offering honor to the woman as to someone who is also a joint heir with you of the gracious gift of life" (1 Pet 3:7).[29] While the author accepts the commonplace that women were "weaker" in the sense of having a more vulnerable constitution,[30] and agrees with other Greco-Roman ethicists that the woman's "weakness" called for consideration, not domination, here he is especially calling attention to another dimension of the wife's identity—"co-heir" of God's gift of life along with her husband, calling upon the husband to reinforce her awareness of her honorable status in this regard in their domestic dealings, rather than live merely from the more hierarchical model of husband and wife relations taught outside the Christian culture.

EMBODYING 1 PETER FOR TODAY'S "ELECT RESIDENT ALIENS"

The author clearly has an agenda. He *wants* to see the addressees continue in the path of discipleship and remain connected to the Christian minority group. His use of the rhetoric of honor and shame, however, cannot be reduced to manipulation. He is not attempting to steer the hearers in a new direction not of their choosing. The hearers had made a conscious decision against continuing in the lifestyle of the people around them. They had rejected that lifestyle—"doing what the Gentiles want"—for what they considered to be a better, more honorable way— "doing what God wants" (1 Pet 4:2–3). The author employs an array of strategies by means of which to help them to arrive at the goal they have set for themselves in their conversion—or, as the author would prefer to put it, that they may arrive at the goal that *God* has set before them in calling them.

The author of 1 Peter attempts to empower them to maintain the new direction that they had chosen in the face of the pressures they are experiencing from without (and potentially internalizing and heeding *within* themselves) that aim to subvert their commitment and make them betray their former insights into what was really true and valuable in life. He stands in a well-attested tradition of philosophical and religious resistance against the tyranny of the majority, and against the coercive pressures the majority (or the dominant culture's representatives) can bring to bear against the will of members of minority cultures. He helps them to find the symbolic and social resources they need to maintain their own moral choices in the face of their neighbors' contrary pressure. Embodying the word and strategies found in 1 Peter would most reliably begin where we find similar social dynamics facing the community of faith.[31]

The author addresses people who have encountered resistance, insult, censure, and even physical abuse because of their commitment to respond to Christ and to do what God commands.[32] A significant portion of the global family of God in many non-Western countries (e.g., India, China, Indonesia, Nigeria, many Islamic countries, and, in its day, the Soviet Union) continue to face censure, discrimination, loss of privilege and means of subsistence, even imprisonment and death, as the dominant and majority cultures in those areas continue to use all the deviancy-control techniques at its disposal to "correct" Christians. 1 Peter may help us to discover avenues by which to support Christians in restricted and hostile environments as they endure society's rejection, insult, scorn, and even violence for their choice to follow Jesus' teachings and pursue God's vision for community. This is also in keeping with the author's own attempt, as a believer writing from one region (Rome) to Christians at a fair distance (Asia Minor), to express the commitment of the global Church to all its members. With global communication being increasingly immediate and accessible, we can put ourselves in contact with the persecuted, encouraging them in their noble contest, making the reality of the church as a social matrix for perseverance felt more keenly through prayer, material support (particularly when the primary supporter of a family is jailed or removed, or when economic privations are a principal means of coercion), and working through diplomacy for the end of religious persecution. We can ask the questions that will give them opportunity to articulate and remember their own reasons for moving out from their former way of life and its association, so as to support their moral faculty of choice in the face of their neighbors' or government's bullying.

As we become involved with them and learn to value their struggles, we will become a voice that lets them know how valued they are by their sisters and brothers worldwide, and we can seek out ways to affirm their dignity. By investigating and telling their stories, spreading the fame of these heroes of faith, we can let them know that their struggle does not go unnoticed, but brings them the admiration of their sisters and brothers throughout the world. This may be more meaningful than we might imagine, since many persecuted churches live in honor and shame cultures that have more in common with the addressees of 1 Peter than with Western culture. In such ways, we may ourselves become more "noble stewards of the manifold gift of God" and the freedom from social shame and hostility that we enjoy (1 Pet 4:10).

ENDNOTES

1. Translations of 1 Peter (and, here, the emphases) are my own.

2. The frequency with which an author returns to a particular topic is underscored as one indication of its importance in the landscape of the community being addressed in Barclay, "Mirror-reading a Polemical Letter," 73–93. Throughout this essay I will simply refer to the "author" without engaging the question of whether this involved the historical Peter. Interested readers may review discussions of authorship in critical commentaries. These positions and supporting literature are briefly surveyed in deSilva, *Introduction to the New Testament*, 844–47.

3. Many first-century Christian communities endured similar verbal and physical assaults on their honor (see, for example, Phil 1:27–30; 1 Thess 1:6; 2:13–14; 3:1–4; 2 Thess 1:4–5; Heb 10:32–34; Rev 2:9–10, 13). It is therefore no surprise, and probably no exaggeration, that the author of 1 Peter can address this phenomenon across so widely distributed an audience.

4. Thus, rightly, Elliott, "Disgraced Yet Graced," 170.

5. For fuller discussions of ancient texts attesting to honor and shame as primary, though by no means not the only, considerations in decision-making, see deSilva, *Depising Shame*, 39–85; *Hope of Glory*, 14–26. As meta-level reflections by insiders on the hierarchies of their own socio-cultural values, the classical rhetorical handbooks (i.e., textbooks on *persuasion*) have been especially instructive in this regard.

6. Plutarch regarded piety toward the gods (and the belief in their rule) as the bedrock of government: "It would be easier to build a city without the ground it stands on than to establish or sustain a government without religion" ("Reply to Colotes" 31; *Moralia* 1125E; translation mine. See the whole paragraph in *Moralia* 1125D–E).

7. Isocrates advises his student: "Revere the gods, both by performing sacrifices and keeping your vows. Honor the gods at all times, but all the more at public festivals. This will give you the reputation for being pious and law-abiding" (*To Demonicus* 13; translation mine).

8. The early Christians struggled to justify participation in idolatry so that they would not have to sever so many important connections with their networks of friends and patrons, their involvement in government, and their good name. This is reflected in 1 Cor 8:1–13; 10:14–22; Rev 2:14–15, 20.

9. MacMullen, *Paganism in the Roman Empire*, 40. Tacitus (*Annals* 15.44) says that Nero was able to scapegoat the Christians for the great fire due to the general unpopularity of the Christians for their "hatred of the human race."

10. The non-Christian Jewish population also had strong reasons for attempting to dissolve through erosion of commitment the sect that had grown up in its midst, but we restrict our attention here to non-Christian Gentiles as they seem to be primarily in view as the aggressors (so also Davids, *First Epistle of Peter*, 8; Michaels, *1 Peter*, xlvi, Elliott, *1 Peter*, 96–97). 1 Pet 4:3–4, for example, speaks of the converts' former way of life—and the aggressors' continuing way of life—as characterized by idolatry, a certain freedom in sexual behavior, and parties involving immoderate eating and drinking, all of which tends to characterize Gentile life rather than typical Jewish practice (even if the author does caricature Gentile life here). Also, no Christian author otherwise speaks of the Jewish heritage as a "futile way of life inherited from one's ancestors" (1 Pet 1:18) or as an "ignorant" way of life (1:14). Paul, who seems quite ready to discard his pre-Christian life, nevertheless maintains that the Jews were always in a privileged position *vis-à-vis* Gentiles specifically because of their knowledge of, and interaction with, the One God (see Rom 3:1–2; 9:4–5).

11. This appears to be the goal even of officially sanctioned persecution (or "deviancy-control"), as Pliny, a governor of Bithynia and Pontus writing some time after 1 Peter (in CE 110–111), expresses a deep satisfaction when his prosecution of those charged with being "Christians" causes a revival of traditional Greek and Roman religion in his province (Pliny *Letters* 10.96).

12. For a discussion of how these techniques are employed by a wide spectrum of Greco-Roman period minority cultures (the Jewish ethnic subculture, Stoic and Cynic philosophical cultures), see deSilva, *Despising Shame*, 86–155; for a discussion of how these techniques are employed across the early Christian movement as represented by select New Testament texts, see deSilva, *Hope of Glory*, 34–202 (chapters on Matthew, John, 1 & 2 Thessalonians, 1 & 2 Corinthians, Hebrews, and Revelation); Elliott, "Disgraced Yet Graced"; Jewett, *Saint Paul Returns to the Movies*; Malina and Neyrey, "Honor and Shame in Luke-Acts"; Moxnes, "Honor, Shame, and the Outside World" (on Romans); Moxnes, "Honour and Righteousness in Romans"; Neyrey,

"Despising the Shame of the Cross" (on John 18–19); Neyrey, *Honor and Shame in the Gospel of Matthew*.

13. See, for example, the comments made in Aristotle, *Rhetorica* 2.6.15, 23; Dio Chrysostom *Orationes* 77/78.21, 25; Plato *Crito* 44C, 46C–47D, 49D; Seneca *De Constantia* 11.2—12.1; 13.2, 5; Epictetus *Dissertationes* 1.22.1–10; 2.24.19; 4.5.22.

14. Martin Hengel (*Crucifixion in the Ancient World*) provides a detailed description of the humiliation involved in crucifixion; see also Neyrey, "Despising the Shame of the Cross."

15. The topic of "mastery of the passions" as an ideal of philosophical ethics is widely attested in Greco-Roman and Hellenistic Jewish literature. See Plato *Respublica* 431A; *Gorgias* 491; *Phaedo* 93–94; Cicero *Tusculanae Quaestiones* 2.22; 3.22; 4.10–11; Plutarch *De Virtute morali* 1–4 (*Moralia* 440D–443D); *Letter of Aristeas* 221; *4 Maccabees*. This was an ideal that the Christian movement was quite intent on fulfilling (see, for example, Gal 5:13–25).

16. The author of Wisdom of Solomon, for example, writes of the pious Jew who held firm in the face of persecution and humiliation by the ungodly: "though in the sight of others they were punished, their hope is full of immortality. Having been disciplined a little, they will receive great good, because God tested them and found them worthy of himself; like gold in the furnace he tried them, and like a sacrificial burnt offering he accepted them" (Wis 3:5–6). The end result of perseverance it to enjoy rewards in God's presence. The author's words resonate also with the Stoic tradition as reflected in Seneca: the wise person "counts even injury profitable, for through it he finds a means of putting himself to the proof and makes trial of his virtue" (*De constantia* 9.3; also *De providentia* 5.10). For a rich introduction to Jewish and Greco-Roman traditions about suffering, see Croy, *Endurance in Suffering*, 77–162.

17. The author does not make it completely explicit, but he says enough for the first-century hearer to *infer* that, because Jesus suffered on behalf of the hearers, and specifically "for their sins" (1 Pet 2:24; see also 3:18), the hearers also ought to be willing to endure shame and suffering for the sake of Jesus' name. This would be part of making a fair return to Jesus for his costly beneficence and faithfulness toward them. On reciprocity as a cardinal social value, and the deployment of these topics in early Christian literature, see deSilva, *Honor, Patronage, Kinship & Purity*, 95–156.

18. This was a common topic in the early church (see also Rom 8:17; Phil 3:10–11; 2 Tim 2:11–12).

19. Rev 20:6 and 22:14 also pronounce "blessed" or "honorable" those who have suffered the world's shaming most intensely (execution in Rev 20:6; those who "wash their robes" are those who endure the "great ordeal," the beast's campaign against godliness, Rev 7:13–14). See the rich discussion of the

meaning of *makarios* in Hanson, "How Honorable! How Shameful!," 81–111; see also deSilva, *Seeing Things John's Way*, 274–84.

20. I disagree here with Elliott (*1 Peter*, 101, 312–313), who regards this as a sign of the legal status of the addressees rather than a metaphorical depiction of their displaced, but unofficial, status. There were, no doubt, actual "resident aliens" among the Christian communities, but these communities would not be comprised exclusively of people of this status.

21. Pitt-Rivers, "Honour and Social Status," 27.

22. The gospels contain many such exchanges, often initiated by Pharisees, Sadducees, or other religious officials against Jesus, whom they regard as an upstart threatening to steal their place in the esteem of the people, and winningly answered or met by Jesus. See, for example, Luke 4:1–13; 5:29–39; 6:1–5, 6–11; 7:39–50; 10:25–28; 11:14–20; 11:37–54; 13:10–17; 14:1–6; 16:14–18; 19:39–40; 20:1–19; 20:20–26, 27–40; 20:41–47. For an analysis of such exchanges in Matthew's Gospel, see Neyrey, *Honor and Shame in the Gospel of Matthew*, 44–52.

23. Elliott ("Disgraced Yet Graced," 171) helpfully compares 1 Peter's advice to the similar course promoted by Plutarch: "'How shall I defend myself against my enemy?' 'By proving yourself good and honorable'" ("How to Profit by One's Enemies" 4; *Moralia* 88B). It will distress the enemy more than being insulted, Plutarch writes, to see you bear yourself with self-control, justice, and kindness toward those with whom you come in contact. The insulted person must use the insult as an occasion to examine his life and rid himself of any semblance of that vice ("How to Profit" 6; *Moralia* 89 D–E).

24. The author returns to this hope in his advice to Christian wives of non-Christian husbands (1 Pet 3:1–6), which ought to be read thoroughly within the context of the author's agenda for appealing to non-Christians by embodying broader social ideals as far as possible without compromise on "essential" matters like idolatry.

25. On the symbolic and social dimensions of the "alternate court of opinion" and its importance for empowering a minority culture to maintain its distinctive values and practices in Greco-Roman philosophical and early Christian literature, see deSilva, *Perseverance in Gratitude*, 171–74; *Despising Shame*, 86–155, 299–340.

26. 1 Pet 2:7 is commonly mistranslated, "To you then who believe, he is precious" (NRSV; see also the KJV, JB, RSV, and NIV), as if the author were continuing to speak about the believers' perception of Jesus, the cornerstone. Translators have tended to read the adjective "precious" (*entimon*), which occurred in verses 4 and 6, into verse 7. The author has deliberately shifted away from the adjective to a related noun "honor" (*timē*) which is the subject of this sentence: "Honor is for you who trust" (compare the CEB: "God

honors you who believe"). In 2:7a, the author is drawing an inference from the end of the quotation of Isa 28:16 in 1 Pet 2:6: "whoever believes in him [here, "Jesus"] will not be put to shame." Honor will be the reward for the Christians' trust and commitment, while their detractors will come to shame (they will "stumble" and "fall," 2:7b).

27.   On the importance of social reinforcement of individual commitment to a particular worldview and ethos, see Berger, *The Sacred Canopy*, chapters 1 and 2.

28.   See, further, deSilva, *Honor, Patronage, Kinship & Purity*, 165–73, 212–26 and the literature cited therein. An especially important primary text is Plutarch's essay, "On Fraternal [and Sororal] Affection."

29.   English translations tend to miss the mark here as well. The NRSV, for example, reads: "Husbands, in the same way, show consideration for your wives in your life together, paying honor to the woman as the weaker sex, since they too are also heirs of the gracious gift of life—so that nothing may hinder your prayers" (1 Pet 3:7; so also the KJV, RSV, NIV, ESV, but contrast the CEB). The verse contains two commands ("show consideration toward your wives" and "give her honor") and two motive clauses ("as a weaker vessel" and "as a fellow heir of life-giving grace"). These translations mistakenly link *both* motives to the second command, which has the effect frankly of making the husband's act of respecting or honoring the wife an act of condescension toward her physical weakness. The Greek clearly links the first motive with the first imperative, and the second motive with the second imperative.

30.   See, for example, Xenophon, *Oeconomicus* 7.22–28.

31.   For more extensive reflections on the applicability of the strategies found in 1 Peter, see deSilva, *Honor, Patronage, Kinship & Purity*, 84–93.

32.   It is their obedience to the commandment to avoid worship of other gods that, in the main, has led to the pressures being brought to bear on them in the household (in the case of wives and slaves) and in the street. The author is *not* speaking about suffering in general, encompassing all disease, chronic illness, domestic abuse, and oppression.

11

Got Good Religion?

The Misuse of Piety to Earn Honor

ROBERT JEWETT

INTRODUCTION

SEVERAL SCHOLARS HAVE NOTICED that an ancient system of honor and shame is visible in Matthew's account of Jesus' teaching about religion.[1] In general these studies overlook the sectarian features of first-century religion. This essay suggests that the question in the black spiritual, "Have you got good religion?"[2] indicates the way forward: bad religion has problematic social consequences. The religion in Massa's house aimed to preserve a discriminatory system of honor and shame that harmed slaves and masters alike and prepared the way to a social catastrophe, which the U.S.A. experienced between 1861–1865, the aftermath of which is still being felt. The "good religion" of "cane break" and "brush arbor" services, organized by black slaves, stressed the egalitarian stream of biblical faith and harbored the hope of a new exodus from slavery.[3] The song perceives Jesus as posing the question about good religion, because the refrain is "Cert'nly, Cert'nly, Cert'nly Lord!"

My thesis is that the bad religion criticized by Jesus and Paul was not just ill-motivated personal behavior but an expression of religio-political programs aimed at achieving social domination. If the entire public could be caused to conform to a pious example of one of the Jewish sects, the law would allegedly be fulfilled and a world empire with

187

its capitol in Jerusalem would come. Acts of public piety had an inner-Israelite consequence of shaming people as unpatriotic if they did not emulate the religion of the right sectarian group. Recipients of charity were shamed as incapable of supporting themselves or aiding others. In various ways, public piety sustained a destructive social hierarchy and a corresponding imperial dream. It thereby sustained hatred of foreigners who did not conform religiously and whose presence in Palestine was thought to pollute the Holy Land. Exposing this false piety of public performance was thus part of Jesus' effort to transform zealous violence that he was certain would lead Israel into a suicidal conflict with Rome. In the work of Paul, a converted Pharisee, we see a continuation of this concern for the social consequences of bad religion, motivated by the desire for public honor and domination. Since Paul's letters precede the writing of the gospel accounts of Jesus' message, and provide an insider's view of the motivation of "bad religion," we discuss some key passages in his letters before turning to the Sermon on the Mount. As background for the viewpoints of both Jesus and Paul, we sketch the evidence of the sectarian challenges they faced.

THE SECTARIAN BACKGROUND OF THE COMPETITION FOR RELIGIOUS HONOR

In first-century Judaism, a number of sectarian groups vied for the loyalty of the nation, each claiming to have the key to the religious behavior required by God. Andrew Overman provides a sketch of the research leading to this generalization, defining "sectarian to mean a group which is, or perceives itself to be, a minority in relation to the group it understands to be the 'parent body' . . . These groups feel alienated from those in authority and often openly denounce or oppose them."[4] The sectarian groups in the period of Jesus and Paul "perceived themselves to be the righteous minority. They rejected, or were rejected by, the parent group."[5] These groups were engaged in hostile vituperation in which the "buzz-words" of "lawless" adversaries and "righteous" ingroup members were typically employed.[6] In the *Psalms of Solomon*, for example, the antagonists of the sectarian group are called "sinners" and "lawless" while group members are "those who fear the Lord."[7] Many other documents in this period reflect "bitter factionalism" and view their conflicts in "rather stark, black-and-white terms. The members of the community were righteous, just, faithful to God, and sure to be vindicated by God

... [their opponents] on the other hand, were corrupt lawbreakers who were far from God, oppressed God's people, and would have no share in the world to come."[8]

The zealot movement reacted violently against Jewish collaborators and Roman occupiers because they failed to conform to the norms of righteousness that the sectarians favored.[9] They advocated freedom from foreign rule and a radical theocratic vision that recognized only God as king, despite that some of their leaders displayed messianic pretensions.[10] Their model was Phineas in Numbers 25, who was "zealous with the zeal of God" in lynching an Israelite who married a foreigner. Murder thus averted divine wrath. The zealots' commitment to redemptive violence was shared with other sectarian groups as well as the Jewish collaborators with Rome, as Torrey Seland has shown.[11] After committing a series of ritual murders of collaborators and other sectarians, various groups of zealots led the revolt against Rome in CE 66–73. The zealots were particularly enraged at the economic deprivation that resulted from Rome's abusive tax system, burning down the tax office in the first year of the rebellion. During the Roman siege of Jerusalem, groups of zealots fought against each other for supremacy and until the end, they all expected divine intervention as the reward of their devotion.[12] The last band of zealots committed suicide on Masada, rather than to fall into the hands of their demonic, Roman besiegers.

The Pharisees taught that perfect obedience to their oral law would usher in the righteous messianic era; their efforts to reform society led to competition with other groups, and to sectarian strife between the Shammai and Hillel groups.[13] Their program was to "build a fence around the law," creating a number of oral regulations to prevent inadvertent offenses.[14] They engaged in a strenuous campaign of public education to inculcate these rules, reinforcing compliance by boycotting violators and denouncing nonconformists. Anthony Saldarini suggests that this movement was a "reformist sect" that sought to change the world;[15] by strenuous adherence to the oral laws reinforcing purity, oaths, Sabbath regulations and tithes, they sought to usher in a new age.[16]

The Essenes argued that adherence to their solar calendar and cultic regulations for the temple would satisfy the conditions of righteousness and bring the messianic age. In a monastic setting they trained an alternate priesthood that would impose these regulations after the holy war annihilated the current temple leadership. As Overman shows, "In

a self-imposed exile, the community through its writings castigated the
Jerusalem leadership and anticipated its vindication by God through a
holy war."[17] They bitterly opposed other Jewish groups engaged in a "cor-
rupted way" and being led by a "spouter of lies," a "wicked priest" whose
supporters were "instruments of violence."[18] In their writings, "sinners
are vilified and assured of judgment, and the righteous are promised
their reward and vindication."[19]

The Sadducees believed that maintaining the purity of the temple
and following the laws of the Pentateuch would satisfy the requirements
of righteousness, disputing particularly with the Pharisees over questions
of purity.[20] As the elite priestly families that collaborated with Rome,[21]
they opposed all of the reformist and revolutionary groups, rejecting all
teachings that went beyond the first five books of Moses. They denied
the doctrines of resurrection, of angels or spirits, of eschatological judgment, and of predestination.[22] As the priestly group that controlled the
temple in Jerusalem, their position of power and wealth was enhanced
by serving as the willing partners of the Roman occupation. Their hated
status is indicated by the fact that the Sadducees and their families were
annihilated in the opening phase of the zealous war against Rome that
started in 67.[23] They had shared with the other groups in first-century
Palestine a vision of their own domination, a discriminatory view of their
competitors, an exalted sense of their own superiority, and a readiness to
employ violence to achieve their goals. The Sadducees no less than their
sectarian opponents sought to "validate their own righteousness" in the
public sphere, in the words of Paul in Rom 10:3.[24]

THE COMPETITION FOR HONOR IN THE LIGHT
OF PAUL'S AUTOBIOGRAPHY

Traditional interpretations of Romans 7 have overlooked the evidence
concerning competition of honor in Paul's description of his former
life as a Pharisee. For centuries, this passage has provided the basis for
theories of the human dilemma as some form of individual weakness in
performing the Jewish law.[25] The idea was that the Pharisaic additions
of oral law to the scriptural commandments were too complicated and
elaborate to obey with exactitude, thus producing bad conscience. No
one, allegedly, was strong enough to obey completely. Fréderic Godet
provided a classic statement of this theory that Romans 7 describes the
conflict between "the Jew such as he ought to be . . . [and] the real Jew,

such as he shows himself in practice."[26] William Sanday and Arthur Cayley Headlam's influential commentary suggested that the dilemma of Romans 7 had been: "felt most keenly when he was a 'Pharisee of the Pharisees.' Without putting an exact date to the struggle which follows, we shall probably not be wrong in referring the main features of it especially to the period before his Conversion. It was then that the powerlessness of the Law to do anything but aggravate sin was brought home to him."[27]

Paul's alleged bad conscience as a Jew unable to obey the whole law was refuted by Krister Stendahl,[28] E. P. Sanders,[29] and a host of others. It is contradicted by the references in Rom 7:13–14 and 9:1–5 to the Jewish law as holy and good; it is even more sharply refuted by Paul's statements in Phil 3:4–6 and Gal 1:14 about his having excelled in the performance of the Jewish law, even to the point of being "blameless." The idea that Paul nevertheless had a bad conscience was a figment of the introspective conscience of the West and of liberal Protestantism of the past century, a view whose vicious stereotype of Jewish religiosity has evoked widespread criticism in the wake of the studies by Stendahl and Sanders. Since most contemporary scholars have abandoned this theory, despite its ongoing appeal in popular understandings and church school materials, another alternative is now frequently advanced: the paralysis of the will in Romans 7 expresses the ongoing power of sin in the life of the converted. Luther's classic formula, "simultaneously justified and a sinner," captures this approach. Yet no matter how widely this theory may be sustained by personal observation and experience in the lives of believers, it stands in chronic tension with Romans 6, which insists that Christians no longer live in sin, that their slavery to sin has been broken by Christ, and that under grace, they are to present their "members to God as instruments of righteousness" (Rom 6:13). Either Romans 6 must be disallowed or a new interpretation for Romans 7 must be found if Romans is to hold together as a coherent argument.

I have suggested an approach to Romans 7 that remains close to the details of Paul's autobiography as explicitly described in Gal 1:13–14 and Phil 3:4–6.[30] There Paul describes himself as a zealous Pharisee, whose perfect performance of the law and religious fanaticism led him to persecute the early followers of Jesus. My hypothesis is that Romans 7 describes the dilemma of a religious fanatic looking back on his career after discovering the destructive error of his ways. He had confronted no barriers in accomplishing the law, but its zealous performance had led him to violence whose full implications only became understandable after encountering the resurrected Christ. Now he can speak of such a dilemma as "zeal without knowledge" (Rom 10:2). In Romans 7, Paul the Christian theologian looks back on his pre-Christian career and lifts up a tendency that was re-emerging in the ethnic and theological conflicts within the Roman congregations.

THE PROBLEM OF ZEAL IN ROMANS

My commentary offers the translation of a key passage as follows: Rom 10:2–3, "For I bear them witness that they have zeal for God, but without acknowledgment. For being ignorant of the righteousness of God, and seeking to validate their own righteousness, they did not submit to the righteousness of God."[31] "Zeal for God" is a technical expression for Jewish piety as described in section I above, implying a "passionate, consuming" desire to do God's will and to defend God's honor "in face of the ungodly acts of men and nations."[32] Elijah was an archetype of this kind of zeal, complaining that "with zeal I have been zealous for the Lord almighty," while others have forsaken the covenant" (1 Kgs 19:10, 14). This is characteristically linked with adherence to the law, as in 1 Macc 2:58 that claims Elijah was "zealous with zeal for the law."[33] Paul's expression "zeal for God" is close to the wording found in *Testament of Asher* 4:5, which describes the righteous as follows: ". . . they live by zeal for the Lord, avoiding what God hates and has prohibited through his commandments, warding off evil by the good."

The great examples of such zealous fervor in the Jewish tradition are Elijah, Phineas, Simeon, Levi, and Mattathias, with violence against nonconformists explicitly sanctioned in a number of texts.[34] The prophetic leader of the Qumran community claims that "according to the measure of my closeness [to God], I was zealous against all evil-doers and men of deceit."[35] Paul describes his former life in Judaism in similar terms as "extremely zealous for the traditions of my fathers" (Gal 1:14) and "as to zeal, a persecutor of the church" (Phil 3:6). Here Paul is dealing with a primary element in his own previous piety.

The explanation that unbelieving Jews were "seeking to validate their own righteousness" implies a competitive stance in which one's "own" accomplishment is being compared with others. As Sanders and others have shown, conformity to the law was not viewed by Jewish teachers as an "entrance requirement"[36] but in George Howard's words, as a confirmation of the Jewish community's "collective righteousness, to the exclusion of Gentiles."[37] Although the reference to "their own righteousness" has usually been understood in an individualistic manner as the sin of "self-righteousness" and pride in one's religious accomplishments, it is more likely a reference to the sense of ethnic or sectarian superiority claimed by Jewish groups[38] as well as by various other groups in the Mediterranean world. Competition for the honor of one's group is the key here. This public competition for religious honor was the motivating center of the "bad religion" criticized by Paul and Jesus.

THE FRUSTRATION OF BAD RELIGION IN ROMANS 7

My exegesis of Romans 7 suggests that the details match Paul's former experience of frustration as a zealot, a frustration only manifest at the moment of his conversion. In Rom 7:5–8 Paul describes how the "passions that were sinful because of the law" led humans to "death." Paul goes on to explain how sin invades and corrupts the law. "I did not know sin except through law. For I was unaware of coveting except that the law said, 'You shall not covet.' But finding foothold through the commandment, the sin worked in me all covetings" (Rom 7:7–8). I prefer to keep the context of the tenth commandment in the forefront; it is not desire as such that is forbidden, but coveting what belongs to others. Paul refers here to a distortion in interpersonal relations that marks the competition for honor in religion. The sin of asserting oneself and one's group at the expense of others[39] fits the intensely competitive environment of Greco-Roman and Jewish culture. This interpretation correlates with the desire for superior performance of the law, which was part of Paul's own past, but it would also include distinctively Gentile forms of competition for honor. Paul's conversion was directly related to his competitive urge to surpass others in enforcing conformity to the cultural and religious laws of his tradition. Paul was convinced that the followers of the martyr Stephen who had broken free from the law should be punished. He was acting out of the zealous ideology that gripped a portion of Judaism in the period before the Jewish-Roman War, in which the heroic model of Phineas in Numbers 25 inspired lynching strategies to cope with evildoers.[40] Paul opposed the Jesus movement because it liberated people from the shameful status of nonconformity religious law, and because its leader, Jesus of Nazareth, had been executed as a lawbreaker and a public threat. Paul's persecution of the church was in direct proportion to the passion with which he maintained his own conformity to the law. In this view, Paul was a kind of first-century Osama bin Laden.

What Paul discovered in the conversion was that Jesus the Sabbath-breaker was Jesus the Messiah. His appearance to Paul proved that he was indeed resurrected, as the disciples were claiming. The resurrection meant that everything Jesus taught and lived and died for was confirmed by God.[41] In an instant, full of grace and judgment, Paul suddenly discovered the truth about himself, and about legalism everywhere. This encounter on the way to Damascus had a series of transforming consequences. Paul discovered his own hostility against God, for in his zeal for the law, he had ended up supporting the crucifixion of the Messiah and the persecution of his followers. There is an unacknowledged level of sin buried at the heart of religious zeal, as he discovered.

Yet at the same time and in the same experience Paul discovered the grace of Christ and the restoration of a proper relationship with God. At the deepest level of his motivations, driven by anxiety about pleasing God and the rest of the world, he was set free by unconditional love. Paul discovered his own calling on the Damascus road. His goal was to become a missionary to the shameful Gentiles who had previously been viewed as the evil influence over Paul's adversaries.[42] He became convinced that the good news about the grace of God rather than conformity to a single code was the means by which the world could be transformed and reunited.

In Rom 7:19–20 we can see how this new perspective on the law, twisted by sin, produced the dilemma of the frustrated zealot. Verse 19 is a reiteration of 7:15b-c, using the language of good and evil. The good that Paul wished to achieve as a persecutor of the church was to advance the rule of the law as a means to usher in the messianic age. He sought to follow the will of God but discovered through the encounter with the risen Lord that he was in fact opposing the will of God as exemplified in the Messiah, Jesus. What verse 19 describes is not an inability to perform the violent deeds that Paul was taught were right, but rather the failure of zealous obedience to produce the good. The last thing he desired was to oppose the Messiah, and this is precisely what he ended up doing.

In Rom 7:20 Paul reiterates verses 17–18 that gave sin the responsibility for moral contradiction. In the light of Romans 1, "the sin dwelling in me" is the human desire to be superior in order to counter the threat of shameful status. A culturally twisted system of competing for honor leads individuals and nations to challenge the honor of God. In this case, the sinful competition for honor dwelling in Paul's zealous behavior was frankly acknowledged in Gal 1:14, the verse that immediately follows his description of persecuting the church: "I advanced in Judaism beyond many among my people of the same age, for I was far more zealous for the traditions of my ancestors." Competition in zeal promised social honor and divine approbation. The shocking discovery on the Damascus road was that such competition was a demonstration of the power of "sin," acting at the very heart of religious devotion. There is no doubt that sin is used here to refer to a cosmic force that drives people to act in certain ways. A demonic social power deriving from a distorted system of honor and shame had been so internalized by Paul so that it "dwelled" within him. This had led him to act as he did. The frustration consisted not in the ability to perform the zealous deeds he had felt were justified, but in the failure of such deeds, motivated by a sinful social system, to achieve the good. Such zeal, in fact, had led him into conflict with the very God he wanted to serve. The basis of this insight lies in the message of Jesus, to which we now turn.

THE SERMON ON THE MOUNT AND THE QUEST FOR PUBLIC HONOR

In Matt 6:1, the admonition, "Beware of practicing your piety before men in order to be seen by them," inaugurates discussions of almsgiving, prayer, and fasting. There is a critical consensus that this opening summary is an editorial heading created by Matthew to introduce the material of 6:2–18[43] or even as much as 6:2—7:11.[44] The formulation is certainly congruent with the material that follows, describing religious activities performed to be praised or seen by others (Matt 6:2, 5, 16). As Warren Carter explains, "In an honor-shame society, one's good reputation, sustained by the approval and esteem of others who have benefited from one's public actions, is important . . . The warning is . . . against making people into spectators by impressing them, or seeking their approval, and sustaining one's own status."[45] The individualistic motivation is explained by Ben Witherington: "In an honor and shame culture, one is always trying to improve one's honor rating."[46] Charles Talbert remains within the individualistic framework in making a distinction between "honor virtue" of proper relationship to God and "honor precedence," which consists of "worldly honor that validates itself before an evaluating public and is based on power, wealth, and other indications of status."[47] There is no hint in these studies that the "bad religion" Jesus criticized had a sectarian, political motivation, or violent social consequences. By viewing the motivation of this piety in the light of Paul's experience as a sectarian performing the law in a publicly exemplary manner, we are better able to grasp the ideological dimensions of this section of the Sermon on the Mount.

In ancient Judaism, "charity was one of the primary obligations of God's people,"[48] firmly established in the law. The admonition in Matt 6:2 that "when you give alms, sound no trumpet before you, as the hypocrites do in the synagogues and in the streets, that they may be praised by men," is an ironic caricature. While no additional evidence has been found of such fanfares[49] celebrating generosity, the trumpet was employed in royal coronations, victory parades and significant religious events, including the famous "last trumpet" announcing the end of the world.[50] Blowing the trumpet would therefore turn almsgiving into a power trip, demonstrating the divinely approved honor of the donor and urging others to do the same, thus bringing God's kingdom nearer. The witty exaggeration serves to deflate the serious intent of such behavior that aimed at evoking emulation and demonstrating the superiority of one's sect. In fact, like Paul the Pharisee who surpassed all his contemporaries in zeal for the law, "they have received their reward" in public esteem and should not expect divine approbation or the advancement of the kingdom of God. The political motivation is reduced to a simple demonstration of social superiority. This is supported by the reference to "hypocrites," which refers to acting a part in a play. As Warren Carter explains, "the term suggests playing a public role or aiding another in accord with God's will, whereas the real inner interest is in one's own honor and reputation. In pursuing one's own honor, the synagogue practice imitates the dominant cultural patterns of reciprocal and conspicuous giving."[51]

The issue of reciprocity involves unequal social relations between donors and recipients. Carter refers to A. R. Hands's analysis of public almsgiving in the Greco-Roman world that locked recipients into patron-client relations that elevated the powerful and locked recipients into shameful dependency.[52] This relates to a central theme in Jesus' ministry, admitting the shamed into honored relationships and overcoming the pain of what Stephen Pattison calls "chronic shame" and "unwanted-ness."[53] This is the rationale of Jesus' witty advice in Matt 6:2, "do not let your left hand know what your right hand is doing." It is not just that "the merit motive of one's achievements is clearly excluded,"[54] but that the integrity and honor of recipients needed to be protected. A secret donation allowed recipients to be aided without being shamed or being forced into social dependency.

In the next verses in Matthew's Gospel, the topic of prayer is intro-duced: "And when you pray, you must not be like the hypocrites; for they love to stand and pray in the synagogues and at the street corners, that they may be seen by men. Truly, I say to you, they have received their reward. But when you pray, go into your closet and shut the door and pray to your Father who is in secret; and your Father who sees in secret will reward you" (Matt 6:5–6). Here Jesus recommends a procedure in stark contrast to normal prayers, which in the context of first-century Judaism were typically public, vocal, and offered from a standing posi-tion.[55] These details are illustrated by Jesus' reference to the two men praying in the temple (Luke 18:9–14). The Pharisee stands and utters his prayer aloud in the same competitive spirit implied in the Sermon on the Mount: "God, I thank thee that I am not like other men, extor-tioners, unjust, adulterers, or even like this tax collector. I fast twice a week, I give tithes of all that I get" (Luke 18:11–12). Most interpreters stress that "motivation" is the central issue;[56] Robert Guelich insisted that "the issue is not public worship . . . but worship for publicity."[57] I believe the issue here is the broader social matter of sectarian competition for honor. Hatred of collaborators with the hated Romans is expressed in the reference to "this tax collector." Religious performances of fasting, almsgiving, and praying were prominent features of the Pharisee pro-gram to demonstrate the superior honor of their sect and to reinforce the conformity that would allegedly lead to the establishment of Israel as the capitol of the world in place of Rome. The stakes here are far larger than an individual male's achievement of public honor.[58] Religion is be-ing misused here in the reinforcement of a system of social superiority, with its ultimate expression in an imperial rule to be established through the annihilation of adversaries.

The antidote suggested by Jesus is both radical and witty: "go into your closet and shut the door and pray to your Father who is in secret." The word translated "closet" is actually the tiny, windowless storage chamber for food supplies and tools that was part of every Palestinian home.[59] It was the last place in which any adult male would want to spend time. This is hyperbole, not a command to establish a new holy spot for communion with God. By laughing at themselves, the spell of public performance for sectarian goals is broken and hearers can begin to reorient their prayers in a healthy direction: toward their heavenly parent who hears in secret. Since the God proclaimed by Jesus welcomes all persons and groups in equal measure, this reorientation involves the abandonment of hostile competition. Thus I suggest a political dimension for the words of Jerome Neyrey, "Not only must they refrain from playing the typical games for gaining honor . . . , the disciples must vacate the playing field, at least in regard to deeds of piety."[60] Bad religion is a political game with lethal social consequences that Jesus was seeking to avert. This is the playing field that followers are advised to vacate while reorienting themselves to the God who will not support violent, sectarian campaigns.

Fasting is the third religious practice discussed in the Sermon on the Mount, and in the first century it had a particularly close association with the national cause. On the Day of Atonement everyone was required to fast in recognition of Israel's sins that had led to disasters (Lev 16:29–34). On the anniversary of the destruction of the temple, several sectarian groups required fasting. The motivation was to mourn for the sins that had allegedly provoked the wrath of God and caused the national defeats. Sackcloth and ashes were worn to indicate grief and repentance for the sins that led to Israel's disasters, sins defined from the perspective of one's sect. Public fasting was thus a form of public propaganda for the views of one's group. Essenes and Pharisees were particularly committed to demonstrative fasting, usually on Mondays and Thursdays,[61] which is reflected in the Pharisee's public boast in Jesus' parable, "I fast twice a week." Such zeal was thought to atone for Israel's sins and thus was able to bring the day of her restoration closer. An early rabbi taught, "He who puts on sackcloth and fasts, let him not lay it off until what he prays for takes place."[62] Thus as Josef Zmijewski concludes, "From the earliest reference to fasting, it possessed an essentially vicarious, expiatory character. Fasting was for the pious an expression of repentance and sorrow for the sins of the nation against God's law."[63] But it was also an aggressive demonstration of the superiority of one's group and of the current sins of the rest of Israel that needed to be removed if her restoration was to be achieved.

The remedy Jesus suggested was to eliminate the possibility of propaganda by rendering fasting completely secret. Again, there is a wry sense of humor expressed in the advice to "anoint your head and wash your face" (Matt 6:17). This not only eliminates all traces of ashes, but also the application of hair oil lends an impression of celebration that replaces the "dismal" expression of grief. Plutarch, for example, advises a bride to oil her hair and wash her face in preparation of her festivities.[64] Fasting is to be done in secret so it "may not be seen by men but by your Father who is in secret; and your Father who will reward you" (Matt 6:18). Once again, if one's religious devotion is directed to the heavenly Abba, who views all persons as his beloved children, there is no longer a need to compete for honor or to assert the superiority of one's group over another. The "reward" is the continuation of the mutuality between God and God's children, a theme that brings us to the question of the relationship between this redirection of religion and Jesus' central message of the kingdom of God.

GOOD RELIGION AND GENEROUS ENTRANCE INTO THE KINGDOM OF GOD

I believe a case can be made that Jesus' distinctive proclamation of the arrival of the kingdom of God and its unconditional inclusion of the unworthy was the basis of his innovative view of religious practices. Although Matthew retains an eschatological concept of the divine kingdom as a strictly future matter,[65] which has caused unending confusion in interpretation, the earliest levels of the Jesus tradition reveal an innovative message concerning the present inbreaking of God's reign.[66] For example, at the beginning of Mark's Gospel, Jesus proclaims "The time is fulfilled, and the kingdom of God is at hand" (Mark 1:15). In the Q source, the poor are told that "yours is the kingdom of God" (Luke 6:20).[67] In Luke 17:21, Jesus tells the Pharisees, "the kingdom of God is in the midst of you."[68] In the controversy over the power of healing, Jesus says, "But if it is by the finger of God that I cast out demons, then the kingdom of God has come upon you" (Luke 11:20).[69] As the distinguished Jewish historian David Flusser has observed, Jesus "is the only Jewish teacher known to us, who proclaimed . . . that the new time of salvation had already begun."[70] Although a scholarly consensus on this point has remained firm over the past sixty years, it has usually not been correlated with Jesus' critique of religious practices.

As we have seen in the Pauline letters and the Sermon on the Mount, a key motivation in the public demonstrations of almsgiving, prayer, and fasting was to encourage the emulation of behavior that would usher in the kingdom of God. Each sectarian group was convinced that the current reign of Satan, visible in their adversaries and the Roman occupation, was due to divine wrath that could only be assuaged by proper religious practice. There was a widespread consensus that if all Israel obeyed the law for a single day, the Messiah would come and Israel's domination of the world would commence. So religious practices were conducted publicly to encourage lawful behavior and to discredit adversaries within Israel itself. If sectarian campaigns were successful, God would allegedly put wrath aside and usher in the messianic kingdom.

If the kingdom of God had already arrived, however, such practices were totally unnecessary. God's realm had arrived without human encouragement, so the current requirement was to receive it with joy and begin to act in accordance with its generous inclusion of all. In fact, the continuation of pious acts that served the goals of hostile propaganda was a sign of resistance against God's mercy, which explains why Jesus devoted considerable effort to clarify the nature of good religion. Unconditional entrance into God's kingdom was the ultimate honor anyone could experience; it addressed the painfully shameful status that afflicted most people in this period of discriminatory, sectarian religion. To persist in pious actions aimed at overcoming a deficit in honor was to discredit the ultimate honor already received. Moreover, Jesus was certain that the continuation of the quest for the perverse honor of domination both in the practice of piety in the public square and in the vision of a messianic kingdom involving Israel's conquest of the world would have disastrous consequences. He lived and died for a kingdom in which all were equally loved and which invited each into an intimate relationship with the heavenly Abba and the Abba's other children.

Unconditional welcome into God's kingdom meant that no one had to perform religiously to be accepted. Proof of piety was no longer required. When someone was motivated to extend generosity to others that he or she had already received by free admission into the kingdom of God, alms needed to be given in such a way as to respect the feelings of recipients. Since almsgiving was no longer needed as proof of one's worthiness, donors were free to consider what was actually needed by others whose equality with oneself had been proven

by the kingdom's invitation to all. Secrecy also served to avoid shaming those whose economic situation was so marginal that they could
not afford to give alms.

If everyone was already welcome into God's kingdom, there was
no longer a rationale to utter prayers in public view. Since prayers now
served to express the new relationship between believers and their loving
parent, they were best uttered in privacy. Disciples were encouraged to
express their requests in the conviction that the heavenly father already
knew what they needed. They could pray in the innocence of children
who know their parent's love is sure. To continue the practice of prayer
as a method of achieving honor was to deny this unconditional affection. Moreover, restricting prayers to the private sphere also avoided
inadvertently shameful comparison with others that was an inevitable
feature of ancient honor systems. Persons with restricted education and
intelligence would inevitably feel shamed when comparing their formulation of prayers with others who were more articulate and adept.

If disciples feel the need to fast, there is no longer a need for public
performance aimed at bringing in the kingdom. They can fast in secret,
devoting their attention not to fellow humans but to the God who has
honored them unconditionally by the gift of affectionate relationship.
Continuing the habit of public fasting would express contempt for this
supreme gift that turns recipients into honorable members of God's
realm. Secrecy also guards non-fasters from shame over their less ascetic behavior. For many members of the kingdom, however, the spirit
of celebration crowded out the need to fast. As Jesus explained his disciples' failure to be as ascetic as the followers of John the Baptist, "Can
you make wedding guests fast while the bridegroom is with them?"
(Luke 5:34).

In all of these examples of pious behavior, the presence of the kingdom of God that accepted everyone as members established a new sense
of freedom that could only be exercised outside of the purview of fellow
humans. The ancient system of honor and shame was so dominant that
extreme measures needed to be taken to preserve this new status as God's
beloved. With the profound respect for each person conveyed through
the message of Jesus, there emerged a right of and need for privacy in
the intimate relation with God. Pious actions needed to be conducted in
secret. This privacy also prevented inadvertent shaming of others who
chose to exercise their religious devotion in different ways and seasons.

When Paul insisted that "For freedom Christ has set us free; stand fast therefore, and do not submit again to a yoke of slavery" (Gal 5:1), he seems to have formulated an idea that Jesus' announcement of the generous arrival of God's kingdom first rendered possible.

THE END OF SATAN'S REIGN

If the Kingdom of God was breaking into history with the ministry of Jesus, it followed that the world must no longer be in the control of demonic powers, as the sectarians believed. In Luke 10:17, Jesus described his vision of the devil's demise: "I saw Satan fall like lightning from heaven."[71] There is a significant consensus that although reported only once in the gospels, this vision concerning the disabling of Satan was an expression of the arrival of God's kingdom on earth that correlates with Jesus' interpretation of healing, found in several locations.[72] This vision fits Jesus' explanation of how it was possible to capture Satan's former possessions: "But if it is by the finger of God that I cast out demons, then the kingdom of God has come upon you. When a strong man, fully armed, guards his own palace, his goods are in peace; but when one stronger than he assails him and overcomes him, he takes away his armor in which he trusted, and divides his spoil" (Luke 11:20–22). Jesus is clearly the stronger man who is enabled to free Satan's captives because the kingdom of God has arrived. The defeat of Satan by divine power had already been accomplished.[73]

This correlates with Jesus' distinctive effort to recognize human responsibility in dealing with the demonic. Having provided an example of freeing people from demonic possession, he sends his disciples out to announce the arrival of God's reign, and they return with the report that "Lord, even the demons are subject to us in your name!" (Luke 10:18). In the temptation story at the beginning of his ministry, Jesus identifies important dimensions of messianic theory as demonic temptations that he decides to resist. The rule of the future messiah over all the kingdoms of the world (Matt 4:8) was a decisive feature of all sectarian groups. Manipulating the future of divine action (Matt 4:5–6) was a goal of sectarian propaganda. Producing bread by a form of social magic was a hope shared by the zealot movement and the Roman civic cult instigated by the Emperor Augustus and his successors. In Jesus' view, these influential religio-political programs were in reality forms of being "tempted by the devil" (Matt 4:1). These insights carry over into Jesus' ministry.

When Peter rejects the messianic plan to face persecution in Jerusalem, Jesus rebukes him with the strange words, "Get behind me, Satan! You are a hindrance to me; for you are not on the side of God, but of men" (Matt 16:23). It is not that Peter was possessed by or led by the devil, but that his messianic views were on "the side ... of men."[74] Humans can become satanic. The demonic becomes a matter of personal responsibility, requiring the weighing of alternatives and the recognition of dangers to be avoided. That humans are capable of very great evils is clearly in view, but they no longer have a demonic alibi.

The fall of Satan has a direct bearing on the public piety in Jesus' day, because each of the sectarian groups perceived their adversaries as satanic agents. This gave their competition in pious deeds a compelling rationale, because in place of mere human strife over superior honor, it established an absolutely compelling need to prevail. No compromise or moderation was morally acceptable. But if Satan had fallen, social competition was reduced to merely human dimensions. The biblical injunctions against pride and social conflicts as well as the normal methods of reconciliation suddenly became relevant. Illness and bad fortune no longer needed to be understood as shameful, demonic possession that isolated sufferers and instilled feelings of shameful helplessness and hopelessness. Finally, if Satan was no longer responsible for all the evil in the world, people could begin to understand the consequences of their own behavior; it even became possible to grasp the presence of hypocrisy in oneself and others.

THE ISSUE OF HYPOCRISY

Jesus' distinctive view of God's kingdom throws light on the term "hypocrite," which we have encountered in Matt 6:3, 5, 7, 16. The word also appears in fourteen other sayings of Jesus and in later Christian writings. The verbs and nouns with the *hypocri–* stem are distinctively Greek terms for public declamations and acting in plays. In contrast to their use by Jesus, in the Greek culture these words never developed "a negative ethical ring"[75] as in the modern term, "hypocrite." Since there was no Hebrew or Aramaic equivalent for "hypocrite" in the sense of play acting or putting on a show,[76] I think it is likely that Jesus used the Greek term in his discourse. If so, the choice of this foreign word would have had a significant rhetorical effect: the very persons demonstrating their extreme conformity to Israel's religion, differentiating themselves thereby from nonconforming Jews and Greek speaking foreigners, were behaving like pagan actors! They were putting on a show just like the performers in the Greco-Roman theaters that pious Jews refused to enter as centers of idolatry and moral corruption. The use of this Greek term evoked a profound and shocking discrepancy between pious deeds and their motivation.

Jesus revolutionary message about free entrance into the kingdom of a loving Abba brought the phenomenon of hypocrisy as play acting in the religious sphere to light for the first time. There is in fact no evidence of the term "hypocrite" being used in this way before Jesus does so. It seems to derive from his central message about the kingdom of God. If God's love is unconditional, each person is honored to the ultimate degree. No pious act could possibly achieve such acceptance. Recipients of such honor are thereby rendered capable of seeing themselves for what they are: unworthy creatures accepted as supremely honorable by a generous divine parent. They no longer needed to perform to be acceptable. They were therefore able to see their prior performances in a clearer light; they could recognize their "self-deception"[77] for the first time because they no longer had to prove their innocent status. Before receiving the message about free entrance into God's kingdom, they had been putting up a pious facade. Their almsgiving, prayers, and fasting had been designed to show their superior virtue as well as the superiority of their sect. They can recognize now that they had been playing a triple game. The competitive culture of honor and shame that marked the entire ancient Mediterranean world had encouraged their individual desire to be more honorable than others as well as their group's struggle for dominance. But the goal of their pious behavior had not been to enter into communion with God, as the actions themselves pretended, but to impress God and the world with their piety. While seeming to act with integrity in relation to God, they were really acting to impress others with their piety and finally to demonstrate the superiority of their sect.

The revolutionary message about the Kingdom of God sweeping the "poor, the maimed, the lame, the blind" (Luke 14:13) as well as the despised wayfarers on "the highways and hedges" (Luke 14:23) into the messianic banquet meant that no one needed to impress anyone anymore. The ultimate "reward" of welcome into the Abba's house had already been granted, which means that when Jesus promises that "your Father who sees in secret will reward you" (Matt 6:6), he's referring to an ongoing relationship experienced in the here and now. As in the parable of the Prodigal Son, welcome to the celebration in the Father's house is the ongoing reward (Luke 15:32). Good religion enjoys the party and thus is enabled to abandon the prestige games that formally beckoned as the key to life.

CONCLUSION

In all three forms of piety in the Sermon on the Mount and in Paul's description of zealous behavior prior to his conversion, we can discern a mixture of the competitive motivation to be more righteous than others as well as the use of pious example to advance sectarian campaigns to bring in the kingdom of God. In both dimensions, religion is perverted into a pillar of domination. These passages reveal a lethal fusion of personal desires for honorable status and sectarian competition under the guise of divine authentication. Bad religion is a terrible thing because it supports unjust social systems and unfair visions of dominance with allegedly divine authority, and in the process it turns its practitioners into hypocrites. A perverse system of honor and shame is particularly destructive when allied with religion and employed in social conflicts. The question, "Have you got good religion?" remains a vital challenge to us all.

ENDNOTES

1. Neyrey, *Matthew*, 1–89; Carter, *Matthew and the Margins*, 158–71; Witherington, *Matthew*, 240; Talbert, *Reading*, 108; Malina and Rohrbaugh, *Synoptic Gospels*; Hanson, "How Honorable! How Shameful!," 81–111.
2. The text of "Cert'nly Lord!" is available in McClain, *Come Sunday*, 120.
3. See Jewett, *Mission and Menace*, chapter 5.
4. Overman, *Matthew's Gospel and Formative Judaism*, 8.
5. Ibid., 15.
6. Ibid., 17.
7. Ibid., 17–18.
8. Ibid., 19.
9. For an account of the hostility of the zealot movement toward other Jewish groups, see Hengel, *Zealots*, 227–28, 359–66.
10. Wandrey, "Zeloten," 8.1832.
11. Seland, *Establishment Violence*, 13–14, 42–74.

12. See Wandrey, "Zeloten," 8.1834.

13. See Saldarini, "Pharisees," 294–303; *Pharisees, Scribes and Sadducees*, 209–11.

14. Baumgarten, "Pharisäer," 6.1262.

15. Saldarini, "Pharisees," 286.

16. Baumgarten, "Pharisäer," 6.1263.

17. Overman, *Matthew's Gospel and Formative Judaism*, 9.

18. The sectarian nature of the Essene movement is described by Collins in "Essenes," 621–22.

19. Overman, *Matthew's Gospel and Formative Judaism*, 10.

20. See Porton, "Sadducees," 892–93; Saldarini, *Pharisees, Scribes and Sadducees*, 302–5.

21. Schröder, "Sadduzäer," 7.732.

22. Ibid.

23. Ibid., 7.732–73.

24. See particularly Overman, *Matthew's Gospel and Formative Judaism*, 8–23.

25. Jewett, "Basic Human Dilemma," 96–109.

26. Godet, *Romans*, 280.

27. Sanday and Headlam, *Romans*, 186.

28. Stendahl, *Paul Among Jews and Gentiles*, 78–96.

29. Sanders, *Paul and Palestinian Judaism*; Sanders, *Paul, the Law, and the Jewish People*.

30. The material in this section is adapted from chapter 7 of *Paul the Apostle to America*; see also my study, *Saint Paul at the Movies*, 21–25, 126–33 and *Romans*, 454–73.

31. See Jewett, *Romans*, 606.

32. Stumpff, "*zelos ktl*," 878; see also Hengel, *Judaism and Hellenism*, 1. 287–309. Significant parallels are found in 1 Macc 2:44–45; 1QS 2:15; 4:4, 10, 17; 1QH 1:5; 2:15, 31; 4:23; 9:3; 14:14.

33. The expression "zeal for the law" or for divine "ordinances" is found in 1 Macc 2:26, 27, 50, 58; 2 Macc 4:2; 1QS 4:4; 9:23; 1QH 14:14; see Hengel, *Judaism and Hellenism*, 1:305–14.

34. See Hengel, *Zealots*, 147–228.

35. *Hodayot/Thanksgiving Psalms* 14:14, cited by Hengel, *Zealots*, 179.

36. Sanders, *Paul, the Law, and the Jewish People*, 36–39.

37. Howard, "Christ the End of the Law," 336.

38. See Sanders, *Paul, the Law, and the Jewish People*, 44–45.

39. In *Romans,* 194, Käsemann refers to "the passion to assert oneself against God and neighbor."

40. See Hengel, *Zealots,* 156–82. For a balancing view, see Rhoads, *Israel in Revolution,* 94–149.

41. See Kim, *Origin,* 73–74.

42. Stendahl, *Paul among Jews and Gentiles,* 9 has stressed that Paul refers to a "call" rather than to a "conversion": "his call brings him to a new understanding of his mission, a new understanding of the law which is otherwise an obstacle to the Gentiles."

43. Luz, *Matthäus,* 321.

44. Zager, *Bergpredigt,* 5.

45. Carter, *Matthew and the Margins,* 158–59.

46. Witherington, *Matthew,* 240.

47. Talbert, *Reading,* 107.

48. Keener, *Matthew,* 209.

49. Luz, *Matthäus,* 323.

50. See Friedrich, "*salpigx ktl,*" 77, 79.

51. Carter, *Matthew and the Margins,* 160.

52. Hands, *Charities and Social Aid,* 26, 77; cited by Carter, *Matthew and the Margins,* 579

53. Pattison, *Shame,* 88–92.

54. Guelich, *Sermon,* 280.

55. Grundmann and Greeven, "*euchomai ktl,*" 786.

56. See, for example, Keener, *Matthew,* 212.

57. Guelich, *Sermon,* 302–3.

58. See Neyrey, *Matthew,* 214–18.

59. Luz, *Matthäus,* 325; Neyrey, *Matthew,* 220–21.

60. Neyrey, *Matthew,* 219.

61. Behm, "*nestis ktl,*" 929–30.

62. Cited by Behm, "*nestis ktl,*" 930.

63. Zmijewski, "*nesteuo ktl,*" 466.

64. See Carter, *Matthew and the Margins,* 171.

65. Becker, "Matthew," 66.

66. See Zager, *Bergpredigt,* 50–54.

67. Eckey, *Lukasevangelium,* I.294–97; Wolter, *Lukasevangelium,* 248–49.

68. Eckey, *Lukasevangelium,* II.741: 'the salvation time is now," translation by Jewett.

69. Ibid., II.531.

70. Flusser, *Jesus in Selbsstzeugnssen*, 87, cited by Zager, *Bergpredigt*, 51; translation by Jewett.

71. See the chapter on this theme in Jewett, *Jesus against the Rapture*.

72. Müller, "Vision und Botschaft," 419–20; Zager, *Bergpredigt*, 53–54; accepted more recently by Eckey, *Lukasevangelium*, I.473–74 and Wolter, *Lukasevangelium*, 385–86.

73. See Wolter, *Lukasevangelium*, 420.

74. See Luz, *Matthäus 1.2*, 489–90.

75. Wilckens, "*hypokrinomai ktl*," 8.563.

76. In "*hypokrinomai ktl*," 8.564, Wilckens notes that *hypocrites* is the Greek term employed in the Septuagint for the Hebrew term *ḥanef* ("wicked, ungodly man"), but that nowhere in the Septuagint or other ancient Jewish writings do these words bear the meaning of play acting or dissembling.

77. See Via, *Self-Deception*, 92–98.

Conclusion

JOHN G. LACEY

I AM BOTH HONORED and humbled at being afforded the opportunity to write the conclusion of this book. Working as part of the editorial team and reading all the authors' contributions has deepened my understanding and appreciation for the dual themes of shame and honor. This essay is a result of my reflection upon the same, and I offer it up to you as an encouragement to share these same themes with others who may be dealing with their own personal shame issues. You can help them find corresponding honor in their relationship with God through Jesus Christ.

The theme of this essay is based upon the lyrics of Billy Joel's song "Shameless." Although it is written as a love song, it speaks to both human and divine relationship components. Drawing upon Joel's lyrics, and some biblical tenets, I hope to unveil how our condition of shame can be transformed into honor by looking to Jesus Christ, "the pioneer and perfecter of our faith" (Heb 12:2).

As in most stories, this one literally starts at the beginning. We find Adam and Eve confronted with their own shame issues in the Garden of Eden. After their disobedience and subsequent fall due to disregard for God's specific intentions about the tree of the knowledge of good and evil (Gen 2:17), the first couple finds themselves confronted with personal shame personified by their nakedness: "Then the eyes of both were opened, and they knew that they were naked; and they sewed fig leaves together and made loincloths for themselves" (Gen 3:7).

Their feeble and futile attempt at covering their shame was compounded in their attempt to hide themselves from God who called to them, "Where are you?" (Gen 3:9). In one of the saddest, most shame-ridden dialogues in Scripture, their resultant shame naturally leads to blame as we read:

> [Adam] said, 'I heard the sound of you in the garden, and I was afraid, because I was naked; and I hid myself.' [God] said, 'Who told you that you were naked? Have you eaten from the tree of which I commanded you not to eat?' [Adam] The man said, '[Eve] the woman whom you gave to be with me, she gave me fruit from the tree, and I ate. (Gen 3:10–12)

With dire consequences for all humanity, the first man and woman exchanged their dual blessing and honor of being created in God's image (Gen 1:27) for opened eyes of consciousness. The resulting fig leaves were a transparent attempt to cover their newfound shame.

As Billy Joel (and Garth Brooks) poignantly sing: "And I'm standing here for all the world to see / There ain't that much left of me / That has very far to fall."[1] Stewing in our juices of sin and shame thanks, in part, to Paul's admonition that "all have sinned" (Rom 3:23) our fall seems less than trivial. Where is the remedy and rescue for our very personal dilemma and crisis with shame? Thankfully, the author of Hebrews comes to our aid by writing:

> Therefore, since we are surrounded by so great a cloud of witnesses, let us also lay aside every weight and the sin that clings so closely, and let us run with perseverance the race that is set before us, looking to Jesus the pioneer and perfecter of our faith, who for the sake of the joy that was set before him endured the cross, disregarding its shame, and has taken his seat at the right hand of the throne of God. (Heb 12:1–2)

In one of the most confounding passages on shame in the entire Bible the Hebrews author informs us that Jesus, the Son of God, "endured the shame of the cross" on behalf of humanity. As David deSilva notes in his essay, the Romans were attempting to use Jesus' crucifixion as a "human billboard advertising the consequences of serious deviation from the dominant culture values." The oppressor (victimizer) hoped to use the oppressed's (victim's) shame to bring others to conformity. Herein, we see how the vehicle of shame encompasses shameful treatment by others.[2]

Yet our sin and shame were somehow nailed there upon that Roman cross on a Palestinian hillside one Friday afternoon once and for all. It seems too impossible, too good to be true. Somehow our shame is placed on God's one and only Son who counts it a "joy" to fulfill his Father's will and purpose as he endured our shame and suffering on that instrument of capital punishment for our behalf. DeSilva goes on to note we are encouraged to "focus on Christ" that we might come to share in his honor.[3]

But wait; there's more to the story. The author of Hebrews notes that Jesus "has taken his seat at the right hand of the throne of God." When Jesus took our shame upon himself on the cross God, in turn, miraculously transformed that shame into honor. The right hand of the throne of God is the place of highest honor and it belongs to the Father's Son, namely Jesus Christ. This is why the Hebrews writer goes to great lengths to extol the supremacy and superiority of God's Son, our Savior:

> He is the reflection of God's glory and the exact imprint of God's very being, and he sustains all things by his powerful word. When he had made purification for sins, he sat down at the right hand of the Majesty on high, having become as much superior to angels as the name he has inherited is more excellent than theirs. (Heb 1:3–4)

Paul even gets in on the act as he notes:

> God put this power to work in Christ when he raised him from the dead and seated him at his right hand in the heavenly places, far above all rule and authority and power and dominion, and above every name that is named, not only in this age but also in the age to come. And he has put all things under his feet and has made him the head over all things for the church, which is his body, the fullness of him who fills all in all. (Eph 1:20–23)

By God's TNT dynamite-power, death was transformed into life as shame morphed into the ultimate honor which Christ, in turn, transferred to his new body—the church! In doing so, our shame-based sin, both committed by us and committed against us, also experienced a transformation into new honor-based life in Christ.

David Rhoads and Sandra Roberts do a wonderful and remarkable job in their essay describing the work of God's grace in our lives. I am deeply indebted to both of them for new insights they have unlocked for me regarding the good news of redemption for the victim and the oppressed. They note that forgiveness is also good news "for those who have been sinned against."[4]

As amazing as this concept might seem, all the shameful aspects of our lives including "the sense of powerlessness, defilement, unworthiness, and alienation"[5] are turned into honor through this Christ event. The apostle Paul understood this profound idea to be true when he wrote to the church in Ephesus:

> But God, who is rich in mercy, out of the great love with which he loved us even when we were dead through our trespasses, made us alive together with Christ—by grace you have been saved—and raised us up with him and seated us with him in the heavenly places in Christ Jesus, so that in the ages to come he might show the immeasurable riches of his grace in kindness towards us in Christ Jesus. (Eph 2:4–7)

Truly, we are seated there "in the heavenly places with Christ" because of God's rich mercy and grace. But you see, there is the rub. God sees us in Christ in this honored position with Jesus Christ, yet we sometimes forget the reality of the gift, how we have been "saved by grace through faith" (Eph 2:8). We continue to live in the reality Paul described so astutely: "We know that the whole creation has been groaning in labor pains until now" (Rom 8:22).

Yes, we sometimes groan in our immediate life-context as we anticipate, by faith, the not-yet future reality of our honored position in the heavenly places with Christ Jesus.

However, it is none other than the apostle John who assures us that better days await us when we will shake off our shame-ridden garden identity of fig leaves and loincloths for an honor-filled identity that is a perfect fit: "Beloved, we are God's children now; what we will be has not yet been revealed. What we do know is this: when he is revealed, we will be like him, for we will see him as he is" (1 John 3:2). Hallelujah, "we are God's children NOW!" God does not focus on our shame, but the honor that is ours as God's adopted children who his Son has taught us to call, "Our Father . . ." More importantly, John tells us "we will be like him." Christ's righteous perfection will be ours, just as his honor is ours. You don't mess with perfection and Christ's perfection will also be ours. John Wesley understood this well as he called Christ-followers to "move on to perfection."

This is our calling, our destiny—to be like Christ in honor and perfection. God transforms our shame into honor through the power of the cross because the Son "endured the cross, disregarding its shame."

You see, I believe Billy Joel gets it right when he says:

> You know it should be easy for a man [person] who's strong
> To say he's [they're] sorry or admit when he's [they're] wrong
> I've never lost anything I ever missed
> But I've never been in love like this . . .
> It's out of my hands
>
> I'm shameless, I don't have the power now
> But I don't want it anyhow
> So I've got to let it go[6]

Shame creates impotence we cannot overcome on our own that makes it nigh on impossible to say we are sorry or admit we are wrong. However, the "power" we so desperately lack is found in God's profound and inexhaustible mercy and grace. You and I have encountered a divine love that will not let us go. When we surrender to that irresistible love and confess, "It's out of our hands," our shame is transformed and we become *shameless* in Christ's honor. In regard to our shame, we can sing with Billy Joel: "I am shameless / Shameless / Shameless . . ."[7]

ENDNOTES

1. Billy Joel, "Shameless."
2. deSilva, "Turning Shame into Honor."
3. Ibid.
4. Rhoads and Roberts, "Justification by Grace."
5. Pattison, "Shame and the Unwanted Self."
6. Billy Joel, "Shameless."
7. Ibid.

Bibliography

Abi-Hashem, Naji. "Peace and War in the Middle East: A Psychopolitical and Sociocultural Perspective." In *Understanding Terrorism: Psychosocial Roots, Consequences, and Interventions*, edited by Fathali M. Moghaddam and Anthony J. Marsella, 69–89. Washington: American Psychological Association Press, 2004.

Afsaruddin, Asma, "Introduction: The Hermeneutics of Gendered Space and Discourse. In *Hermeneutics and Honor: Negotiating Female "Public" Space in Islamic/ate Societies*, edited by Asma Afsaruddin, 1–28. Cambridge: Harvard University Press, 1999.

Alter, Robert. *The Art of Biblical Narrative*. New York: Basic Books, 1981.

Atran, S., and J. Stern. "Small Groups Find Fatal Purpose Through the Web." *Nature* 437 (2005) 620–21.

Atran, S. "A Failure of Imagination." *Studies in Conflict and Terrorism* 29/3 (2006) 285–300.

Augsburger, David W. *Pastoral Counseling Across Cultures*. Philadelphia: Westminster, 1986.

Aune, David, editor. *Rereading Paul Together: Protestant and Catholic Perspectives on Justification*. Grand Rapids: Baker, 2006.

Barclay, John M. G. "Mirror-Reading a Polemical Letter: Galatians as a Test Case." *Journal for the Study of the New Testament* 31 (1987) 73–93.

Barclay, John M. G. *Obeying the Truth: Paul's Ethics in Galatians*. Minneapolis: Fortress, 1988.

Batson, C. D., N. Ahmad, and E. Stocks. "Benefits and Liabilities of Empathy-Induced Altruism." In *The Social Psychology of Good and Evil*, edited by Arthur G. Miller, 359–85. New York: Guilford, 2004.

Baumgarten, Albert I. "Pharisäer." In *Religion in Geschichte und Gegenwart*, edited by Hans Dieter Betz, 6:1262–63. 4th ed. Tübingen: Mohr/Siebeck, 2003.

Becker, Hans-Jürgen. "Matthew, the Rabbis and Billerbeck on the Kingdom of Heaven." In *The Sermon on the Mount and Its Jewish Setting*, edited by Hans-Jürgen Becker and Serge Ruzer, 57–69. Cahiers de la Revue biblique 60. Paris: Gabalda, 2005.

Bedford, Olwen, and Kwang-Kuo Hwang. "Guilt and Shame in Chinese Culture: A Cross-cultural Framework from the Perspective of Morality and Identity." *Journal for the Theory of Social Behavior* 33 (2003) 127–43.

Behm, Johannes. "*nestis ktl.*" In *Theological Dictionary of the New Testament*, edited by Gerhard Kittel, 4:924–35. Translated and edited by Geoffrey W. Bromiley. Grand Rapids: Eerdmans, 1967.

Bergen, Wesley J., "The Prophetic Alternative: Elisha and the Israelite Monarchy." In *Elijah and Elisha in Socioliterary Perspective*, edited by Robert B. Coote, 127–37. Semeia Studies. Atlanta: Scholars, 1992.

Berger, Peter L. *The Sacred Canopy: Elements of a Sociological Theory of Religion*. Garden City, NY: Doubleday, 1967.

Berlin, Ira. *Many Thousand Gone: The First Two Centuries of Slavery in North America*. Cambridge, MA: Belknap, 1990.

Blass, Thomas, editor. *Obedience to Authority: Current Perspectives on the Milgram Paradigm*. Mahwah, NJ: Erlbaum, 1999.

Blassingame, John W. *The Slave Community: Plantation Life in the Antebellum South*. New York: Oxford University Press, 1972.

Blassingame, John W., editor. *Slave Testimony: Two Centuries of Letters, Speeches, Interviews, and Autobiographies*. Baton Rouge: Louisiana State University Press, 1977.

Bleibtreu, Erika. "Grisly Assyrian Record of Torture and Death." *Biblical Archaeologist Reader* 17 (1991) 53–61, 75.

Bloomquist, Karen L., and Wolfgang Greive, editors. *The Doctrine of Justification: Its Reception and Meaning Today*. LWF Studies 2003/2. Geneva: Lutheran World Federation, 2003.

Bowles, Samuel, and Herbert Gintis. "Social Capital and Community Governance." *Economic Journal* 112 (2002) 419–36.

Braaten, Carl E. *Justification: The Article by Which the Church Stands or Falls*. Minneapolis: Fortress, 1990.

Bradshaw, John. *Healing the Shame that Binds You*. Deerfield Beach: Health Communications, 1988.

Braithwaite, John. "Rape, Shame, and Pride." *Journal of Scandinavian Studies in Criminology and Crime Prevention* 7 (2006) 2–16.

Braxton, Brad Ronnell. *No Longer Slaves: Galatians and African American Experience*. Collegeville, MN: Liturgical, 2002.

British Government. "Intelligence and Security Committee Report into the London Terrorist Attacks on 7 July 2005." Available from the House of Commons Stationery Office (2006).

Broucek, Francis. *Shame and the Self*. New York: Guilford, 1991.

Brown, Brené. "Shame Resilience Theory: A Grounded Theory Study on Women and Shame." *Families in Society* 87 (2006) 43–52.

Bruner, Jerome. *Child's Talk*. New York: Norton, 1983.

Bushman, B., R. Ridge, E. Das, C. Key, and G. Busath. "When God Sanctions Killing: Effect of Scriptural Violence on Aggression." *Psychological Science* 18.3 (2007) 204–7.

Bushman, B., and R. Baumeister. "Does Self-Love or Self-Hate Lead to Violence?" *Journal of Research in Personality* 36 (2002) 543–45.

———. "Threatened Egotism, Narcissism, Self-Esteem, and Direct and Displaced Aggression: Does Self-Love or Self-Hate Lead to Violence?" *Journal of Personality and Social Psychology* 75 (1998) 219–29.

Camp, Claudia. "1 and 2 Kings." In *The Women's Bible Commentary*, edited by Carol A. Newsom and Sharon H. Ringe, 102–16. Lousiville: Westminster John Knox, 1992.

Campbell, K., J. Bossom, T. Goheen, C. Lakey, and M. Kernis. "Do Narcissists Dislike Themselves 'Deep Down Inside'?" *Psychological Science* 18 (2007) 227–29.

Capps, Donald. *The Child's Song*. Louisville: Westminster John Knox, 1995.

———. *The Depleted Self*. Minneapolis: Fortress, 1993.

Carpenter, Delores, editor. *African American Heritage Hymnal*. Chicago: GIA Publications, 2001.

Carter, Warren. *Matthew and the Margins: A Socio-Political and Religious Reading.* Journal for the Study of the New Testament Supplement Series 204. Sheffield: Sheffield Academic, 2000.

Chenu, Bruno. *The Trouble I've Seen: The Big Book of Negro Spirituals.* Valley Forge, PA: Judson, 2003.

Clines, David J. A. "Michal Observed: An Introduction to Reading her Story." In *Telling Queen Michal's Story: An Experiment in Comparative Interpretation,* David J. A. Clines and Tamara C. Eskenaszi, 24–63. Journal for the Study of the Old Testament Supplement 119. Sheffield: JSOT Press, 1991.

Cogan, Mordechai. *I Kings.* Anchor Bible 10. New York: Doubleday, 2001.

Cogan, Mordechai, and Hayim Tadmor. *II Kings.* Anchor Bible 11. New York: Doubleday, 1988.

Collins, John J. "Essenes." In *Anchor Bible Dictionary* 2 (1992) 621–22.

Cone, James H. *The Spirituals and the Blues.* New York: Seabury, 1972.

Cooley, Charles H. *Human Nature and the Social Order.* New York: Scribner, 1922.

Courlander, Harold. *A Treasury of Afro-American Folklore.* New York: Marlowe, 1976.

Crook, Zeba. "Honor, Shame, and Social Status Revisited." *Journal of Biblical Literature* 128 (2009) 591–611.

Croy, N. Clayton. *Endurance in Suffering.* Cambridge: Cambridge University Press, 1998.

Crozier, W. Ray. *Blushing and the Social Emotions: The Self Unmasked.* New York: Palgrave Macmillan, 2006.

Cushman, Philip. *Constructing the Self: Constructing America: A Cultural History of Psychotherapy.* Cambridge: Da Capo, 1995.

Cutlip, William D., and Marl R. Leary. "Anatomic and Physiological Bases of Social Blushing: Speculations from Neurology and Psychology." *Behavioral Neurology* 6 (1993) 181–85.

Davids, Peter H. *The First Epistle of Peter.* New International Commentary on the New Testament. Grand Rapids: Eerdmans, 1990.

Davies, W. D., and Dale C. Allison. *Matthew: A Commentary.* London/New York: T & T Clark, 2004.

Davis, Joyce M. *Martyrs: Innocence, Vengeance and Despair in the Middle East.* New York: Palgrave, 2003.

De Botton, Alain. *Status Anxiety.* New York: Vintage International, 2005.

de Jong, Corine Dijk and Peter J. and Madelon L. Peters. "The Remedial Value of Blushing in the Context of Transgression and Mishaps." *Emotion* 9 (2009) 287–91.

deSilva, David A. *Despising Shame: Honor Discourse and Community Maintenance in the Epistle to the Hebrews.* Rev. ed. Studies in Biblical Literature 21. Atlanta: Society of Biblical Literature, 2008. (Original publication: Society of Biblical Literature Dissertation Series 152; Atlanta: Scholars, 1995.)

deSilva, David A. *Honor, Patronage, Kinship & Purity: Unlocking New Testament Culture.* Downers Grove, IL: InterVarsity, 2000.

———. *The Hope of Glory: Honor Discourse and New Testament Interpretation.* Collegeville, MN: Liturgical, 1999. Reprinted, Eugene: Wipf & Stock, 2009.

———. *An Introduction to the New Testament: Contexts, Methods & Ministry Formation.* Downers Grove, IL: InterVarsity, 2004.

———. *Perseverance in Gratitude: A Socio-Rhetorical Commentary on the Epistle "to the Hebrews."* Grand Rapids: Eerdmans, 2000.

————. *Seeing Things John's Way: The Rhetoric of the Book of Revelation*. Louisville: Westminster John Knox, 2009.

Dewey, John. *Experience and Nature*. Chicago: Open Court, 1925.

Donaldson-Pressman, Stephanie, and Robert Pressman. *The Narcissistic Family: Diagnosis and Treatment*. San Francisco: Jossey-Bass, 1994.

Dost, Ayer, and Bilge Yagmurlu. "Are Constructiveness and Destructiveness Essential Features of Guilt and Shame Feelings Respectively?" *Journal for the Theory of Social Behavior* 38 (2008) 109–29.

Douglass, Frederick. *My Bondage and My Freedom*. Edited with an Introduction by William L. Andrews. Blacks in the New World. Urbana: University of Illinois Press, 1987.

————. *Narrative of the Life of Frederick Douglass, An American Slave*. New York: Signet, 1968.

Douglas, Mary. *Purity and Danger*. London: Routledge & Kegan Paul, 1969.

DuBois, W. E. B. *The Souls of Black Folk*. 1903. Reprinted, New York: Fawcett, 1961.

Eckey, Wilfried. *Das Lukasevangelium: Unter Berücksichtigung seiner Parallelen. Teilband I. Lk 1,1—10,42*. Neukirchen-Vluyn: Neukirchener, 2004.

Eckey, Wilfried. *Das Lukasevangelium. Unter Berücksichtigung seiner Parallelen. Teilband II. Lk 1,11,1—24,53*. Neukirchen-Vluyn: Neukirchener, 2004.

Eisenberg, Nancy, Carlos Valiente, and Claire Champion. "Empathy-Related Responding: Moral, Social, and Socialization Correlates." In *The Social Psychology of Good and Evil*, edited by Arthur G. Miller, 386–415. New York: Guilford, 2004.

Elison, Jeff, Randy Lennon, and Steven Pulos. "Investigating the Compass of Shame: The Development of the Compass of Shame Scale." *Social Behavior and Personality* 34 (2006) 221–38.

Elison, Jeff, Steven Pulos, and Randy Lennon. "Shame-Focused Coping: An Empirical Study of the Compass of Shame." *Social Behavior and Personality* 34 (2006) 161–68.

Elliott, John H. "Disgraced Yet Graced. The Gospel According to 1 Peter in the Key of Honor and Shame," *Biblical Theology Bulletin* 24 (1994) 166–78.

————. "The Evil Eye and the Sermon on the Mount: Contours of a Pervasive Belief in Social Scientific Perspective." *Biblical Interpretation* 2 (1994) 51–84.

————. "The Evil Eye in the First Testament: The Ecology and Culture of a Pervasive Belief." In *The Bible and the Politics of Exegesis: Essays in Honor of Norman K. Gottwald on His Sixty-Fifth Birthday*, edited by David Jobling et al., 147–59. Cleveland: Pilgrim, 1991.

————. "The Fear of the Leer: The Evil Eye from the Bible to Li'l Abner." *Forum* 4.4 (1988) 42–71.

————. "Matthew 20:1–15: A Parable of Invidious Comparison and Evil Eye Accusation." *Biblical Theology Bulletin* 22 (1992) 52–65.

————. "Paul, Galatians and the Evil Eye." *Currents in Theology and Mission* 7 (1990) 262–73.

————. *1 Peter*. Anchor Bible 37B. New York: Doubleday, 2000.

Elman, Pearl, "Deuteronomy 21:10–14: The Beautiful Captive Woman." *Women in Judaism* 1 (1997): http://wjudaism.library.utoronto.ca/index.php/wjudaism/article/view/166/277.

Exum, J. Cheryl. *Fragmented Women*. Valley Forge, PA: Trinity, 1993.

Fanon, Frantz. *Black Skin, White Mask.* Translated by Charles Lam Markman. New York: Grove, 1967.

Feshbach, S. "The Dynamics and Morality of Violence and Aggression." *American Psychologist* 26 (1971) 281–92.

Fisher, Miles Mark. *Negro Slave Songs in the United States.* 1953. New York: Russell & Russell, 1968.

Fleishman, Joseph. "Legal Innovation in Deuteronomy XXI 18–20." *Vetus Testamentum* 53 (2003) 311–27.

Flusser, David. *Jesus in Selbstzeugnissen und Bilddokumenten.* Rowohlts Monographien 140. Reinbek bei Hamburg: Rowohlt, 1978.

Fontan, V. "Polarization between Occupier and Occupied in Post-Saddam Iraq: Colonial Humiliation and the Formation of Political Violence." *Terrorism and Political Violence* 18.2 (2006) 217–38.

Forbes, Christopher. "Comparison, Self-Praise, and Irony: Paul's Boasting and the Conventions of Hellenistic Rhetoric." *New Testament Studies* 32 (1986) 1–30.

Forde, Gerhard O. *Justification by Faith—A Matter of Life and Death.* Philadelphia: Fortress, 1982.

Fossum, Merle, and Marilyn Mason. *Facing Shame: Families in Recovery.* New York: Norton, 1986.

Foster, George M. "The Anatomy of Envy: A Study in Symbolic Behavior." *Current Anthropology* 13 (1972) 165–202.

Freud, Sigmund. *The Future of an Illusion.* Garden City: Doubleday Anchor, 1964.

Friedrich, Gerhard. "*salpigx ktl.*" In *Theological Dictionary of the New Testament*, edited by Gerhard Friedrich, 7:71–88. Translated and edited by Geoffrey W. Bromiley. Grand Rapids: Eerdmans, 1971.

Galpaz-Feller, Pnina. "Hair in the Bible and in Ancient Egyptian Culture: Cultural and Private Connotations." *Biblische Notizen* 125 (2005) 75–94.

Gardner, Carol B., and William P. Gronfein. "Reflections on Varieties of Shame Induction, Shame Management, and Shame Avoidance in Some Works of Erving Goffman." *Symbolic Interaction* 28.2 (2005) 175–82.

Garsiel, Moshe, "Revealing and Concealing as a Narrative Strategy in Solomon's Judgment (1 Kings 3:16–28)." *Catholic Biblical Quarterly* 64 (2002) 229–47.

Gates, Henry Louis Jr., editor. *The Classic Slave Narratives.* New York: Mentor, 1987.

Ghosh, Amitav. "The Relations of Envy in an Egyptian Village." *Ethnology* 32 (1983) 211–23.

Gilligan, James. "Shame, Guilt and Violence." *Social Research* 70 (2003) 1149–80.

———. *Violence—Reflections on a National Epidemic.* New York: Vintage, 1997.

Ginges, Jeremy, and Scott Atran. "Humiliation and Inertia Effects: Implications for Understanding Violence and Compromise." *Journal of Cognition and Culture* 8 (2008) 281–94.

Giordano, Christian. "Mediterranean Honour Reconsidered." *Anthropological Journal on European Cultures* 10 (2001) 39–44.

Goffman, Erving. *The Presentation of Self in Everyday Life.* New York: Anchor, 1959.

———. *Relations in Public: Microstudies of the Public Order.* New York: Basic Books, 1971.

———. *Stigma: Notes on the Management of Spoiled Identity.* Englewood Cliffs: Prentice-Hall, 1963.

Godet, Fréderic. *Commentary on St. Paul's Epistle to the Romans*. Translated by A. Cusin, revised and edited by T. W. Chambers. New York: Funk & Wagnalls, 1883.

Goldberg, Carl. *Understanding Shame*. Northvale: Aronson, 1991.

Goodliff, Paul. *With Unveiled Face: A Pastoral and Theological Exploration of Shame*. London: Darton, Longman & Todd, 2005.

Gregersen, Niels Henrik et al., editors. *The Gift of Grace: The Future of Lutheran Theology*. Minneapolis: Fortress, 2005.

Greven, Philip. *Spare the Child*. New York: Vintage, 1992.

Grundmann, Walter, and Heinrich Greeven. *"euchomai ktl."* In *Theological Dictionary of the New Testament*, edited by Gerhard Kittel, 2:775–808. Translated and edited by Geoffrey W. Bromiley. Grand Rapids: Eerdmans, 1964.

Guelich, Robert A. *The Sermon on the Mount: A Foundation for Understanding*. Waco: Word, 1982.

Guthrie, Donald. *The Letter to the Hebrews: An Introduction and Commentary*. Grand Rapids: Eerdmans, 1983.

Hafez, Mohammed M. *Manufacturing Human Bombs: The Making of Palestinian Suicide Bombers*. Washington, DC: United States Institute of Peace, 2006.

Hagedorn, Anselm C. "Guarding the Parents' Honour—Deuteronomy 21.18–21." *Journal for the Study of the Old Testament* 88 (2000) 101–21.

Hagedorn, Anselm C., and Jerome H. Neyrey. "'It Was Out of Envy That They Handed Jesus Over' (Mark 15.10): The Anatomy of Envy and the Gospel of Mark." *Journal for the Study of the New Testament* 69 (1998) 15–56.

Halliday, Michael A. K. *Language as a Social Semiotic: The Social Interpretation of Language and Meaning*. Baltimore: University Park Press, 1978.

Hands, A. R. *Charities and Social Aid in Greece and Rome*. Ithaca, NY: Cornell University Press, 1968.

Hanson, K. C. "How Honorable! How Shameful! A Cultural Analysis of Matthew's Makarisms and Reproaches." *Semeia* 68 (1996) 83–114.

Hartling, L., and D. Luchetta. "Humiliation: Assessing the Impact of Derision, Degradation, and Debasement." *Journal of Primary Prevention* 19.4 (1999) 259–78.

Hassan, N. "An Arsenal of Believers." *The New Yorker* (November 19, 2001) 36–41.

Hedges, Chris. *American Fascists: The Christian Right and the War on America*. New York: Free Press, 2006.

Henderson, Glen. *Treasures of Darkness*. Atlanta: GH Group, 2009.

Hengel, Martin. *Crucifixion in the Ancient World and the Folly of the Message of the Cross*. Translated by J. Bowden. Philadelphia: Fortress, 1977.

———. *Judaism and Hellenism*. Translated by John Bowden. Philadelphia: Fortress. 1974.

———. *The Zealots: Investigations into the Jewish Freedom Movement in the Period from Herod I until 70 A.D.* Translated by D. Smith. Edinburgh: T. & T. Clark, 1989.

Hens-Piazza, Gina. "Forms of Violence and the Violence of Forms: Two Cannibal Mothers before a King (2 Kings 6:24–33)." *Journal of Feminist Studies in Religion* 14 (1998) 91–104.

———. *Nameless, Blameless, and Without Shame: Two Cannibal Mothers before a King*. Collegeville, MN: Liturgical, 2003.

Hindle, Steve. "Dependency, *Shame* and Belonging: Badgering the Deserving Poor, c.1550–1750." *Cultural & Social History* 1 (2004) 6–35.

Hobbs, T. R. *2 Kings*. Word Bible Commentary 13. Waco: Word, 1985.

Hoffman, Bruce. *Inside Terrorism*. New York: Columbia University Press, 1998.

Holladay, William L. *Jeremiah 1: A Commentary on the Book of the Prophet Jeremiah Chapters 1—25*. Hermeneia. Philadelphia: Fortress, 1986.

Hollander, John. "Honour Dishonorable: Shameful Shame." *Social Research* 70 (2003) 1061–74.

Hollander, Martha. "Losses of Face: Masaccio, Rembrandt, and the Drama of Shame." *Social Research* 70 (2003) 1327–50.

Hoppe, Leslie J. *There Shall Be No Poor among You: Poverty in the Bible*. Nashville: Abingdon, 2004.

Houlden, James L. *Ethics and the New Testament*. Oxford: Oxford University Press, 1973.

Howard, George E. "Christ the End of the Law: The Meaning of Romans 10:4ff." *Journal of Biblical Literature* 88 (1969) 331–37.

Huggins, Nathan Irvin. *Black Odyssey: The African-American Ordeal in Slavery*. New York: Pantheon, 1977.

Jacobs, Harriet. *Incidents in the Life of a Slave Girl*. Reprint of the 1861 edition by the Academic Affairs Library, the University of North Carolina at Chapel Hill, 1998.

Jewett, Robert. "The Basic Human Dilemma: Weakness or Zealous Violence (Romans 7:7–25 and 10:1–18)." *Ex Auditu* 13 (1997) 96–109.

————. *Jesus against the Rapture: Seven Unexpected Prophecies*. Philadelphia: Westminster, 1979.

————. *Letter to Pilgrims: A Commentary on the Epistle to the Hebrews*. New York: Pilgrim, 1981.

————. *Paul the Apostle to America: Cultural Trends and Pauline Scholarship*. Louisville: Westminster John Knox, 1994.

————. *Romans: A Commentary*. Hermeneia. Minneapolis: Fortress, 2007.

————. *Saint Paul at the Movies: The Apostle's Dialogue with American Culture*. Louisville: Westminster John Knox, 1993.

————. *Saint Paul Returns to the Movies: Triumph over Shame*. Grand Rapids: Eerdmans, 1999.

Jewett, Robert, with Ole Wangerin. *Mission and Menace: Four Centuries of Religious Zeal in America*. Minneapolis: Fortress, 2008.

Johnson, James Weldon, and J. Rosamond Johnson. *The Books of American Negro Spirituals*. 2 vols. New York: Viking.

Jones, Arthur C. *Wade in the Water: The Wisdom of the Spirituals*. Maryknoll, NY: Orbis, 1993.

Jones, James W. *Blood that Cries Out From the Earth: The Psychology of Religious Terrorism*. New York: Oxford University Press, 2008.

————. "Eternal Warfare: Violence on the Mind of American Apocalyptic Christianity." In *The Fundamentalist Mindset: Psychological Perspectives on Religion, Violence and History*, edited by Charles B. Strozier et al., 91–103. New York: Oxford University Press, 2010.

————. *Terror and Transformation: The Ambiguity of Religion in Psychoanalytic Perspective*. London: Routledge, 2002.

Juergensmeyer, Mark. *Terror in the Mind of God: The Global Rise of Religious Violence*. Berkeley: University of California Press, 2000.

Käsemann, Ernst. *Commentary on Romans*. Translated by Geoffrey W. Bromiley. Grand Rapids: Eerdmans, 1980.

Kaufman, Gershen. *The Psychology of Shame*. New York: Springer, 1989, 1993.

———. *Shame: The Power of Caring*. Rochester: Shenkman, 1985.

Kaufman, Gershen, and Lev Raphael. "Shame as Taboo in American Culture." In *Forbidden Fruits: Taboos and Tabooism in Culture*, edited by Ray Browne, 57–64. Bowling Green: Bowling Green University Press, 1984.

Keener, Craig S. *A Commentary on the Gospel of Matthew*. Grand Rapids: Eerdmans, 1999.

Khosrokhavar, Farhad. *Suicide Bombers: Allah's New Martyrs*. Translated by David Macey. London: Pluto, 2005.

Kim, Seyoon. *The Origin of Paul's Gospel*. Wissenschaftliche Untersuchungen zum Neuen Testament 2/4. Tübingen: Mohr/Siebeck, 1981.

Kitayama, Shinobu, et al. "Culture, Self and Emotion: A Cultural Perspective on 'Self-Conscious' Emotions." In *Self-Conscious Emotions: The Psychology of Shame, Guilt, Embarrassment and Pride*, edited by June P. Tangney and Kurt W. Fisher, 439–64. New York: Guilford, 1995.

Kohut, Heinz. "Forms and Transformations of Narcissism." In *The Search for the Self: Selected Writings of Heinz Kohut*, edited by Paul H. Ornstein, 1:427–60. New York: International Universities Press, 1978.

———. *The Restoration of the Self*. Madison: International Universities Press, 1977.

———. *Self Psychology and the Humanities*. Edited by Charles Strozier. New York: Norton, 1985.

———. "Thoughts on Narcissism and Narcissistic Rage." Pp. 360–400 in *The Psychoanalytic Study of the Child*. New York: Quadrangle, 1973.

Konrath, S., B. Bushman, and W. Campbell. "Attenuating the Link Between Threatened Egotism and Aggression." *Psychological Science* 17 (2006) 995–1001.

Kritzman, Lawrence, editor. *Michel Foucault: Politics, Philosophy, Culture*. London: Routledge, 1988.

LaBarbera, Robert. "The Man of War and the Man of God: Social Satire in 2 Kings 6:8—7:20." *Catholic Biblical Quarterly* 46 (1984) 637–51.

Lang, Bernhard. "The Social Organization of Peasant Poverty in Biblical Israel." In *Anthropological Approaches to the Old Testament*, edited by Bernhard Lang, 93–99. Issues in Religion and Theology 8. Philadelphia: Fortress, 1985.

Lanner, Laurel. "Cannibal Mothers and Me: A Mother's Reading of 2 Kings 6.24—7.20." *Journal for the Study of the Old Testament* 85 (1999) 107–16.

Lakoff, George. *Women, Fire, and Dangerous Things*. Chicago: University of Chicago, 1990.

Lasine, Stuart. "Jehoram and the Cannibal Mothers (2 Kings 6:24–33): Solomon's Judgment in an Inverted World." *Journal for the Study of the Old Testament* 50 (1991) 27–53.

———. "The Riddle of Solomon's Judgment and the Riddle of Human Nature in the Hebrew Bible." *Journal for the Study of the Old Testament* 45 (1989) 61–86.

Leggitt, John S., and Raymond W. Gibbs Jr. "Emotional Reactions to Verbal Irony." *Discourse Processes* 29 (2000) 1–24.

Lewis, Helen Block, editor. *The Role of Shame in Symptom Formation*. Hillsdale: Erlbaum, 1987.

———. *Shame and Guilt in Neurosis*. New York: International Universities Press, 1971.

Lewis, Michael. *Shame: The Exposed Self*. New York: Free Press, 1992.

Lieven, Anatol. *America Right or Wrong: An Anatomy of American Nationalism.* New York: Oxford University Press, 2004.

Lifton, Robert Jay. *Destroying the World to Save It: Aum Shinrikyō, Apocalyptic Violence, and the New Global Terrorism.* New York: Henry Holt-Owl, 2000.

Li. Li, et al. "Impacts of HIV/AIDS Stigma on Family Identity and Interactions in China." *Families, Systems and Health* 26 (2008) 432–42.

Lincoln, Bruce. "Treatment of Fingernails and Hair Among the Indo-Europeans." *History of Religions* 16 (1977) 351–62.

Lindner, Evelin. *Making Enemies: Humiliation and International Conflict.* Foreword by Morton Deutsch. Westport, CT: Praeger, 2006.

Long, Burke O. *2 Kings.* Forms of the Old Testament Literature 10. Grand Rapids: Eerdmans, 1991.

Lovell, John Jr. *Black Song: The Forge and the Flame: The Story of How the Afro-American Spiritual Was Hammered Out.* New York: Macmillan, 1972.

Luz, Ulrich. *Das Evangelium nach Matthäus. 1. Teilband. Mt 1–7.* Zurich: Bensinger, 1985.

———. *Das Evangelium nach Matthäus. 2. Teilband. Mt 8–17.* Zurich: Bensinger, 1990.

Lynd, Helen Merrell. *On Shame and the Search for Identity.* New York: Harcourt Brace, 1958.

McClain, William B. *Come Sunday: The Liturgy of Zion.* Nashville: Abingdon, 1990.

MacMullen, Ramsey. *Paganism in the Roman Empire.* New Haven: Yale University Press, 1981.

McNish, Jill L. *Transforming Shame: A Pastoral Response.* New York: Routledge, 2004.

Mackie, Scott D. "Confession of the Son of God in Hebrews." *New Testament Studies* 53 (2007) 114–29.

Malina, Bruce J. "Limited Good and the Social World of Early Christianity." *Biblical Theology Bulletin* 8 (1979) 162–76.

———. *The New Testament World: Insights from Cultural Anthropology.* 3rd ed. Louisville: Westminster John Knox, 2001.

———. *The Social World of Jesus and the Gospels.* London: Routledge, 1996.

Malina, Bruce J., and Jerome H. Neyrey, "Honor and Shame in Luke-Acts: Pivotal Values of the Mediterranean World." In *The Social World of Luke-Acts: Models for Interpretation,* edited by Jerome H. Neyrey, 25–66. Peabody, MA: Hendrickson, 1991.

Malina, Bruce J., and Richard L. Rohrbaugh. *Social Science Commentary on the Synoptic Gospels.* Minneapolis: Fortress, 1992.

Marcus, David. "Juvenile Delinquency in the Bible and the Ancient Near East." *Journal of the Ancient Near Eastern Society of Columbia University* 13 (1981) 31–52.

Margalit, Avishai. *The Decent Society.* Cambridge: Harvard University Press, 1996.

Mattes, Mark C. *The Role of Justification in Contemporary Theology.* Grand Rapids: Eerdmans, 2004.

Matthews, Victor H. "The Anthropology of Clothing in the Joseph Narrative." *Journal for the Study of the Old Testament* 65 (1995) 25–36.

———. "Entrance Ways and Threshing Floors: Legally Significant Sites in the Ancient Near East." *Fides et Historia* 19 (1987) 25–40.

———. *Old Testament Turning Points: The Narratives That Shaped a Nation.* Grand Rapids: Baker Academic, 2005.

Matthews, Victor H., and Don C. Benjamin, *Old Testament Parallels: Laws and Stories from the Ancient Near East*. 3rd ed. Mahwah, NJ: Paulist, 2006.

Matthews, Victor H., and Don C. Benjamin. *Social World of Ancient Israel, 1250–587 BCE*. Peabody, MA: Hendrickson, 1993.

Mead, George Henry. *Mind, Self, and Society*. Chicago: University of Chicago Press, 1934.

Mellon, James, editor. *Bullwhip Days: The Slaves Remember, An Oral History*. New York: Avon, 1988.

Michaels, J. Ramsey. *1 Peter*. Word Biblical Commentary 49. Waco: Word, 1988.

Milgram, Stanley. *Obedience to Authority: An Experimental View*. New York: Harper & Row, 1974.

Miller, Alice. *For Your Own Good: The Roots of Violence in Child-Rearing*. London: Virago, 1987.

Miller, Patrick D. *The Ten Commandments*. Interpretation. Louisville: Westminster John Knox, 2009.

Miller, P., and N. Eisenberg. "The Relation of Empathy to Aggression and Externalizing/Antisocial Behavior." *Psychological Bulletin* 103 (1988) 324–44.

Miller, William Ian. *Humiliation and Other Essays on Honor, Social Discomfort, and Violence*. Ithaca, NY: Cornell University Press, 1993.

Moxnes, Halvor. "Honor, Shame, and the Outside World in Paul's Letter to the Romans." In *The Social World of Formative Christianity and Judaism: Essays in Tribute to Howard Clark Kee*, edited by Jacob Neusner et al., 207–18. Philadelphia: Fortress, 1988.

———. "Honour and Righteousness in Romans," *Journal for the Study of the New Testament* 32 (1988) 61–77.

Müller, Ulrich B. "Vision und Botschaft. Erwägungen zur prophetischen Struktur der Verkündigung Jesu." *Zeitschrift für Theologie und Kirche* 74 (1977) 416–48.

Nathanson, Donald. *Shame and Pride: Affect, Sex, and the Birth of the Self*. New York: Norton, 1992.

Neyrey, Jerome H. "Despising the Shame of the Cross," *Semeia* 68 (1996) 113–37.

———. *Honor and Shame in the Gospel of Matthew*. Louisville: Westminster John Knox, 1998.

Nicolson, Ronald. *A Black Future? Jesus and Salvation in South Africa*. Philadelphia: Trinity, 1990.

Nussbaum, Martha. *Hiding from Humanity: Disgust, Shame, and the Law*. Princeton: Princeton University Press, 2004.

Oakley, J. W. "Hypocrisy in Matthew." *Irish Biblical Studies* 7 (1985) 118–35.

Overman, J. Andrew. *Matthew's Gospel and Formative Judaism: A Study of the Social World of the Matthean Community*. Minneapolis: Fortress, 1990.

Painter, Nell Irvin. "Soul Murder and Slavery: Toward a Fully Loaded Cost Accounting." In *U.S. History As Women's History: New Feminist Essays*, edited by Linda K. Kerber et al., 125–46. Chapel Hill: University of North Carolina Press, 1995.

Pape, Robert A. *Dying to Win: The Strategic Logic of Suicide Terrorism*. New York: Random House, 2005.

Pargament, K., G. Magyar, E. Benore, and A. Mahoney. "Sacrilege: A Study of Loss and Desecration." *Journal for the Scientific Study of Religion* 44 (2005) 59–78.

Pargament, K., K. Trevino, A. Mahoney, and I. Silberman. "They Killed Our Lord: The Persecution of Jews as Desecrators of Christianity as a Predictor of Anti-Semitism." *Journal for the Scientific Study of Religion* 46 (2007) 143–48.

Parker, Robert. *Miasma: Pollution and Purification in Early Greek Religion.* Oxford: Oxford University Press, 1983.

Patterson, Orlando. *Slavery and Social Death: A Comparative Study.* Cambridge: Harvard University Press, 1987.

Pattison, Stephen. *The Challenge of Practical Theology: Selected Essays.* London: Kingsley, 2007.

————. *Shame: Theory, Therapy, Theology.* Cambridge: Cambridge University Press, 2000.

Patton, John. *Is Human Forgiveness Possible?* Nashville: Abingdon, 1985.

Pickett, Raymond. *The Cross in Corinth: The Social Significance of the Death of Jesus.* Sheffield: Sheffield Academic, 1997.

Pilch, John J. "Secrecy in the Mediterranean World: An Anthropological Perspective." *Biblical Theology Bulletin* 24 (1994) 151–57.

Pitt-Rivers, Julian. "Honour and Social Status." In *Honour and Shame: The Values of Mediterranean Society,* edited by J. G. Peristiany, 21–77. London: Weidenfeld & Nicolson, 1965.

Porton, Gary G. "Sadducees." In *Anchor Bible Dictionary* 5 (1992) 892–93.

Post, Jerrold M. *The Mind of the Terrorist: The Psychology of Terrorism from the IRA to Al-Qaeda.* New York: Palgrave Macmillan, 2007.

Post, Jerrold M., E. Sprinzak, and L. Denny. "The Terrorists in Their Own Words: Interviews with 35 Incarcerated Middle Eastern Terrorists." *Terrorism and Political Violence* 15 (2003) 171–84.

Post, J., K. Ruby, and F. Shaw. "The Radical Group in Context." *Studies in Conflict and Terrorism* 25.1 (2002) 73–100.

Probyn, Elspeth. *Blush: Faces of Shame.* Sydney: University of New South Wales, 2005.

Raskin, R., and H. Terry. "A Principal-Components Analysis of the Narcissistic Personality Inventory." *Journal of Personality and Social Psychology* 54 (1988) 890–902.

Rawick, George P., editor. *The American Slave: A Composite Biography.* 19 vols. Westport, CT: Greenwood, 1972–1979.

Reader, Ian. *Religious Violence in Contemporary Japan: The Case of Aum Shinrikyo.* London: Curzon, 2000.

Redles, David. "Ordering Chaos: Nazi Millennialism and the Quest for Meaning." In *The Fundamentalist Mindset: Psychological Perspectives on Religion, Violence, and History,* edited by Charles B. Strozier et al., 156–74. New York: Oxford University Press, 2010.

Rendsburg, Gary A. "The Guilty Party in 1 Kings iii 16–28." *Vetus Testamentum* 48 (1998) 534–41.

Rhoads, David. *Israel in Revolution: 6–74 C. E. A Political History Based on the Writings of Josephus.* Philadelphia: Fortress, 1976.

Roberts, J. Deotis. *Liberation and Reconciliation.* Philadelphia: Westminster, 1971.

Rogers, Molly. *Delia's Tears: Race, Science, and Photography in Nineteenth-Century America.* New Haven: Yale University Press, 2010.

Rosenthal, Joel. "The French Path to Jihad." *Policy Review* 139 (October-November, 2006) 39–59.

Sachs, Stuart. *Hebrews through a Hebrew's Eyes: Hope in the Midst of a Hopeless World.* Messianic Jewish Resources International. Baltimore: Lederer, 1995.

Sakenfeld, Katharine D. *Just Wives? Stories of Power and Survival in the Old Testament and Today.* Louisville: Westminster John Knox, 2003.

Saldarini, Anthony J. "Pharisees." *Anchor Bible Dictionary* 5 (1992) 294–303.

———. *Pharisees, Scribes and Sadducees in Palestinian Society: A Sociological Approach.* Wilmington, DE: Glazier, 1988.

Salzberger, Ronald P., and Mary C. Turck, editors. *Reparations for Slavery: A Reader.* Lanham, MD: Rowman & Littlefield, 2004.

Sanday, William, and Arthur C. Headlam. *A Critical and Exegetical Commentary on the Epistle to the Romans.* Edinburgh: Clark, 1895. 5th ed. 1902. Reprinted 1958, 1962.

Sanders, E. P. *Paul and Palestinian Judaism: A Comparison of Patterns of Religion.* Philadelphia: Fortress, 1977.

———. *Paul, the Law, and the Jewish People.* Philadelphia: Fortress, 1983.

Scheff, Thomas. *Catharsis in Healing, Ritual, and Drama.* Berkeley: University of California Press, 1979.

———. *Emotions, the Social Bond, and Human Reality.* Cambridge: Cambridge University Press, 1997.

———. "Looking-Glass Self: Goffman as Symbolic Interactionist." *Symbolic Interaction* 28 (2005) 147–66.

———. "Shame and Conformity: The Difference-Emotion System." *American Sociological Review* 53 (1988) 395–406.

———. "Shame and Related Emotions: An Overview." *American Behavioral Scientist* 38 (1995) 1053–59.

———. "The Structure of Context: Deciphering *Frame Analysis.*" *Sociological Theory* 23 (2005) 368–85.

———. "The Taboo on Coarse Emotions." *Review of Personality and Social Psychology* 5 (June 1984) 156–69.

———. "Toward a Sociological Model of Consensus." *American Sociological Review* 32 (1967) 32–46.

———. *What's Love Got to Do with It?* Denver: Paradigm, 2010.

Scheff, Thomas J., and Suzanne M. Retzinger *Emotions and Violence: Shame and Rage in Destructive Conflicts.* Lexington, MA: Lexington, 1991.

———. *Emotions and Violence: Shame and Rage in Destructive Conflicts.* Lexington, MA: Lexington, 1991.

Schneider, Carl. *Shame, Exposure, and Privacy.* New York: Norton, 1987.

Schröder, Bernd. "Sadduzäer." In *Religion in Geschichte und Gegenwart,* edited by Hans Dieter Betz, 7:732–33. 4th ed. Tübingen: Mohr/Siebeck, 2004.

Scroggs, Robin. *Paul for a New Day.* 1977. Reprinted, Eugene, OR: Wipf & Stock, 2002.

Shweder, Richard A. "Toward a Deep Cultural Psychology of Shame." *Social Research* 70 (2003) 1109–30.

Seland, Torrey. *Establishment Violence in Philo and Luke: A Study of Non-Conformity to the Torah and Jewish Vigilante Reactions.* Biblical Interpretation Series 13. Leiden: Brill, 1995.

Sennett, Richard. *Authority.* London: Faber & Faber, 1993.

Smith, Archie Jr. *Navigating the Deep River: Spirituality in African American Families.* Cleveland: United Church Press, 1997.

Smith, Wilfred C. *The Meaning and End of Religion.* New York: Harper & Row, 1978.

Sonsino, Rifat. *Motive Clauses in Hebrew Law*. Society of Biblical Literature Dissertation Series 45. Chico: Scholars, 1980.

Spelman, Elizabeth V. "The Virtue of Feeling and the Feeling of Virtue." In *Feminist Ethics*, edited by Claudia Card, 213–32. Lawrence: University Press of Kansas, 1991.

Staubli, Thomas, and Silvia Schroer. *Body Symbolism in the Bible*. Collegeville, MN: Liturgical, 2001.

Steinsaltz, Adin. *Biblical Images: Men and Women of the Book*. New York: Basic Books, 1984.

Stendahl, Krister. *Paul Among Jews and Gentiles and Other Essays*. Philadelphia: Fortress, 1976.

Stern, J. "Anatomy of Terror." A lecture presented at a conference on "The Psychology of Fundamentalism," at the Chicago Institute of Psychoanalysis, February, 25, 2006.

Stern, Jessica. *Terror in the Name of God: Why Religious Militants Kill*. New York: Ecco, 2003.

Strozier, Charles B., David M. Terman, James W. Jones, and Katharine A. Boyd, editors. *The Fundamentalist Mindset: Psychological Perspectives on Religion, Violence, and History*. New York: Oxford University Press, 2010.

Strozier, Charles B. *Apocalypse: On the Psychology of Fundamentalism in America*. Boston: Beacon, 1994.

Strecker, Georg. *Die Bergpredigt. Ein exegetischer Kommentar*. Göttingen: Vandenhoeck & Ruprecht, 1984.

Stuhlmacher, Peter. *Revisiting Paul's Doctrine of Justification: A Challenge to the New Perspective*. With an essay by Donald A. Hagner. Downers Grove, Il: InterVarsity, 2001.

Stumpff, Albrecht. "*Zelos, ktl.*" In *Theological Dictionary of the New Testament*, edited by Gerhard Kittel, 2:877–88 Translated and edited by Geoffrey W. Bromiley. Grand Rapids: Eerdmans, 1964.

Tangney, June P., and Ronda L. Dearing. *Shame and Guilt*. New York; London: Guilford, 2002.

Talbert, Charles H. *Reading the Sermon on the Mount: Character Formation and Decision Making in Matthew 5–7*. Columbia: University of South Carolina Press, 2004.

Tamez, Elsa. *The Amnesty of Grace: Justification by Grace from a Latin American Perspective*. Translated by Sharon Ringe. Nashville: Abingdon, 1991.

Taylor, Gabriele. *Pride, Shame, and Guilt: Emotions of Self-Assessment*. Oxford: Clarendon, 1985.

Terman, David M. "Fundamentalism and the Paranoid Gestalt." In *The Fundamentalist Mindset: Psychological Perspectives on Religion, Violence, and History*, edited by Charles B. Strozier et al., 47–61. New York: Oxford University Press, 2010.

Tigay, Jeffrey H. *Deuteronomy*. JPS Torah Commentary. Philadelphia: Jewish Publication Society, 1996.

Tillich, Paul. *The Eternal Now*. New York: Scribner, 1963.

Tomkins, Silvan S. *Affect/Imagery/Consciousness*. Volume 3. New York: Springer, 1992.

Triandis, Harry C. "Cross-Cultural Studies in Individualism and Collectivism." In *Nebraska Symposium on Motivation 1989*, edited by R. A. Diensbier and J. J. Berman, 41–133. Lincoln: University of Nebraska Press, 1990.

Twenge, Jean M., and W. Keith Campbell. *The Narcissism Epidemic: Living in the Age of Entitlement*. New York: Free Press, 2009.

Via, Dan O. Jr. *Self-Deception and Wholeness in Paul and Matthew*. 1990. Reprinted, Eugene, OR: Wipf & Stock, 2005.

Victoroff, J. "The Mind of the Terrorist: A Review and Critique of Psychological Approaches." *Journal of Conflict Resolution* 49 (2005) 3–42.

Volkan, Vamik D. *Bloodlines: From Ethnic Pride to Ethnic Terrorism*. Boulder, CO: Westview, 1997.

Walcott, Peter. *Envy and the Greeks: A Study of Human Behavior*. Warminster: Ares & Phillips, 1978.

Wandrey, Irena. "Zeloten." In *Religion in Geschichte und Gegenwart*, edited by Hans Dieter Betz, 8:1832–34. 4 ed. Tübingen: Mohr/Siebeck, 2005.

Watson, Philip. *Let God Be God! An Interpretation of the Theology of Martin Luther*. Philadelphia: Muhlenburg, 1949.

Websdale, Neil. *Familicidal Hearts: The Emotional Style of 211 Killers*. Oxford: Oxford University Press, 2010.

Weimann, Gabriel. *Terror on the Internet*. Washington, DC: United States Institute of Peace, 2006.

Wesley, John. *The Works of John Wesley*. Reprinted from the 1872 edition issued by the Wesleyan Methodist Book Room, London. 14 vols. Grand Rapids: Baker, 1990.

Westbrook, Raymond, and Bruce Wells. *Everyday Law in Biblical Israel: An Introduction*. Louisville: Westminster John Knox, 2009.

Westerholm, Stephen. *Perspectives Old and New on Paul: The "Lutheran" Paul and His Critics*. Grand Rapids: Eerdmans, 2004.

Westhelle, Vitor. *The Scandalous God: The Use and Abuse of the Cross*. Minneapolis: Fortress, 2006.

Wharton, Barbara. "The Hidden Face of Shame: The Shadow, Shame, and Separation." *Journal of Analytical Psychology* 35 (1990) 279–99.

Willis, Timothy M. *The Elders of the City: A Study of the Elders-Laws in Deuteronomy*. Atlanta: Society of Biblical Literature, 2001.

Wilckens, Ulrich. "*hypokrinomai ktl*" Pp. 559–71 in volume 8.of Gerhard Friedrich, editor. *Theological Dictionary of the New Testament*, edited by Gerhard Friedrich, 8:559–71. Translated and edited by Geoffrey W. Bromiley. Grand Rapids: Eerdmans, 1972.

Wimberly, Edward P. *Practical Theology in the Wesleyan Spirit*. Atlanta: Unpublished manuscript, 2010.

———. *Relational Refugees: Alienation and Reincorporation in African American Churches and Communities*. Nashville: Abingdon, 2000.

Witherington, Ben III. *Matthew*. Smyth & Helwys Bible Commentary. Macon, GA: Smyth & Helwys, 2006.

Wolter, Michael. *Das Lukasevangelium*. Handbuch zum Neuen Testament 5. Tübingen: Mohr/Siebeck, 2008.

Worthington, Everett L. Jr. "Unforgiveness, Forgiveness, and Reconciliation and Their Implications for Societal Interventions." In *Forgiveness and Reconciliation*, edited by Raymond G. Helmick and Rodney L. Petersen, 161–82. Foreword by Desmond M. Tutu. Philadelphia: Templeton Press, 2001.

Wright, David P. "Music and Dance in 1 Sam 6." *Journal of Biblical Literature* 121 (2001) 201–25.

Wright, N. T. *Justification: God's Plan and Paul's Vision*. Downers Grove, IL: IVP Academic, 2009.

Wurmser, Leon. *The Mask of Shame*. Northvale, NJ: Aronson, 1994.

Yancey, Philip. *What's So Amazing about Grace?* Grand Rapids: Zondervan, 1997.

Zager, Werner. *Bergpredigt und Reich Gottes*. Neukirchen-Vluyn: Neukirchener, **2002**.

Zinn, Howard. *A People's History of the United States*. New York: HarperCollins, 1995.

Zmijewski, Josef. "*nesteuo ktl.*" In *Exegetical Dictionary of the New Testament*, edited by Horst Balz and Gerhard Schneider, 2:465–67. Grand Rapids: Eerdmans, 1991.

POPULAR SONGS

The Beatles. "You've Got to Hide Your Love Away." On *Help!* Parlophone, 1968.

Harvey, P. J. "Shame is the Shadow of Love." On *Uh huh her*. Universal Music Canada, 2004.

Joel, Billy. "Shameless." On *Storm Front*. Columbia Records, 1989.

Rich, Tony. "Nobody Knows." On *Words*. LaFace/Arista, 1996.

Urban, Keith. "Tonight I Wanna Cry." On *Be Here*. Capitol Records, 2004.

Index of Ancient Documents

2 Samuel (cont.)

14:5	141
15:1–6	134
15:3–4	136
15:3	136

1 Kings

1:33–35	141
3:16–28	135–36
3:16	136
19:10	192
19:14	192
22	140

2 Kings

6:21–23	137
6:24—7:20	133–38
6:27	137
6:28	137
6:30–31	137
6:31	137
6:32	137
6:33	136–37
7:1–2	137
7:3–15	130–33
7:4	133
7:5	133
7:9	133
7:10–12	133
7:16	133
11:12	141
19:26	126

Job

1:20	127
31:38–39	140

Psalm

19:1	150
25:1–3	130
117:22	167
119:1–6	124
119:31	124
119:46	124
119:80	124
127:1	113

Proverbs

3:34	179
10:23	119
11:12	119
14:28	150
18:2	119
19:26	124–25
23:19–21	125
25:2	154
25:23	119
25:27–28	124
28:24	124
29:15	125

Isaiah

20:2–6	126
28:16	167, 177, 186
47:3	140

Jeremiah

3:3	131
13:26	140
16:6	127
19:9	135
29:11	113
31:10–14	139
50:11–13	140

Ezekiel

5:10	135

Amos

2:8	128

Zephaniah

3:5	125

~

APOCRYPHA AND PSEUDEPIGRAPHA

Letter of Aristeas

221	184

≈

GRECO-ROMAN LITERATURE

Shame factor - Thanksgiving

Chapters 7, 8, 9